EDINBURGH
CityMap

CONTENTS

Key to Map Symbols	2 - 3
Key to Map Pages	4 - 5
Route Planning Map	6 - 7
City Centre Map	8 - 9
Main Mapping	10 - 77
Airport Map	78 - 79
Index to Streets	80 - 95
Index to Places of Interest	95 - 100

First Edition: Published by Nicolson Maps 2000
© 2000 Nicolson Maps

Created and designed by the XYZ Digital Map Company Ltd in conjunction with Nicolson Maps.

CityMap © 1999 XYZ Digital Map Company Ltd, (Part derived from Cities Revealed®
Orthophotography © 1998 Geoinformation Group Ltd).

Motorway *Autobahn* Autoroute	
Slip Road *Auf- / Ausfahrt* sortie	
Primary Dual Carriageway *zweispurige Hauptstraße* route nationale (voie express)	
Primary Road *zweispurige Hauptstraße* route nationale	
Slip Road *Auf- / Ausfahrt* sortie	
A Dual Carriageway *zweispurige A-Straße* route départementale (voie express)	
A Road *A-Straße* route départementale	
Slip Road *Auf- / Ausfahrt* sortie	
B Dual Carriageway *zweispurige B-Straße* voie communale (voie express)	
B Road *B-Strafle* voie communale	
Slip Road *Auf- / Ausfahrt* sortie	
Other Dual Carriageway *sonstige zweispurige Straße* autres voies express	
Other Road *sonstige Straße* autres routes	
Tunnel *Tunnel* Tunnel	
Minor Road *Nebenstraße* voie secondaire	
Track *Fahrweg* piste	
Pedestrian *Fußgängerweg* piéton	
Railway *Eisenbahn* chemin de fer	
Rail Siding *Abstellgleis* voie de garage	
Footpath *Fußgängerweg* sentier	
Cycle Path *Fahrradweg* voie cyclable	
Ward Boundary *Wahlbezirks-Grenze* limite de canton	

Postcode Sector Boundary *Postleitzahl-Grenze* limite de secteur postal

Land Uses / *Land* / Terrain

	Urban *Stadtgebiet* urbain
	Pedestrian *Fußgänger* piéton
	Loch,Dock *See,Dock* lac
	Marsh *Sumpf* marécage
	Sewage ,Water Works *Abwasser, Wasserwerk* égouts, service d'eau
	Beach *Strand* plage
	Dockland *Dockgebiet* port
	Car Park *Parkplatz* parking
	Prison, Hospital Grounds *Gefängnis, Krankenhaus-Gelände* terrain de prison, terrain de hopîtal
	School , College Grounds *Schule, Hochschul-Gelände* terrain de école, terrain de université
	Military Base *Militär-Standort* base militaire
	Woodland *Waldgebiet* bois
	Nursery *Gärtnerei* pépiniére
	Rural *Ländliches Gebiet* rurale
	Park *Park* parc
	Open Space *Offenes Gelände* espace publique
	Sports Grounds *Sportplatz* terrains de sport
	Cemetery *Friedhof* cimitiére
	Allotments *Schrebergärten* jardins potages
	Sand, Gravel Pit *Sand, Kiesgrube* carriére de sable, gravier

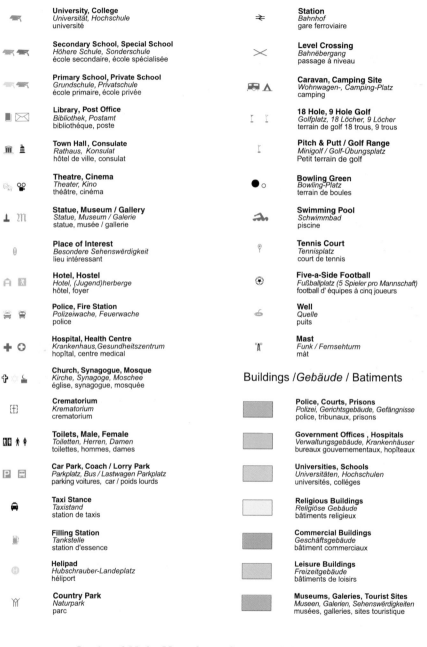

University, College
Universität, Hochschule
université

Station
Bahnhof
gare ferroviaire

Secondary School, Special School
Höhere Schule, Sonderschule
école secondaire, école spécialisée

Level Crossing
Bahnëbergang
passage à niveau

Primary School, Private School
Grundschule, Privatschule
école primaire, école privée

Caravan, Camping Site
Wohnwagen-, Camping-Platz
camping

Library, Post Office
Bibliothek, Postamt
bibliothéque, poste

18 Hole, 9 Hole Golf
Golfplatz, 18 Löcher, 9 Löcher
terrain de golf 18 trous, 9 trous

Town Hall, Consulate
Rathaus, Konsulat
hôtel de ville, consulat

Pitch & Putt / Golf Range
Minigolf / Golf-Übungsplatz
Petit terrain de golf

Theatre, Cinema
Theater, Kino
théâtre, cinéma

Bowling Green
Bowling-Platz
terrain de boules

Statue, Museum / Gallery
Statue, Museum / Galerie
statue, musée / gallerie

Swimming Pool
Schwimmbad
piscine

Place of Interest
Besondere Sehenswërdigkeit
lieu intéressant

Tennis Court
Tennisplatz
court de tennis

Hotel, Hostel
Hotel, (Jugend)herberge
hôtel, foyer

Five-a-Side Football
Fußballplatz (5 Spieler pro Mannschaft)
football d' équipes à cinq joueurs

Police, Fire Station
Polizeiwache, Feuerwache
police

Well
Quelle
puits

Hospital, Health Centre
Krankenhaus,Gesundheitszentrum
hopîtal, centre medical

Mast
Funk / Fernsehturm
màt

Church, Synagogue, Mosque
Kirche, Synagoge, Moschee
église, synagogue, mosquée

Buildings /*Gebäude* / Batiments

Crematorium
Krematorium
crematorium

Police, Courts, Prisons
Polizei, Gerichtsgebäude, Gefängnisse
police, tribunaux, prisons

Toilets, Male, Female
Toiletten, Herren, Damen
toilettes, hommes, dames

Government Offices , Hospitals
Verwaltungsgebäude, Krankenhäuser
bureaux gouvernementaux, hopîteaux

Car Park, Coach / Lorry Park
Parkplatz, Bus / Lastwagen Parkplatz
parking voitures, car / poids lourds

Universities, Schools
Universitäten, Hochschulen
universités, colléges

Taxi Stance
Taxistand
station de taxis

Religious Buildings
Religiöse Gebäude
bâtiments religieux

Filling Station
Tankstelle
station d'essence

Commercial Buildings
Geschäftsgebäude
bâtiment commerciaux

Helipad
Hubschrauber-Landeplatz
héliport

Leisure Buildings
Freizeitgebäude
bâtiments de loisirs

Country Park
Naturpark
parc

Museums, Galeries, Tourist Sites
Museen, Galerien, Sehenswërdigkeiten
musées, galleries, sites touristique

Scale of Main Mapping - Approx. 1:10,000

0   0.1   0.2   0.3   0.4   0.5   0.6   0.7   0.8   0.9   1 kilometre

0                        $^1/_4$ $^1/_2$ statute mile

Cramond
Island

10-11

Granton
A901
Trinity
New

A90
Muirhouse
Pilton
A903

Cramond
Silverknowes
16-17
18-19
Warr

Craigiehall
Davidson
Mains
Drylaw
B9085
Inverleith
B901

Barnton
A902

Clermiston
Blackhall
Craigleith
B900
Comely Bank

24-25
26-27
Ravelston
A90
28-29
Newtow

Turnhouse
Murrayfield
Dalry
Old

⊕
Edinburgh Airport
(see pages 78-79)
A902
B701
Corstorphine
A8
Gorgie
40-41
42-43
Merchiston

A8
38-39
Stenhouse
A70
A702

A720
B701
A71
Longstone
Morningside

M8
Sighthill
Craiglockhart
52-53

48-49
50-51
A702

A71
Wester
Hailes

Baberton
Colinton
Mains

Juniper
Green
Colinton
Oxgangs

58-59
60-61
B701
62-63
Fairmile

Currie
A720
Swanston

70-71

Balerno

A70

A702

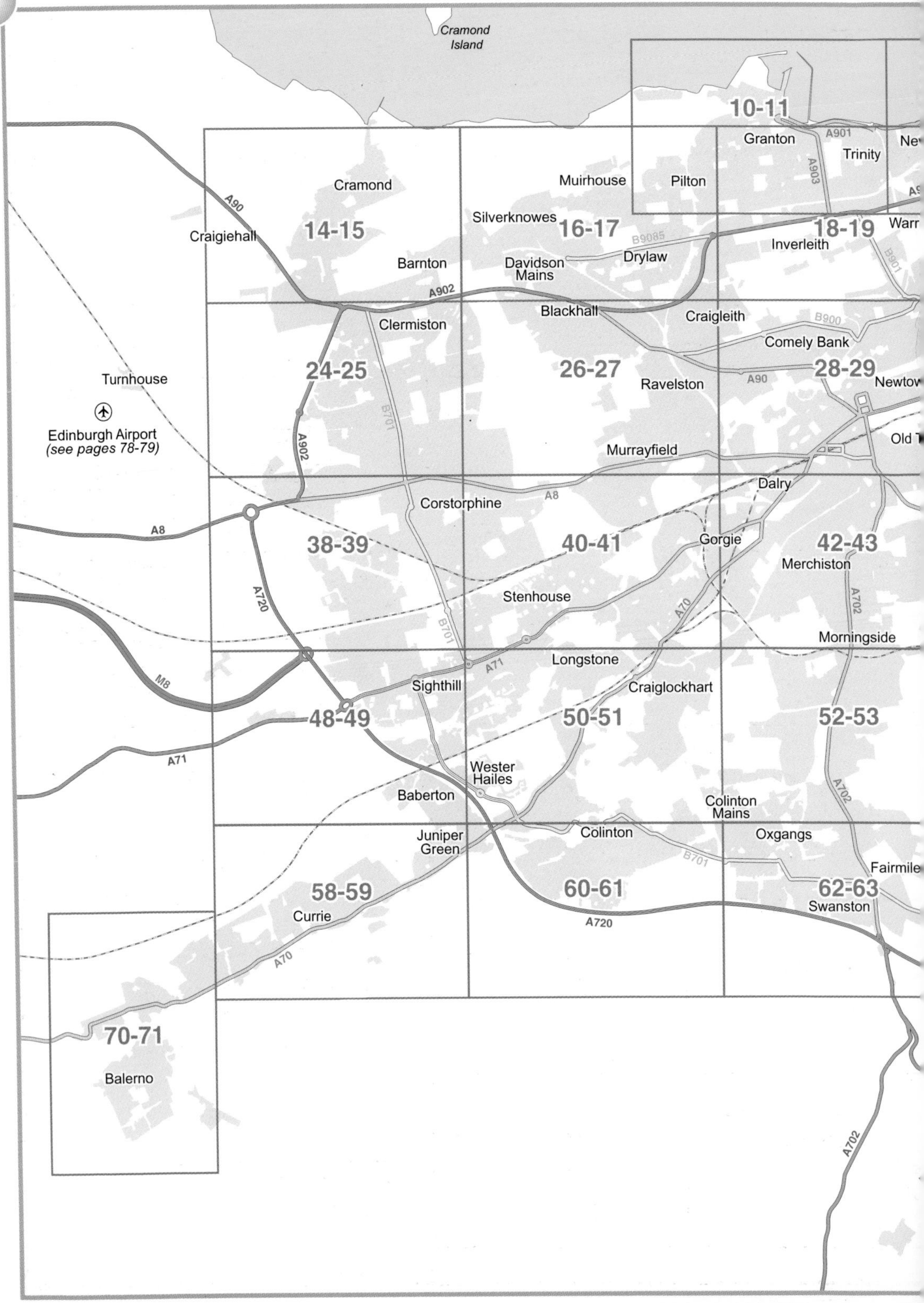

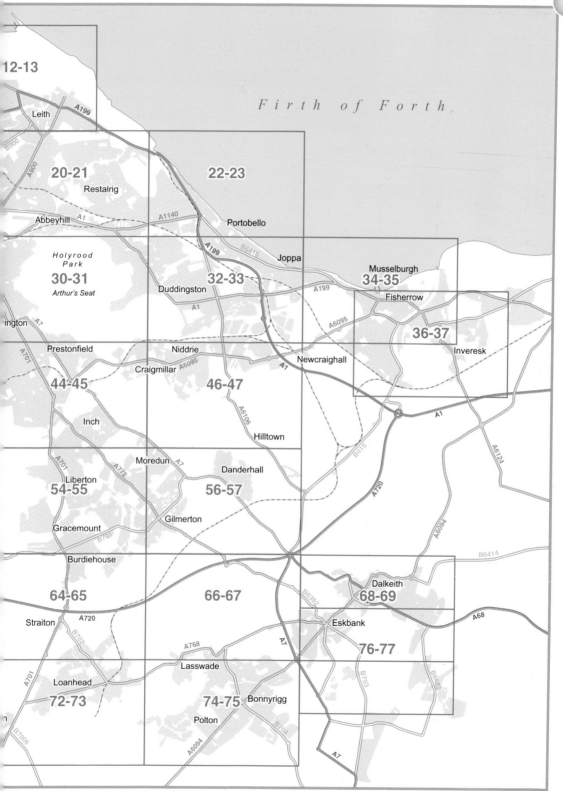

12-13

Leith

Firth of Forth

20-21

Restalrig

Abbeyhill

22-23

Portobello

A199

Joppa

Holyrood Park

30-31

Arthur's Seat

Duddingston

32-33

Musselburgh

34-35

Fisherrow

36-37

Inveresk

ington

Prestonfield

Niddrie

Craigmillar

44-45

46-47

Newcraighall

Inch

Hilltown

Moredun

Danderhall

Liberton

54-55

56-57

Gracemount

Gilmerton

Burdiehouse

Dalkeith

64-65

66-67

68-69

Straiton

Eskbank

76-77

Lasswade

Loanhead

72-73

74-75

Bonnyrigg

Polton

Firth of Forth

Newhaven Harbour
Newhaven
Newhaven Heritage Museum
The Former Royal Yacht Britannia
Britannia Visitor Centre
Scottish Executive
Leith
Clan Tartan Centre
Leith Victoria
Warriston
St Mark's Park
Leith Waterworld
Warriston Park
Leith Links
Eastern General
Craigentinny Public Golf Course
Playhouse
Easter Road (Hibernian FC)
London Road
Restalrig
Lochend Park
Portrait Gallery
Calton Hill
Abbeyhill
Meadowbank Sports Centre
Portobello
Portobello Swimming Pool
Newtown
Waverley Station
Regent Road
Palace of Holyroodhouse
Scottish Parliament (Open 2001)
Dynamic Earth
Joppa
Edinburgh Castle
St Giles
Museum of Childhood
Old Town
National Museums
Holyrood Park
Arthur's Seat
251m
Meadowfield Park
Figgate Burn Park
Portobello Road
Joppa Road
Musselburgh
Joppa Quarry Park
Milton Road East
Royal Infirmary
The Meadows
Bruntsfield Links
Melville Drive
Royal Commonwealth Pool
Milton Road West
Duddingston
Portobello Public Golf Course
Newington
Royal Hospital For Sick Children
Prestonfield Golf Course
Duddingston Loch
Duddingston
Golf Course
Milton Road
Edinburgh Leisure
Prestonfield
Peffermill Road
Niddrie
UCI
Astley Ainslie
Peffermill Sports Ground
Craigmillar
Niddrie Main Road
Jack Kane Sports Centre
Newcraighall Road
Edinburgh Fort Retail Park
Newcra
Whitehill Street
Cameron Toll Shopping Centre
Old Dalkeith Road
The Inch Park
Craigmillar Castle
New Royal Infirmary of Edinburgh (Open 2001)
Blackford Pond
Inch
Blackford Hill
Craigmillar Park Golf Course
of Braid
Liberton Golf Course
Hilltown
Braid Hills Golf Course
Gilmerton Road
Moredun
Danderhall
Newton
Braid Hills
Mortonhall Golf Course
Liberton
Liberton Park
Liberton Hospital
Southfield Hospital
Gracemount
Ferniehill Drive
Gilmerton
airmilehead
Princess Margaret Rose
Mortonhall Caravan Park
Captain's Road
Gilmerton Dykes St
Newton St
Drum Street
Sheriffhall Roundabout
Frogston Road West
Frogston Road East
Burdiehouse Burn Park
Burdiehouse
Gilmerton Road
Gilmerton Junction
Edinburgh Butterfly World
Old Dalk
Lasswade Junction
Kings Acre

NW Circus Pl.
Christopher North House
Gloucester Pl.
Royal Circus
Circus Place
Circus Gdns.
Royal Circus
NE Circus Pl.
SE Circus Pl.
Great
Northumberland St. NE La.
Northumberland St.
Nthum Pl.
Nelson St.
Dublin Meuse
Dublin Street
Broughton Market
Albany St.

Darnaway St.
India Street
Gloucester Lane
Jamaica St La Nth.
Jamaica St.
Jamaica Mews
Jamaica St La Sth.
Heriot Row
Northumberland St. NW La.
Northumberland St. SW La.
Northumberland St. SE La.
Abercromby Place
Royal Scots Club
Robert Louis Stevenson's House
Queen St Gdns E
Gardens
York P
Dublin Street Lane South

Wemyss Pl.
Queen
Street
Queen St Gdns W
BBC Scotland
St. David St.
St. Andrew
Scottish National Portrait Gallery
St. Andrew Square Bus Station
Clyde Street
N. Clyde St.
St. Andrew's

Albyn Place
Wemyss Pl Mews
Queen
Street
Frederick St.
Hanover St.
St. Andrew
Street
Henry Dundas
Square
St. Andrew St.
Royal Bank
Register House
New Register House
West
Royal Bank Head Office
Register
Royal British

Sth Charlotte St.
Spain
Philippines
Hill St La Nth.
Hill Street
Hill St La Sth.
Nth Castle St.
Frederick's House
Switzerland
Netherlands
George Hotel
Royal Society of Edinburgh
Thistle St La NE
Thistle St La SE
Thistle St La SW
Thistle St La NW
Thistle
Street
George IV
Rose Street
Rose St Sth La.
Jenners
Meuse Lane
Old Waverley
Scottish Tartans
David Livingstone

Sir Alexander Graham Bell's House
Norway
Thomas Chalmers
Monaco
Freemasons Hall
Rose St Nth La.
Rose Street
Rose St Sth La.
George
Street
Pitt
Rose St N
Sweden
Finland
Mount Royal
Adam Black
John Wilson
Waverley Market
Scott Monument

Roxburghe
Rose St Nth La.
Rose St Sth La.
Royal Overseas League
The New Club
A8
Princes Street
Allan Ramsay
Royal Scots Greys
Royal Scottish Academy
Spanish Civil War
East Princes Street Gdns.
Waverley Bridge
Waver Statio
Market

Sth Charlotte St.
Sir Alexander Graham Bell's House
Hope St La.
James Simpson
Dean Ramsay
The Call
Thomas Guthrie
Ross Theatre
West Princes
Street Gardens
The Mound
National Gallery of Scotland
Black Watch
Bank of Scotland HQ
North Bank St.
City Chambers
Cockbu
Tattoo Office
Stree
Station

St. John's
St. Cuthbert's
Ross Fountain
Robert Louis Stevenson
Edinburgh Castle
Mills Mount Battery (1pm Gun)
St. Margaret's Chapel
Scottish United Services
Palace
Ensign Ewart's Grave
William Wallace
Robert Bruce
Ramsay Gdn.
Camera Obscura
Scottish Parliament (Temp)
Castlehill
Esplanade
The Hub
Upper Bow
Lawnmarket
Ramsay Ln.
The Writers' Museum
Gladstone's Land
High Court
St. Giles Cathedral
Parliament Square
High Courts
Heart of Midlothian
Mercat Cross
Signet
Melbourne
High Street
Alexan
Cenotaph

Lothian Road
A702
Castle Terrace
King's Stables Road
King's Bridge
Castle Rock
Johnston Terrace
Castle Inn
Thistle Inn
Cowgatehead
Magdalen Chapel
Victoria Street
Central Library
National Library of Scotland
Cowg
George Bridge
Candlemaker Row
Merchant St
Sheriff Court
Chan

Standard Life
Cambridge St.
Traverse Theatre
Usher Hall
Royal Lyceum
Cornwall St.
King's Stables Road
Lady Wynd
Argyle House
King's Stables La.
White Hart Inn
Grassmarket
Apex International
Brown's
Greyfriars Bobby
Greyfriars Kirk
Greyfriars Pl.
National of.S
Bristo Port

Festival Square
Grindlay Street
Spittal Street
Spittal St La.
Western Bar
Lady Lawson St.
West Port
Edinburgh College of Art
George Heriot's
Forrest Hill
Bedlam Theatre
Oddfellows Hall
Bristo Pl.
Teviot Place

The Filmhouse
Cineworld Parking
Main Point
Bread Street
Bread St Nth Ln.
Point
Royal Mail HQ
High Riggs
Lauriston Street
Lothian & Borders Fire Brigade HQ
Heriot Place
Keir Street
McEwan Hall
University M School
Char

ABC Cinema
Semple Street
East Fountainbridge
Riego St.
Gilmore Park
Lauriston Place
Lawson Street
Chalmers
Blood Donor Centre
Lauriston Terr.
Lauriston Place
Georg
Edin

Thornybauk
Dunbar St.
Glen Street
Earl Grey St.
Ponton St.
Tollcross
Tollcross
Brou
Lauriston Park
Simpsons
Princess Alexandra Eye Pavilion
Royal Infirmary
Archibald Pl.

Index to Numbered Close Names

#	Name	#	Name
1	Mylne's Court	29	Paisley Close
2	Anderson's Close	30	Chalmer's Close
3	James Court	31	South Gray's Close
4	Riddell's Close	32	Hyndford's Close
5	Lady Stair's Close	33	Trunk's Close
6	Fisher's Close	34	Fountain Close
7	Wardrop's Court	35	Baron Maule's Close
8	Advocate's Close	36	Tweeddale Court
9	Warriston's Close	37	World's End Close
10	Barrie's Close	38	Gullan's Close
11	Craig's Close	39	Pirrie's Close
12	Borthwick's Close	40	Chessel's Court
13	Old Assembly Close	41	Old Playhouse Close
14	Anchor Close	42	Gladstone Court
15	Covenant Close	43	Sugar House Close
16	Burnet's Close	44	Hammermen's Entry
17	Old Stamp Office Close	45	Bakehouse Close
18	Bell's Wynd	46	Wilson's Court
19	Lyon's Close	47	Bull's Close
20	New Assembly Close	48	Dunbar's Close
21	Jackson's Close	49	Crighton's Close
22	Stevenlaw's Close	50	Little Lochend Close
23	Fleshmarket Close	51	Lochend Close
24	Hastie's Close	52	Campbell's Close
25	Carrubber's Close	53	Reid's Close
26	North Gray's Close	54	Vallence's Entry
27	Morrison's Close	55	White House Close
28	Bailie Fyfe's Close		

Sealcarr Street

Chestnut Street

West Shore Road

West Harbour

EH5 1

New Broompark

Granton Park Avenue

West Granton

Gran

Lidl P

West Granton Road

Queensberry

Granton

Wardieburn

Wardieburn Road

Blackadd

Caroline Pk. Grv.

Royston Mains Close

Royston Mains Green

Pilton Drive North

Wardieburn Gdns.

Water Front
Redevelopment Area

West Granton Road

Granton Mains Wynd

Granton Mains E.

Royston Mains Street

Royston Mains Avenue

Royston Mains Crescent

West Pilton March

Royston Mains Place

Granton
Mains Bank

Granton
Mains Gait

Granton
Mains Vale

Granton
Mains Brae

Granton
Mains Court

Granton Mains Avenue

Crewe Road North

Crewe

Royston

Boswall Parkway

Pilton Drive

Pilton Park

Pilton

West Pilton Drive

West Pilton Loan

West Pilton Green

West Pilton Terrace

West Pilton Rd.

Crewe Bank

Royston

Crewe Crescent

Pilton Place

Pimiehall

West Pilton Lea

West Pilton Street

West Pilton Gdns.

Ferry Road Drive

Crewe Road West

Crewe Loan

Crewe Place

Crewe Grove

Crewe Terrace

Pilton Loan

Pilton Cres.

Pilton Bank

West Pilton Crossway

Craigmuir

4 4

West
Pilton Rise

West Pilton

West Pilton Park

West Pilton Neighbourhood Centre

P

Inchcolm
Court

Inchgarvie
Court

Inch.

Place

West Pilton

Pilton Avenue

EH

Telford

Crewe

Ainslie Park
Leisure Centre

Pilton Dr.

Pilton Park

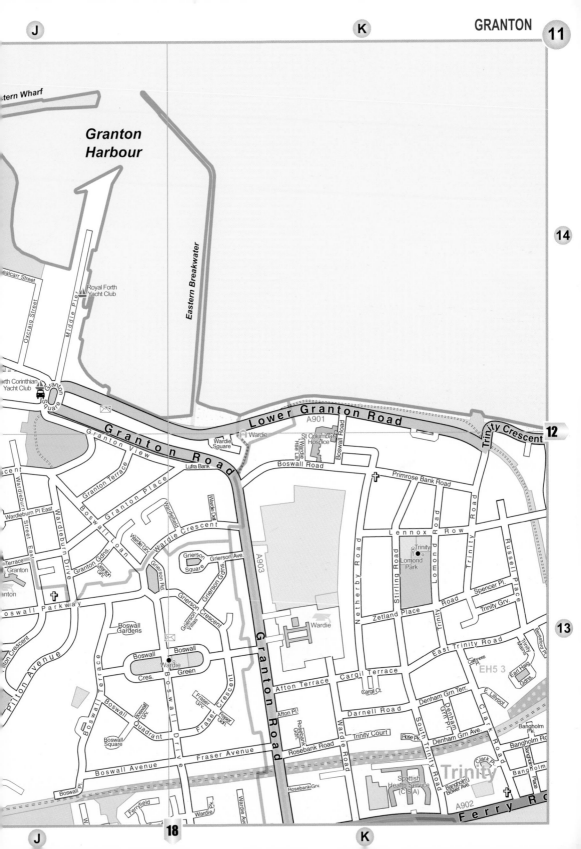

Eastern Wharf

Granton Harbour

Royal Forth Yacht Club

Sealcarr Street

Oxcraig Street

Middle Pier

Eastern Breakwater

North Corinthian Yacht Club

Granton Square

Lower Granton Road

A901

Trinity Crescent

Wardie Square

Wardie

St Columba's Hospice

Wardie Hse La.

Boswall Road

Primrose Bank Road

Granton View

Granton Road

Lufra Bank

Boswall Road

Granton Terrace

Granton Place

Lennox Row

Lomond Road

Trinity Road

Russell Place

Wardieburn Pl East

Wardieburn Street East

Boswall Loan

Granton Drive

Wardiefield

Wardle Cr.

Wardie Crescent

Marine Dr.

Netherby Road

Stirling Road

Trinity

Lomond Park

A903

Crescent

Terrace

Granton

Granton Gdns.

Granton Crescent

Grierson Square

Grierson Ave.

Grierson Gdns.

Spencer Pl.

Trinity Grv.

Boswall Parkway

Grierson Rd.

Grierson Crescent

Grierson Villas

Zetland Place

Trinity Road

Appleton Avenue

Boswall Crescent

Boswall Terrace

Boswall Gardens

Boswall Green

Wardie

Cargil Terrace

Cargil Ct.

East Trinity Road

Caithness

Earl Haig Gdns.

EH5 3

Boswall Cres.

Wardie Green

Boswall Gro.

Afton Terrace

Darnell Road

Denham Grn Terr.

Denham Grn Pl.

Bangholm Pk.

Boswall Square

Boswall Quadrant

Fraser Grv.

Fraser Crescent

Afton Pl.

Rosebank Gdn.

South Trinity Road

Denham Grn Ave.

Bangholm Ter.

Boswall Drive

Fraser Avenue

Rosebank Road

Wardie Road

Trinity Court

Rose Pk.

Denham Grn Ave.

Clark Road

Bangholm

Boswall Avenue

Rosebank Grv.

Trinity

Bangholm Bower Ave.

Fernfield

Wardie Pk.

Wardie Ave.

Scottish Health Service (CSA)

A902

Ferry Rd

14

12

13

L

M

14

Western Harb

Next
Generation
Club

Travel
Inn

Brewers
Fayre

Newhaven

EH6 6

P

Newhaven
Harbour

Harry
Ramsden's

Newhaven
Heritage
Museum

P

Chancelot
Mills

Cruise Ship
Terminal

The F
Royal
Brita

P

Britannia
Visitor Centre

Pier Place

Fishmarket
Sq.

Newhaven Place

11

Starbank Road

A901

Newhaven Main Street

Peacock

Victoria

Annfield Terr.

Ocean Drive

North Leith Sands

Andrew
Wood
Ct.

Willowbank

Row

Whale Brae

Michael's Brae

New La.

Annfield Street

A901

Lindsay Road

Laverockbank
Ave

Laverockbank Cres.

Archer's
Brae

Park Road

Derby St.

Jessfield Terr.

Hawthornvale

Lindsay Rd

Lindsay St.

Portland St.

Laverockbank
Gdn.

Park Rd

Park Pl.

South
Pk.

Belvedere
Pk.

Stanley Road

Dudley Bank

Nth Hillhousefield

Bathfield

Hamburn

Portland

Laverockbank Terrace

Giraffield Road

Mayville
Grv.

Mayville
Gdn.

Mayville
Grv.
South

West
Cherrybank

Dudley Crescent

Dudley

Dudley Grv.

Knoxland

Cannon Wynd

Fort House

North Fort Street

Lindsay Pl.

Argyle St.

Hopefield Terr.

Laverockbank
Grv.

Roseville Gdns.

Craighall Cres.

Trinity Academy

Trinity

Dudley Terr.

Dudley Gardens

Newhaven Road

EH6 4

Fort

Hawthornbank

Newton St.

Lapicide Pl.

Madeira St.

Prince Regent St.

East Trinity Road

Cromwell Gdns.

Granville

Grandfield

Craighall Gardens

Victoria Park

Summerside

Summerside Place

Summerside Street

Dudley Ave. Sth

Industry La.

Madeira Pl.

Thomas
Morton
Hall

13

Beresford Ave.

Beresford Gdns.

Lixmount Ave.

Lixmount Gdns.

Craighall Rd

Craighall Terr.

Holy
Cross

Trinity
Academy
Annex

Victoria
Park

A-Haven
Townhouse

Ferry Road

Trafalgar
Lane

South Fort Street

Ferry Road

Clar
Tartar
Cent

Clark Avenue

Bangholm
View

Bangholm
Grv.

Gosford Place

Victoria Park

Bonnington Terr.

Trafalgar St.

Pitt Street

West Bowling Green Street

Bangholm
Loan

Bangholm
Villas

Bangholm La.

Chancelot Terr.

Bonar
Pl.

Connaught Place

Agnew Terr.

Bonnington Grove

Mulberry Pl.

Graham St.

W. Ferry Rd

Chancelot
Cres.

Dalmeny Road

Newhaven Rd

Bonnington Ave.

Anders

Connaught Pl.

Whitingford

Milnacre

Water of Leith

19

L

M

14

Leith Docks

Imperial Dock

Ocean Terminal
(Opens 2001)

Ocean Drive

Victoria Dock

Albert Dock

Scot FM

EH6 7

Edinburgh Dock

Victoria Quay

Scottish
Executive

P

Malmaison

P

Tower Pl

Tower Street

Lorne

Commercial Street

A199

Sandport

Dock Place

Shore

Timber
Bush

Timber Bsh

Citadel
Court

Dock Street

Bernard St.

Baltic St.

Coburg   Street

Quayside St

Sandport Place

Cornwall Wynd

Shore

Sandport St

Seaport St

Robert
Burns

Broad Wynd

Portugal
Place

Assembly St

Cadiz St

Salamander   Street

A199

Rose
Garden

Sheriff Pl
Mill Lane
Sheriff
Bank

Mill Lane

Sheriff Brae

Parliament St

Henderson Street

Water St

Maritime
Lane

Maritime

Queen
Charlotte
Lane

Cadiz St

Coburg St

Bath Road

Poplar Lane

Salamander Place

Carron Pl

Great Junction Street

Cables Wynd

Giles Street

Henderson St

Toibooth Wynd

Shore Pl

Scotch Malt
Whisky Society

Gaits St

Spiers Street

Kirkgate

Queen
Charlotte St

Johns La.

Coalhill La.

Constitution Street

A900

Mitchell St.

Leith
'D' Division HQ

Bernard St

Johns Place

Links Place

Links Gdns La.

Links Gdns

Yardheads

Anthony St

Junction Pl

Anthony
St

Corving Pl

Leith Victoria

P

Leith Links

Carmore

McNair

Links

A901

20

M   N

13

East Craigie Farm

River Almond

Scotland

A90

Cramond
Bridge
Cotts.

Cramond Brig Toll

Cramond
Brig

P

Dowie's Mill Lane

Inveralmond
Gate

Inveralmond Drive

Cra

Peggy's Mill Road

Avon Road

Avo

Grv.

Avon Place

Essex Rd.

Essex Road

Essex Brae

Essex Rd.

Essex Pk.

Essex Road

Temple's Cran'

Ewerland

Brae Park

Brae Park Road

Cara

Braehead
Cres.

Braehead Drive

Braehead
Row

Almond
Court
West

Almond
Court
East

Braehead
Pk.

Avenue

Braehead Drive

Braehead Loan

Braehead Grove

Braehead View

Br

Queensferry R

A90

Braehead Road

Road

almond Road

Strathalmond
Green

Strathalmond
Court

almond Park

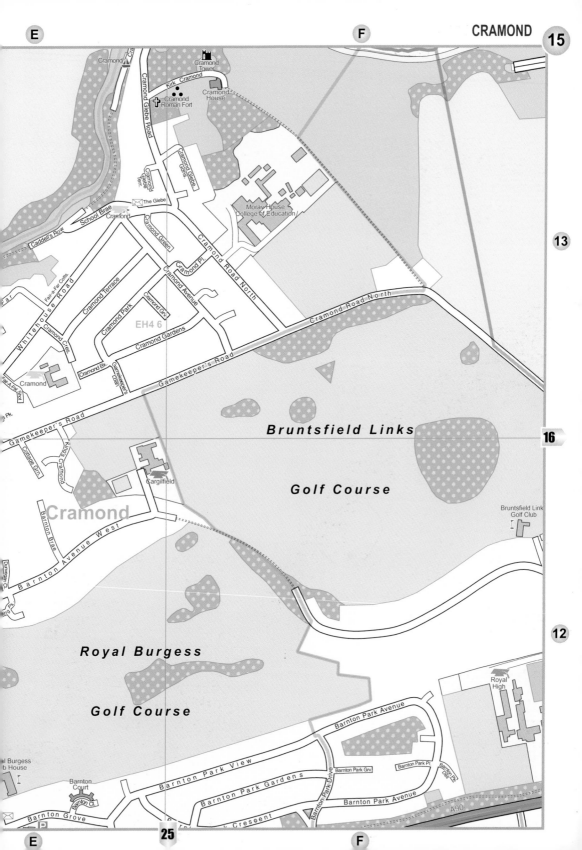

Cramond
Cramond Tower
Kirk Cramond
Cramond House
Cramond Roman Fort
Cramond Glebe Road
Cramond Glebe Terr.
Cramond Glebe
Cramond Glebe Gdns.
The Glebe
School Brae
Cramond
Caddell's Row
Cramond Green
Cramond Pl.
Cramond Road North
Moray House College of Education
Whitehouse Road
Fair-a-Far Cotts
Cramond Rd
Cramond Terrace
Cramond Park
Cramond Cres.
Cramond Avenue
Cramond Grn.
EH4 6
Cramond Gardens
Cramond Bk.
Gamekeeper's Loan
Cramond
Gamekeeper's Road
Cramond Road North

Gamekeeper's Road

Bruntsfield Links

Kings Cramond
Cottage Grn.
Cargilfield

Golf Course

Bruntsfield Link Golf Club

Barnton Brae
Cramond
Barnton Avenue West
Donegal Ct.
Barnton

Royal Burgess

Golf Course

Royal High
Barnton Park Avenue
Royal Burgess Club House
Barnton Court
Barnton Ct.
Barnton Park View
Barnton Park Grv.
Barnton Park Pl.
Barnton Park Gardens
Barnton Park Drive
Barnton Park Avenue
Barnton Grove
A90
Crescent

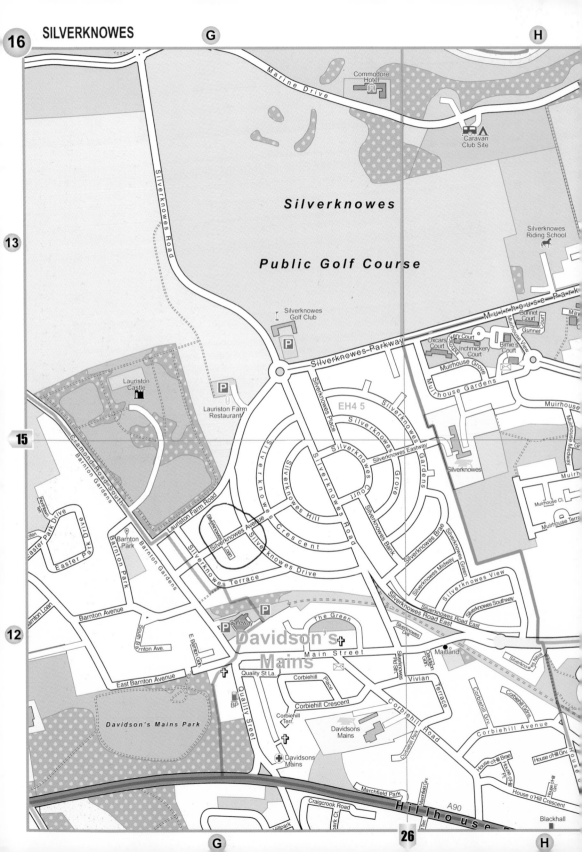

G

H

13

15

12

G

H

26

Marine Drive

Commodore Hotel

Caravan Club Site

Silverknowes

Public Golf Course

Silverknowes Riding School

Silverknowes Road

M·u·i·r·h·o·u·s·e·-·P·a·r·k

Silverknowes Golf Club

Silverknowes-Parkway

Oxcars Court

Inchmickery Court

Gunnet Court

Gunnet

Muirhouse View

May

Birnie's Court

Muirhouse Grove

Muirhouse

EH4 5

Silverknowes Place

Silverknowes Court

Silverknowes Grove

Silverknowes Road

Silverknowes Eastway

Silverknowes Gardens

Muirhouse Gardens

Silverknowes

Muirhouse Medway

Muirh

Lauriston Castle

Lauriston Farm Restaurant

Cramond Road South

Barnton Gardens

Silverknowes Hill

Silverknowes Co

Silverknowes Bank

Muirhouse Cl.

Muirhouse Terra

Silverknowes Avenue

Silverknowes Loan

Silverknowes Drive

Silverknowes Crescent

Silverknowes Brae

Silverknowes Midway

Silverknowes Green

Silverknowes View

Northlaw Terr.

Easter Park Drive

Park Drive

Lauriston Farm Road

Barnton Park

Barnton Gardens

Silverknowes Terrace

Silverknowes Road East

Silverknowes Road East

Silverknowes Southway

Garden

Barnton Avenue

E Barnton Gdn.

The Green

Silverknowes Dr.

Silverknowes Neuk

Barnton Loan

Sth. Barnton Ave.

Safeway

BP

E Barnton Avenue

Quality Street

Quality St La.

Davidson's Mains

Main Street

Corbiehill Place

Corbiehill Crescent

Corbiehill Terr.

Maitland

Davidson Gait

Vivian Terrace

Corbiehill Road

Corbiehill Gns.

Corbiehill Gro.

Corbiehill Avenue

Davidson's Mains Park

Davidsons Mains

Davidsons Mains

Corbiehill Park

Craigcrook Road

Marchfield Park

Marchfield Gve.

Hillpark

Craigcrook Pl.

House o'Hill Brae

House o'Hill Grv.

House o'Hill Pl.

House o'Hill Gdn.

House o'Hill Crescent

House o'Hill R

Blackhall

H·i·l·l·h·o·u·s·e

A90

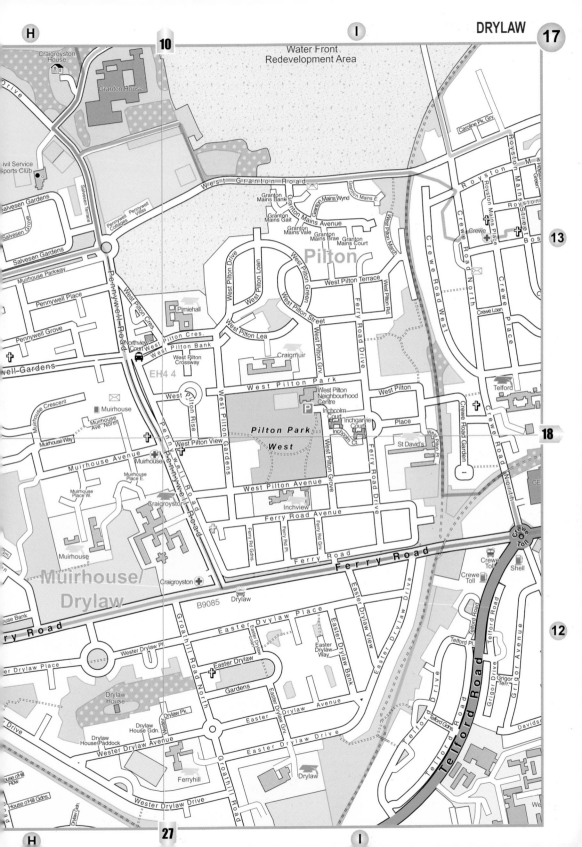

BOSWALL

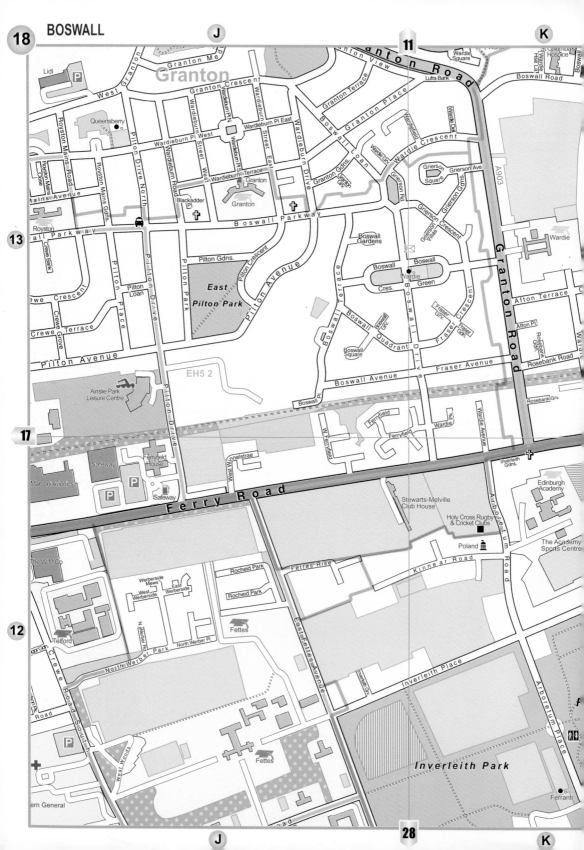

Granton

Lidl

Queensberry

West Granton

Granton Mey

Granton Crescent

Royston Mains Road

Royston Mains Gdns.

Royston Mains Close

Mains Avenue

Pilton Drive North

Wardieburn Pl. North

Wardieburn Street West

Wardieburn Pl West

Wardieburn Road

Wardieburn Terrace

Wardieburn Pl East

Wardieburn Street East

Wardieburn Drive

Granton View

Granton Terrace

Granton Place

Boswall Loan

Granton Gdns.

Granton Gdns.

Wardiefield

Wardie Cres.

Wardie Grv.

Wardie Crescent

Grierson Rd.

Grierson Crescent

Grierson Gdns.

Grierson Square

Grierson Ave.

Grierson Villas

Wardie Dell

GRANTON ROAD

A903

Boswall Road

Lufra Bank

Wardie Square

St Columba's Hospice

Wardie

Blackadder Pl.

Granton

Granton

Boswall Parkway

13

Royston

Crewe Bank

Crewe Crescent

Pilton Place

Pilton Loan

Pilton Gdns.

Pilton Crescent

East Pilton Park

Pilton Drive

Pilton Avenue

Boswall Gardens

Boswall Terrace

Boswall Terrace

Boswall Quadrant

Boswall Square

Boswall Pl.

Boswall

Boswall Green

Boswall Cres.

Wardie

Boswall Grv.

Boswall Drive

Fraser Crescent

Fraser Grv.

Fraser Grv.

Afton Terrace

Wardie

Afton Pl.

Rosebank Cres.

Rosebank Road

Rosebank Grv.

Crewe Grove

Crewe Terrace

Pilton Avenue

EH5 2

Ainslie Park Leisure Centre

Boswall Avenue

Fraser Avenue

Wardie Avenue

Wardie Pk.

17

W. Ferryfield

Ferryfield

Ferryfield

Inverleith Gdns.

Crynelstrae

West

Safeway

Ferryfield House

Marconi Avionics

Safeway

Edinburgh Academy

Ferry Road

Stewarts-Melville Club House

Holy Cross Rugby & Cricket Clubs

Poland

The Academy Sports Centre

Arboretum Road

The W M Co

Werberside Mews

West Werberside

East Werberside

Rocheid Park

Rocheid Park

Fettes Rise

Kinnear Road

Inverleith Place

12

Telford

N. Werber Rd.

North Werber Pl.

North Werber Park

Fettes

East Fettes Avenue

Inverleith Grv.

Inverleith Place

Arboretum Place

Crewe Road South

West Woods

Fettes

Inverleith Park

Ferranti

Western General

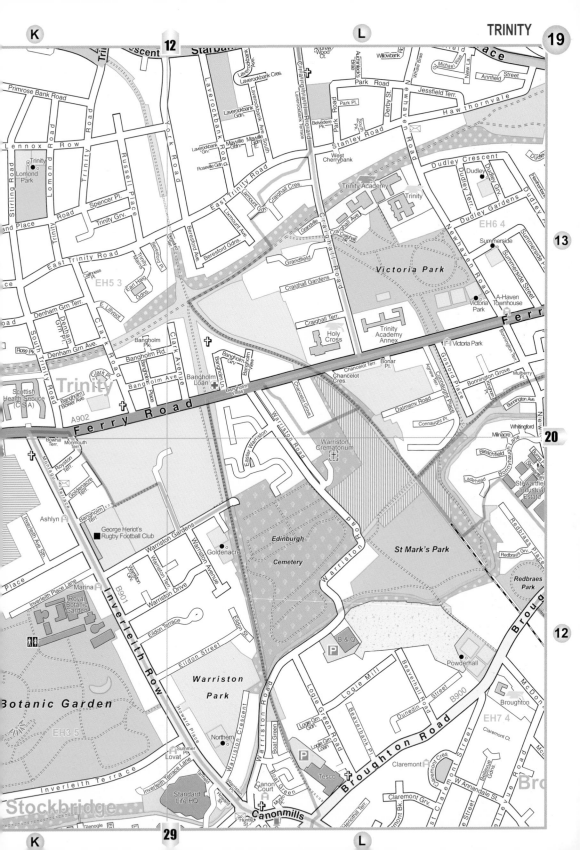

Primrose Bank Road

Trinity Road

Starbank

Laverockbank Cres.

Park Road

Willowbank

Michael's

New La.

Annfield Street

Laverockbank Ave.

Laverockbank Gdn.

Park Pl.

Derby St.

Jessfield Terr.

Hawthornvale

Lennox Row

York Road

Russell Place

Trinity Road

Belvedere Pk.

South Pk.

Stanley Road

Newhaven Road

Lomond Road

Spencer Pl.

Mayville Gdns.

Rosevale Gdns.

West Cherrybank

Trinity Academy

Trinity

Dudley Crescent

Dudley

Dudley Grv.

Dudley Gardens

Dudley Terr.

EH6 4

Trinity Grv.

Laverockbank Grv.

Beresford Ave.

Craighall Cres.

Lixmount Gdns.

Craighall Ave.

Craighall Bk.

Summerside

Summerside St.

East Trinity Road

Beresford Gdns.

Grandfield

Victoria Park

Summerside Pl.

EH5 3

Trinity Mains

Calmess Rd.

Earl Haig Gdns.

Craighall Gardens

Victoria Park

A-Haven Townhouse

Denham Grn Terr.

E. Lillyput

Grandfield

Craighall Terr.

Holy Cross

Trinity Academy Annex

Victoria Park

Bonnington Terr.

Gosford Place

Bonnington Grove

Mulberry Pl.

Denham Grn Ave.

Bangholm Pk.

Bangholm Rd.

Bangholm Grv.

Bangholm View

Chancelot Terr.

Chancelot Cres.

Bonar Pl.

Connaught Place

Bonnington Ave.

Rose Pk.

Clark Road

Clark Avenue

Bangholm Loan

Bangholm Villas

Bangholm Ln.

Chancelot Grove

Dalmeny Road

Agnew Terr.

Connaught Pl.

Whitingford

Scottish Health Service (C S A)

Trinity

Bangholm Place

Bangholm Bower Ave.

Clark Rd.

Ferry Road

Milnacre

Bleachfield

Ferry

EH5 3

A902

Ferry Road

Warriston Crematorium

Ladehead

Stewartfield Industrial Estate

Bowhill Terr.

Monmouth Terr.

Royston Terr.

Easter Warriston

Warriston Road

20

Montagu Terrace

Goldenacre Terr.

Bangholm Terr.

Ashlyn

Inverleith Ave Sth.

George Heriot's Rugby Football Club

Warriston Gardens

Goldenacre

Warriston Terr.

Edinburgh Cemetery

Warriston Road

St Mark's Park

Redbraes Place

Redbraes Grv.

Place

Inverleith Place Lane

Marina

B901

Warriston Grv.

Warriston Drive

Warriston Avenue

Eldon Terrace

Eldon St.

Redbraes Park

12

Royal Botanic Garden

Inverleith Row

Eldon Street

B & Q

Powderhall

Broughton

Botanic Garden

Warriston Park

Northern

Warriston Crescent

Howard Place

Warriston Road

Boat Green

Logie Mill

Logie Green Road

Logie Gm Loan

Braeheaden Road

Braeheaden St.

Dunedin St.

B900

Broughton

McDon

EH7 4

EH3 5

Summer Pl.

Lovat

P

Canon Court

Boat Green

Tesco

Broughton Road

Claremont Cres.

Claremont Ct.

Claremont

Bellevue Gdns.

Inverleith Terrace

Inverleith Terrace Lane

Standard Life HQ

Canonmills

Huntly St.

Claremont Grv.

W Annandale St.

Bro

Stockbridge

Glenogle

29

13

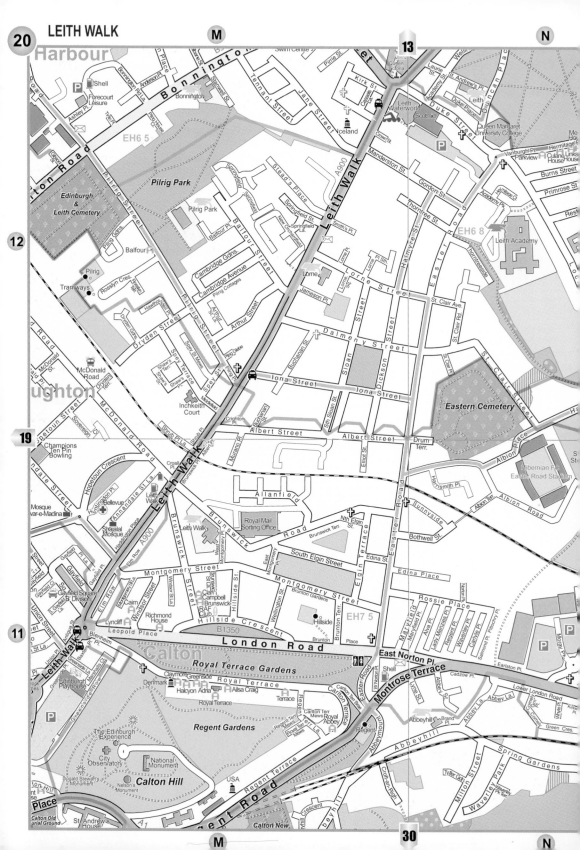

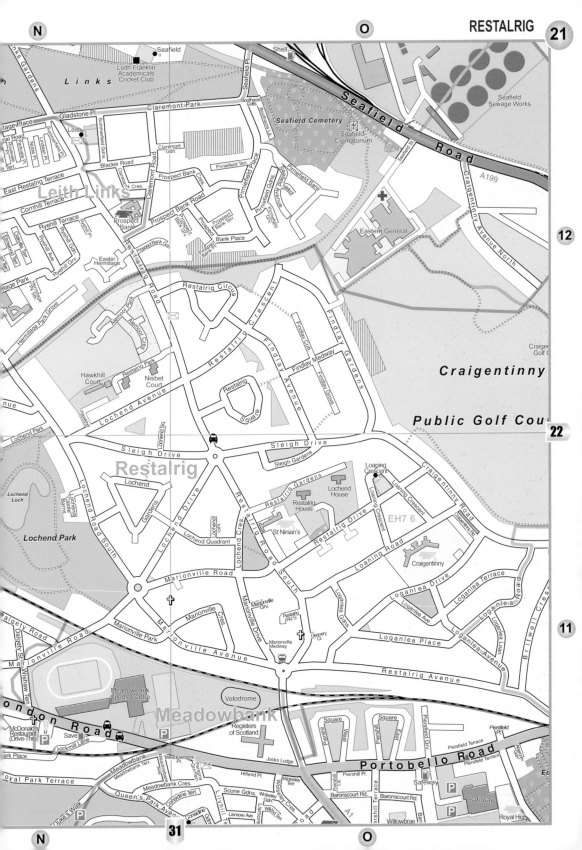

12

22

11

P Q

12

21

11

Seafield Recreation Ground

P

Matalan

Fillyside Road

Seafield Way

Edinburgh Cat & Dog Home

Fillyside Terrace

Fillyside Avenue

Nantwich Drive

Craigentinny Avenue

A199

Seafield Road East

Promenade

Stapeley Avenue

Craigentinny Road

Craigentinny Avenue

Christie Miller Avenue

Sydney Terrace

Sydney Pl.

Sydney Pk

Vandeleur Avenue

Vandeleur Pl.

Kekewich Avenue

Bryce Grv.

Bryce Avenue

Wakefield Avenue

Golf Avenue

Portobello

Craigentinny Crescent

Christie Miller Pl.

Christie Miller Grv.

Vandeleur Grv.

Craigentinny Grv.

Craigentinny

Craigentinny Pl.

Ellwyn

Moira Terr.

Moira Terrace

Moira Terrace

Moira Park

Inchview Terrace

Inchview Terrace

College Ct.

Portobello Road

Parker Avenue

Parker Road

Parker Terr.

Farrer Terrace

West Telferton

East Telferton

Bailiefield Road

Fishwives' Causeway

London Road Foundry

Fishwives' Causeway

Edinburgh & Portobello Cemetery

A1140

Mountcastle

Mount

King's Road

King's Pl.

Hillcoat Ln.

Hillcoat Pl.

Electra Pl.

Westbank Loan

Westbank Street

Westbank Place

Great Cannon Bank

Portobello Indoor Bowls Leisure Club

P

Pitz Five-a-Side

Jet

Bridge Street

William Jameson Pl.

Brickfield

Harbour Pl.

Law Pl.

Figgate

B6415

32

F i r t h   o f

F o r t h

12

11

Beach Lane
Tower Pl.
one.
Pagoda Bank
Sen 1
Towerbank
Mc Main
Wilson's Pl.
P r o m e

14

Cammo Crescent

Cammo Home Farm

Cammo Grove

Cammo Gardens

Cammo Hill

Cammo Bree

Cammo Parkway

Cammo Pl

Cammo Bank

Cammo Grove

EH4 8

Cammo Walk

P

Cammo Country Park

11

Lennie Hill

ouse

ourse

City of Edinburgh

Cammo Walk

Civic Amenity Site

Maybury Road

A902

North Bughtlin

Bughtlin Green

Bughtlin Dr

Bughtlin

Gdn

Bughtlin

Ln

Bughtlin

Havfield

Almond Grn

M-a y-b-u-r-y

Almond Sq.

Burr

10

Craigs Road

Scottish Agricultural Science Agency

Craigievar

Craigs Road

West Craigs

West Craigs Farm

Craigmount

Turnhouse Road

Meadowfield Farm

West Craigs Industrial Estate

Maybury Road

A902

North

N. Gvle

West Cr

ST JOHN BAPTIST

ST NINIANS ROAD

CORSTORPHINE

EH12 8AL

MASS 9.30

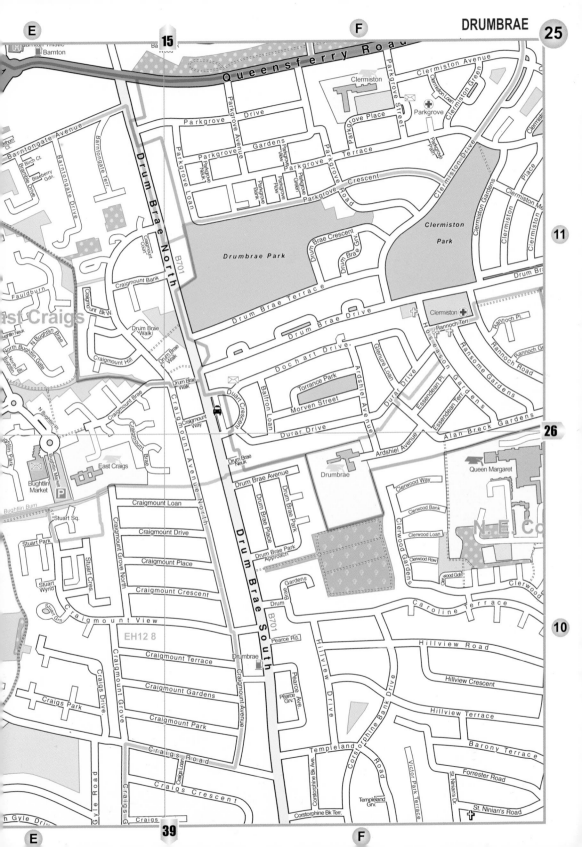

CORSTORPHINE HILL

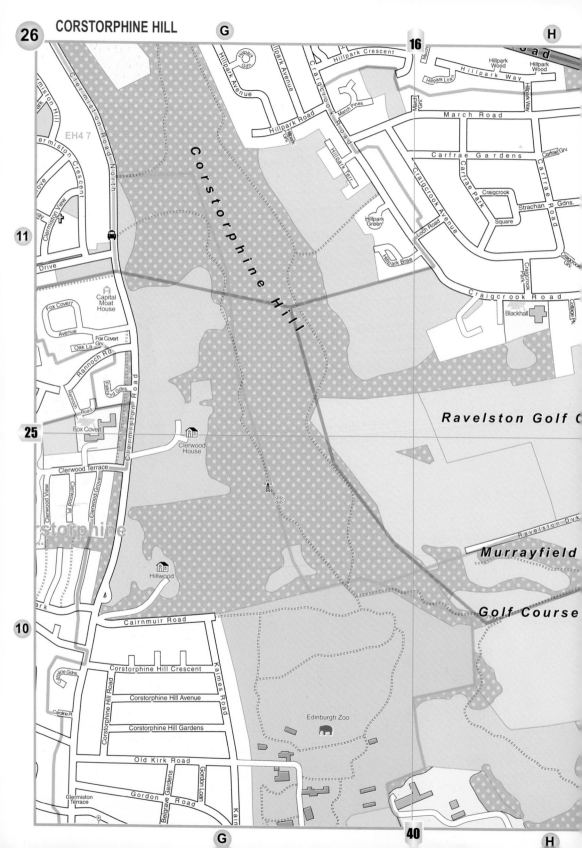

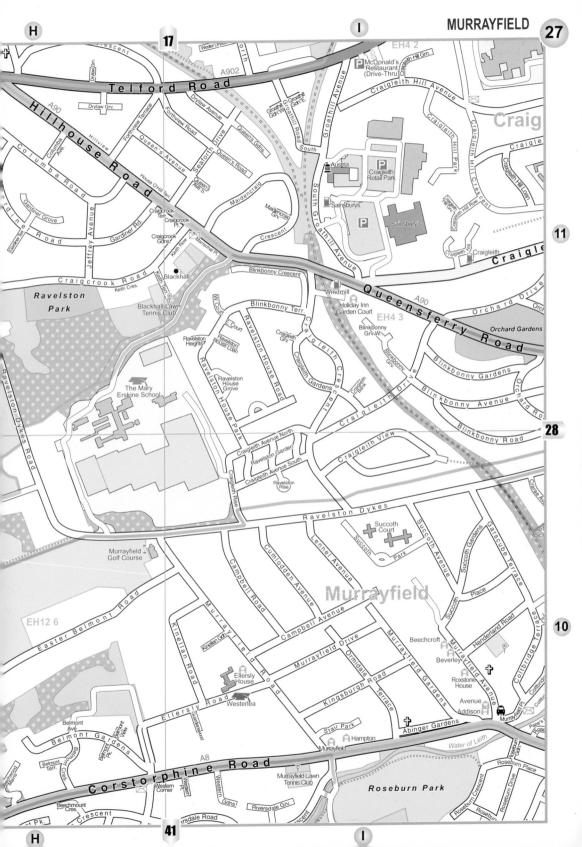

H   17   I

EH4 2

P McDonald's Restaurant (Drive-Thru)

Wester Drylaw Place North

A902

Telford Road

Craigleith Hill Avenue

Craigleith Hill Grn.

Craig

Drylaw Grn.

Drylaw Grv.

A90

Hillhouse Road

Drylaw Avenue

Forthview Terrace

Forthview Road

Hillview

House O'Hill Terr.

Seaforth Drive

Queen's Gdns.

Queen's Avenue

Queen's Road

Groathill Gdns. W.

Groathill Gdns. E.

Groathill Road South

Groathill Avenue

Craigleith Hill Park

Craigleith Hill Crescent

Craigleith Hill Loan

Craigle

Columba Road

Columba Ave.

Gardiner Grove

Gardiner Road

Jeffrey Avenue

Gardiner Rd.

Craigcrook Terr.

Craigcrook Pl.

Craigcrook Gdns.

Maidencraig Crescent

Maidencraig Grv.

Austria

P Craigleith Retail Park

Sainsburys

P Sainsbury's

Craigleith Hill Row

Craigleith

11

Keith Row

Marischal Pl.

Keith Cres.

Keith Terr.

Blackhall

Craigcrook Road

Blinkbonny Crescent

Windmill

Queensferry Road

A90

Orchard Drive

Orch

Ravelston Park

Blackhall Lawn Tennis Club

W. Court

Blinkbonny Terr.

E. Court

Blinkbonny Grv.

Holiday Inn Garden Court

EH4 3

Blinkbonny Grv. W.

Craigleith Crescent

Orchard Gardens

Ravelston Heights

Ravelston House Loan

Craigleith Grv.

Craigleith Gardens

Craigleith Bank

Blinkbonny Drive

Blinkbonny Gardens

Orchard Road

The Mary Erskine School

Ravelston House Grove

Ravelston House Road

Blinkbonny Avenue

28

Ravelston Dykes Road

Craigleith Avenue North

Ravelston Garden

Craigleith Avenue South

Ravelston Rise

Craigleith View

Blinkbonny Road

Ravelston Dykes

Succoth Court

Succoth Park

Succoth Gardens

Succoth Avenue

Garscube Terrace

St. Sch

Craigs Av.

Murrayfield Golf Course

Campbell Road

Cumlodden Avenue

Lennel Avenue

Succoth Place

Henderland Road

Coltbridge Terrace

10

EH12 6

Easter Belmont Road

Kinellan Road

Kinellan Gdns.

Murrayfield Road

Campbell Avenue

Murrayfield Avenue

Murrayfield Gardens

Beechcroft

Beverley

Murrayfield Avenue

Roxstone House

Coltb

Ellersly House

Westerlea

Ellersly Road

Gordon

Murrayfield Drive

Ormidale Terrace

Kingsburgh Road

Stair Park

Addison

Avenue

Murrayfield Pl.

Pape's

Belmont Ave.

Belmont Gardens

Belmont Pk.

Belmont View

Belmont Terr.

Bishop

Beechmount Mains

A8

Corstorphine Road

Western Corner

Western Gdns.

Abinger Gardens

Hampton

Murrayfield

Water of Leith

Roseburn Place

Roseburn

Beechmount Cres.

Crescent

Riversdale Road

Riversdale Grv.

Murrayfield Lawn Tennis Club

Roseburn Park

Roseburn Crescent

Roseburn Drive

St. Pk.

H   41   I

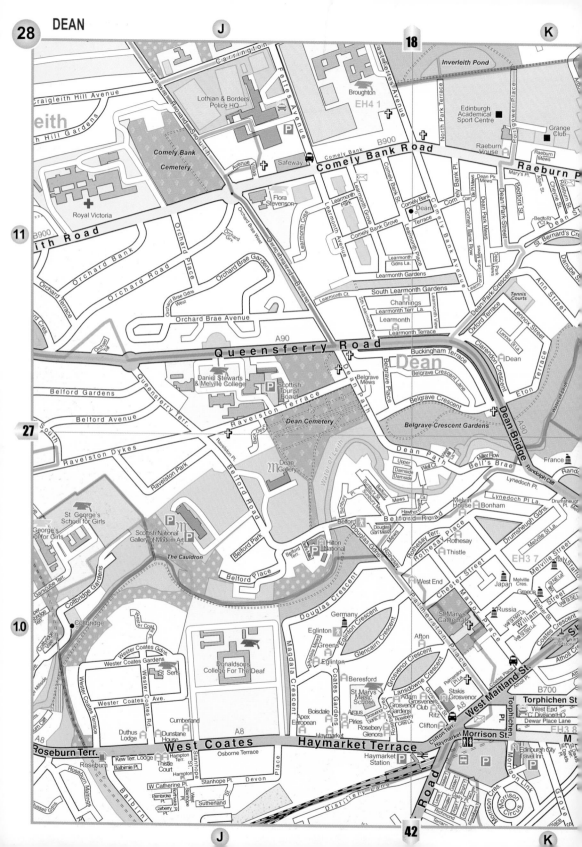

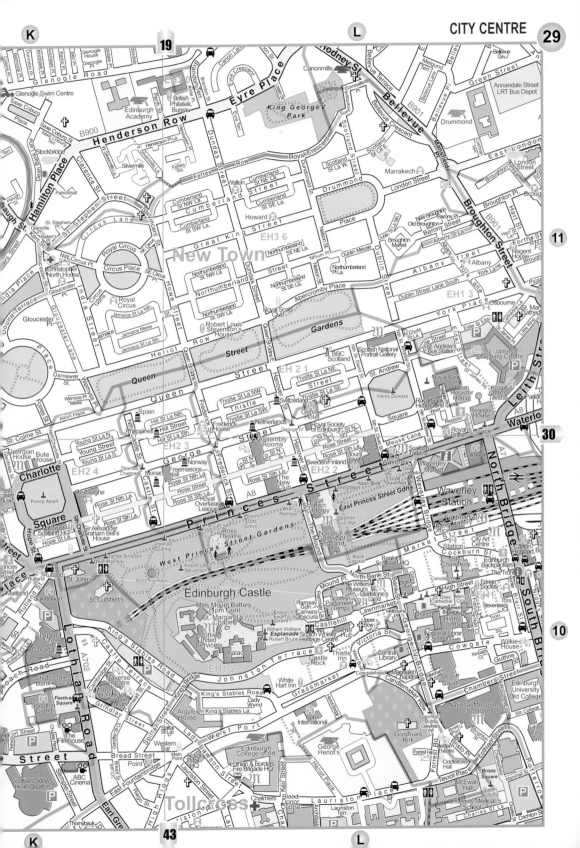

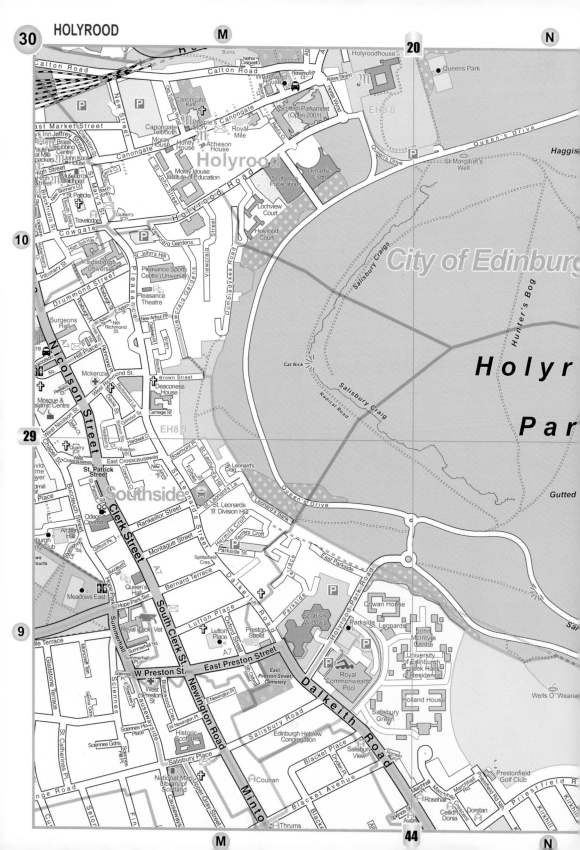

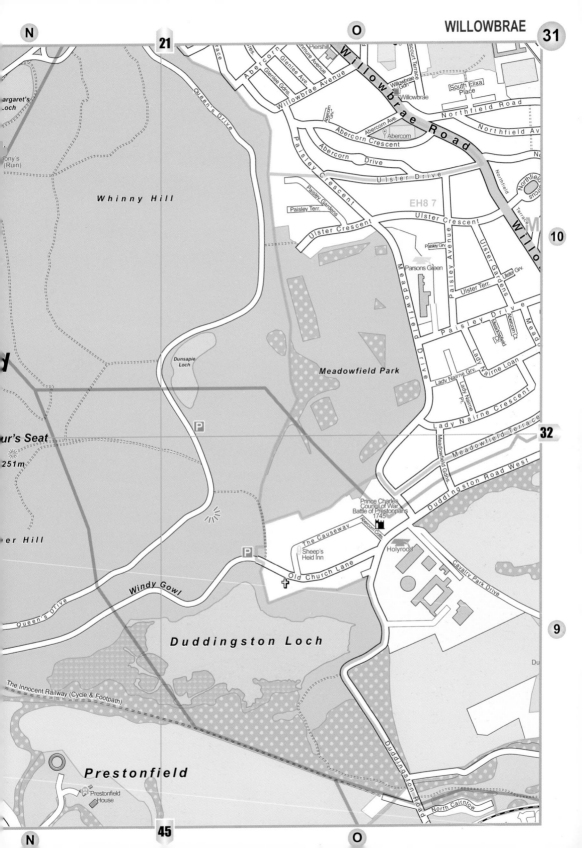

10

Margaret's
Loch

Tony's
(Ruin)

Whinny Hill

Piershill
South Terrace

Willowbrae
Scout Centre

Willowbrae

South Elixa
Place

Abercorn Terrace

Glenlee Ave

Glenlee Gdns

Willowbrae Avenue

Willowbrae Gdns

Abercorn Ave.

Abercorn Crescent

Abercorn Gro't

Abercom

Abercorn Drive

Willowbrae Road

Northfield Road

Northfield Av

Ulster Drive

Northfield

Northfield

Paisley Crescent

Queen's Drive

Paisley Gardens

Paisley Terr.

EH8 7

Ulster Crescent

Paisley Gardens

Ulster Crescent

Ulster Gardens

Willo

Paisley Grv.

Parsons Green

Meadowfield Drive

Paisley Avenue

Ulster Terr.

Ulster Grv.

Dunsapie
Loch

Meadowfield Park

Lady Nairne Grv.

Lady Nairne Loan

Paisley Drive

Abercorn Ct.

Meadowfield

Meadowd

P

Lady Nairne Pl.

Lady Nairne

Lady Nairne Crescent

ur's Seat

251m

Meadowfield Terrace

Meadowfield Gdns

32

Duddingston Road West

Prince Charles
Council of War
Battle of Prestonpans
1745

The Causeway

P

Sheep's
Heid Inn

Holyrood

Duddingston Road

Cavalry Park Drive

er Hill

Old Church Lane

Windy Gowl

9

Queen's Drive

Duddingston Loch

Du

The Innocent Railway (Cycle & Footpath)

Duddingston Road

Prestonfield

Prestonfield
House

North Cairntow

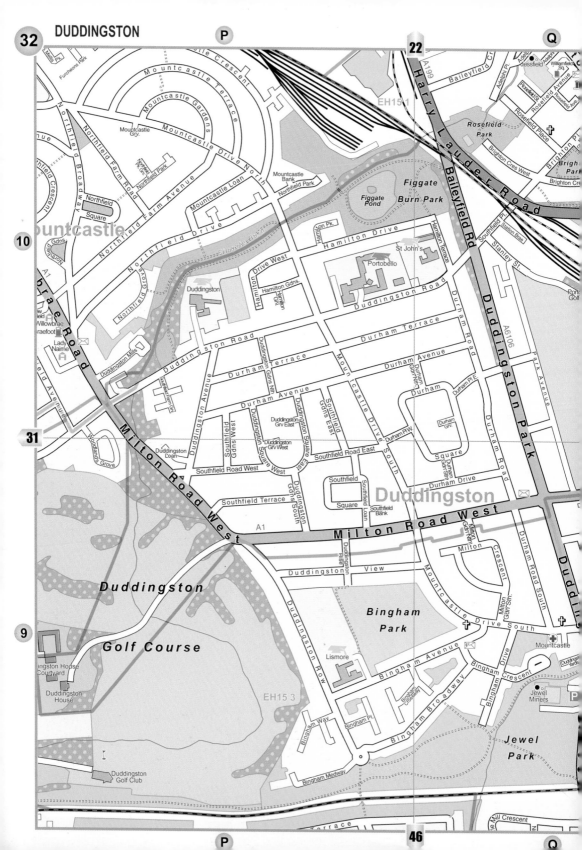

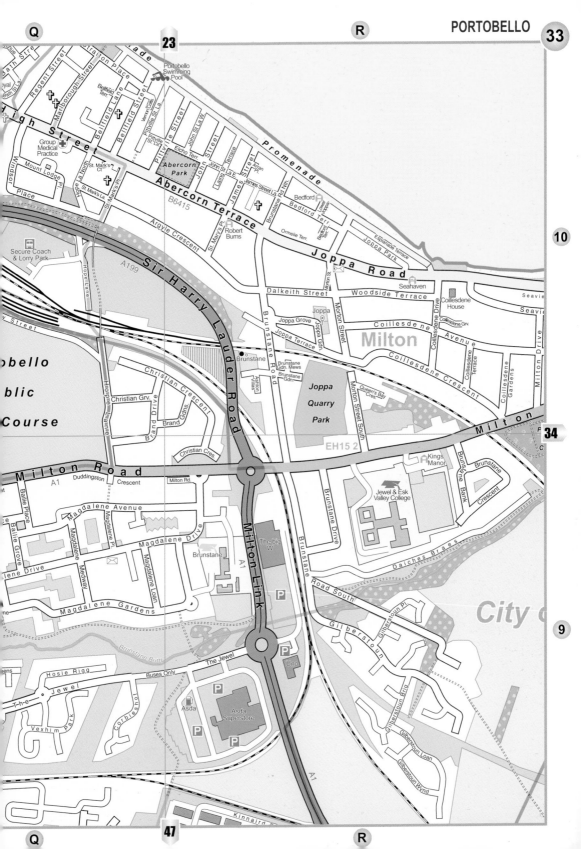

10

Firth

Joppa Pans Rockville

M u s s e l b u r g h   R o a d B6415

Terrace

w Crescent

Seaview

Eastfield

Coillesdene Avenue

Milton Terrace

Eastfield Gdns.

Terrace

Cassidy Pl

Coillesdene Loan

ene Loan

Milton Gn.

A199

oad East

R o a d   E a s t

E d i n b u r g h   R o a d A199

33

obello

metery

Bournstane Burn

Newhailes

Maitland Park Road

Maitland Avenue

Crescent

Maitland St

Newhailes Avenue

Dalrymple Cres.

P

Fishe

Har

Fi

Ya

Sh

of Edinburgh

Musselburgh

West

Newhailes
Mansion House
(NTS)

Fisherrow
Industrial
Estate

Bog Park Rd

A

F

9

A6095

N e w h a i l e s   R o a d

Stoneyhill Drive

Stoneyhill Ct.

Stoneyhill Terrace

Stoneyhill Gv.

Stoneyhill Rise

Stoneyhill Wynd

Stoneyhill Avenue

Stoneyhill Place

B

Mu
Ru

Claybowes Place

Claybowes Drive

Stoneybank Ga

Stoneyhill Cres.

Wanton
Walls Farm

Niddrie

Claybowes
Way

Whitehill Ave

Stoneybank Drive

t Newcraighall Rd.

Denholm Road

Claykn

Stoneyhill

10

F o r t h

lburgh North

Fisherrow Links

Fisherrow Links
Pitch & Putt

Musselburgh

Musselburgh Links
The Old Golf Course
(Public)

Goose Grn Pl

Goose Green Crescent

Goose Green Ave.

Balcarres Road

Balcarres Place

Goose Green Road

Mount Lothian Terrace

New Street

Musselburgh
Racecourse

Promenade
Clerks Row

Beach Lane

Bush St
Bush Terr.

Links Avenue

Links View

Links Street

Downie Place

Ladywell

Eskside Mews

Eskside East

James St.

Millhill Lane

Millhill

Loretto

New Street

New Street

Lochend Rd North

Fishers Wynd

Gracefield Crt

Watts La

Campie La

Loretto
Junior

North High Street

Eskside West

Kers Wynd

Musselburgh
Arms

Loretto

Orth HIGH STREET

Havelston
House

Lochend Rd South

South Street

Bridge Street

Ladywell Way

Eskbridge

A199

Save

Musselburgh

Newbigging

Musselburgh

Town Hall

Musselburgh

Market Street

Campie Gdn

Campie Road

Hercus Loan

West Holmes Gardens

Eskside West

Mall Avenue

Dalrymple Loan

Museum
of Dolls &
Art Exhibits

Musselburgh

Musselburgh
Burgh

Mansfield Road

Mansfield Pl.

Mansfield Avenue

Mansfield
Court

Kilwinning Place

Kilwinning St.

Kilwinning
Terrace

Newbigging

Loretto

Loretto

Wanless Court

King St.

9

Olive Bank
Park

Campie

Stoneyhill
Farm Road

Belfield Ave

Bellfield
Court

Eskside West

Inveresk
Road

Esk Mill
Villas

Station Road

Eskbank Road

Eskview Terrace

Eskview Avenue

Eskview Grove Road

Eskview
Crescent

Riverside Gdn

B6415

Station Road

Inveresk Road

A6124

Musselburgh

Rothesay Place

Newbigging

Pi

Michael's Avenue

Musselburgh
Sports Centre

Musselburgh

Musselburgh

Inveresk House

Inveresk Cemetery

Inveresk Village

Musselburg

Central

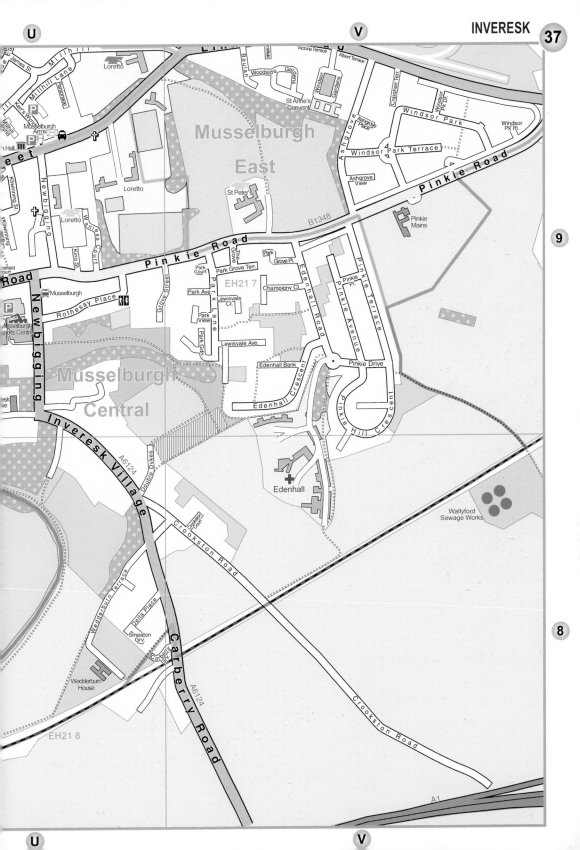

U V

9

8

Victoria Terrace
Albert Terrace
Beulah
Woodside
Windsor
Gardens
St Anne's
Convent
Craighall Terr.
Windsor
Pk. Pt.
Windsor Park
Ashgrove
Ashgrove
Place
Windsor
Pk. Pt.

Musselburgh
East

Windsor Park Terrace

Ashgrove
View

Pinkie Road

St Peter's

B1348

Pinkie
Mains

Loretto
Kers Wynd
James St.
Millhill Lane
Panmurepl

Millhill

P
Musselburgh
Arms
P PH
Hall

Kilwinning St.

Newbigging

King St.

Loretto

Loretto

Wanless Court

Road

Newbigging

P
Musselburgh
Sports Centre

Musselburgh

Rothesay Place

Grove Street

Pinkie Road

Park
Court
Park Grove Terr.
The
Grove
Park
Grove Pl.

EH21 7

Park Ave.

Park
Lane
Lewisvale
Ct.

Park
View

Champigny Ct.

Edenhall Road

Pinkie
Pl.

Pinkie Terrace

Pinkie Avenue

Park Gdn.

Lewisvale Ave.

Edenhall Bank

Pinkie Drive

Edenhall Crescent

Edenhall Crescent

Pinkie Hill Crescent

Pinkie Hill Crescent

Musselburgh

Central

Inveresk Village

A6124

Double Dykes

Edenhall

Wallyford
Sewage Works

Crookston Road

Wedderburn Terrace

Delta Place

Smeaton Gdv.

Carberry Gdv.

Carberry Road

A6124

Wedderburn
House

EH21 8

Crookston Road

A1

U V

D

E

West Craigs Avenue

The Courts Edge

Crescent

S Maybury

North Gyle Grove

N Gyle Terr

North Gyle Grove

N Gyle Farm Grove

North Gyle T

Maybury
Stakis Casino

Craigmount

Maybury

Gyle Park Gardens

9

EH12 9

Gogar Roundabout

Gogar Roundabout

Royal Scot

Great Mills DIY

The Gyle Centre

Gogarbrae Syke

Park Club

Gogar Park House

Gogar Burn

Gogarloch Syke

Gogarloch

P

South-Gyle-Broadway

Gogarloch

Scottish Equitable Head Office

Lochside

Redheughs Rigg

John Menzies

C-i-t-y B-y-p-a-s-s

A720

Lochside Avenue

Crescent

Redheughs Avenue

Ritz Bar & Grill

Lochside Place

Millburn Tower

Oracle

Midland Bank

Royal Bank of Scotland

British Energy

Bank

8

Gogar Station Road

Edinburgh Park
(Opens 2000)

Gogarburn Poultry Farm

D

E

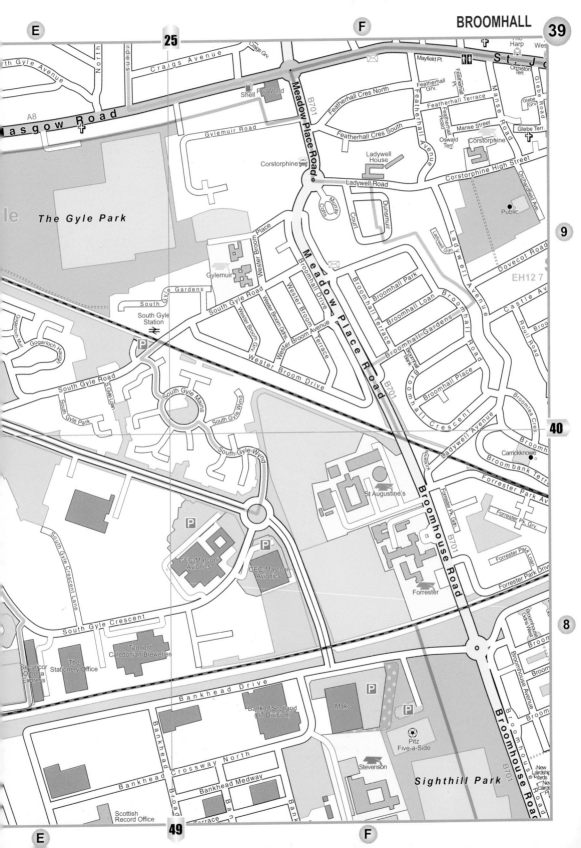

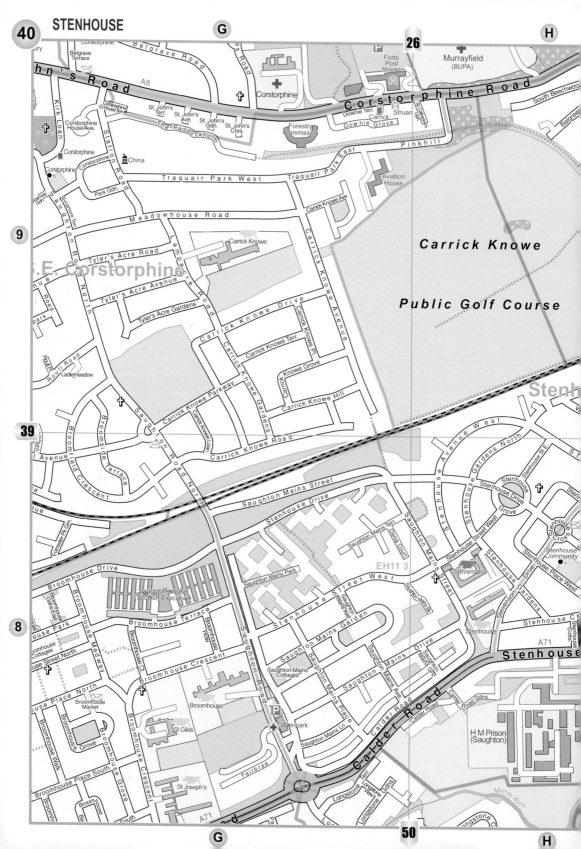

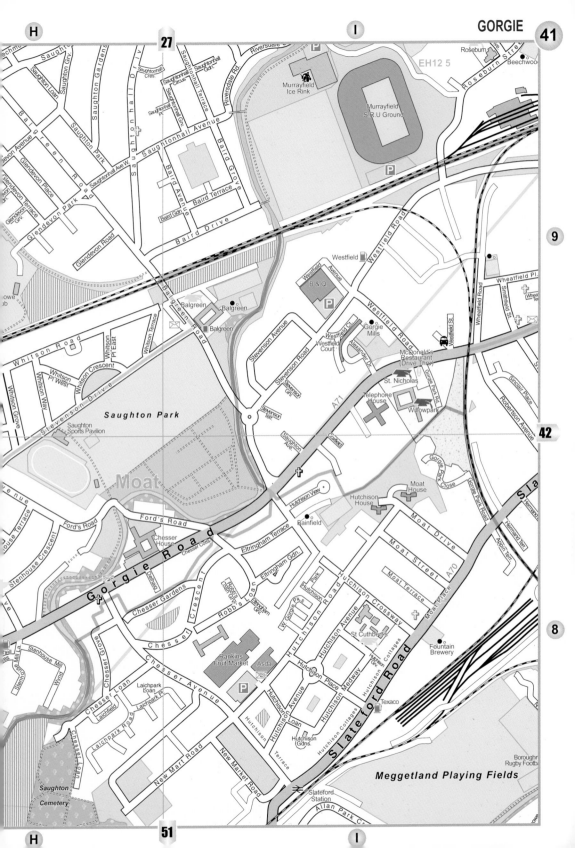

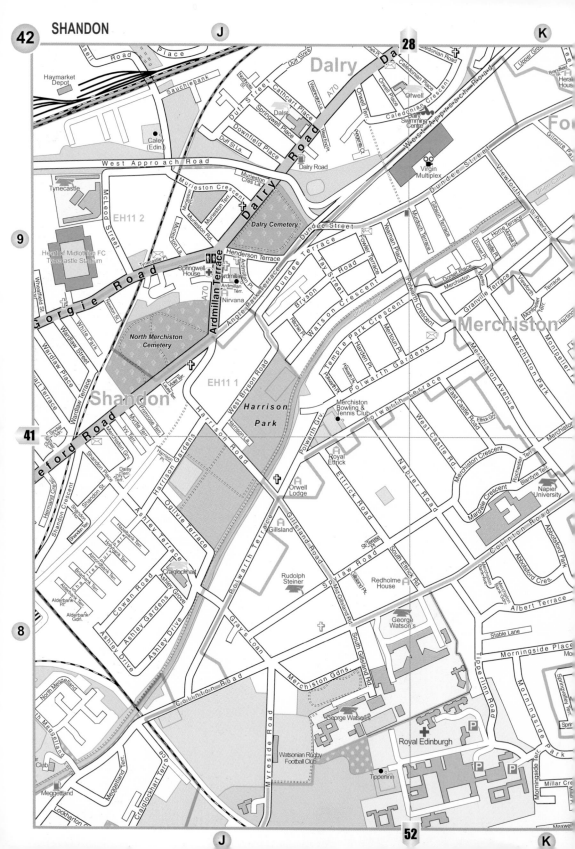

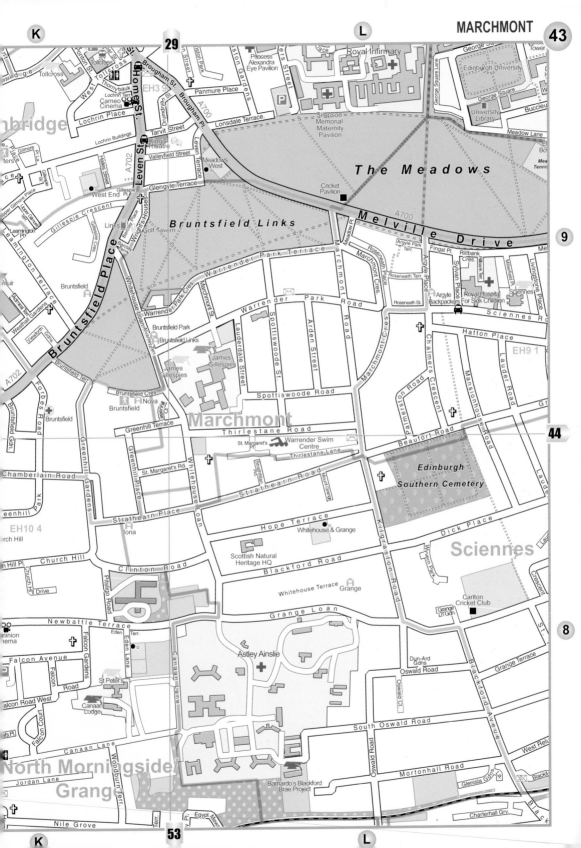

Tollcross
West Tollcross
Home St.
Brougham St.
Panmure Place
Lonsdale Terrace.
Princess Alexandra Eye Pavilion
Royal Infirmary
George St
Edinburgh University
George Square
University Library
Meadow Lane
Buccleu

Cameo Cinema
Thornybauk
Lochrin Terr.
Lochrin Place
Tarvit Street
Drumdryan
EH3 9
Leven St.
Simpson Memorial Maternity Pavilion

Lochrin Buildings
Gilmore Pl
King's Theatre
Valleyfield Street
Leven Terrace
Meadows West

West End Place
Glengyle Terrace
The Meadows

Gillespie Crescent
Gillespie Cres.
Golf Tavern
Wright's Houses
Cricket Pavilion

Leamington Ph
Links
Bruntsfield Links
Melville Drive
A700

Bruntsfield
Whitehouse Loan
Warrender Park Terrace
Argyle Park Terr.
Roseneath Place
Fingal Pl.
Rillbank Cres.
Black Terr.
Millerfield Pl.
Livingstone Place
Sciennes Pl

Westhall Gardens
Warrenderpark Cres.
Warrender Park
Marchmont St.
Marchmont Cres.
Roseneath Terr.
Roseneath St.
Argyle Place
Argyle Backpackers
Royal Hospital For Sick Children
Sciennes
Sciennes R

Forbes Road
Bruntsfield Terr.
Bruntsfield Park
Bruntsfield Links
Lauderdale Street
Warrender Park Road
Spottiswoode St.
Arden Street
Marchmont Road
Marchmont Cres.
Chalmers Crescent
Hatton Place
EH9 1
Lauder Road

A702
Bruntsfield Gdn.
Wrentham Cres.
James Gillespies
James Gillespies
Spottiswoode Road
Palmerston Road
Manslionhouse Road

Bruntsfield
Nova
Bruntsfield
Marchmont
Thirlestane Road
Beaufort Road
44

Greenhill Terrace
St. Margaret's
Warrender Swim Centre
Thirlestane Lane
Edinburgh Southern Cemetery

Chamberlain Road
Greenhill Gardens
Greenhill Place
St. Margaret's Rd.
Whitehouse Loan
Strathearn Road
Mount Grange
Dick Place

Greenhill Park
Strathearn Place
Iona
EH10 4
Church Hill
Hope Terrace
Whitehouse & Grange
Sciennes
Wyvern Park
Crescent

Church Hill Pl.
Church Hill Drive
Clinton Road
Pitsligo Road
Scottish Natural Heritage HQ
Blackford Road
Whitehouse Terrace
Grange
Carlton Cricket Club
Grange Ln Gdn
Kilgraston Road

8

Dominion Cinema
Newbattle Terrace
Falcon Gardens
Eden Terr.
Eden Lane
Canaan Lane
Astley Ainslie
Dun-Ard Gdns
Oswald Road
Grange Terrace
Blackford Avenue

Falcon Avenue
St Peter's
Canaan Lodge
Oswald Ct

Falcon Court
South Oswald Road
West Relu

Canaan Lane
Woodburn Terr.
North Morningside/
Grange
Barnardo's Blackford Brae Project
Mortonhall Road
Glenisla Gdns
Blackfor

Jordan Lane
Nile Grove
Egypt Mews
Charterhall Grv.

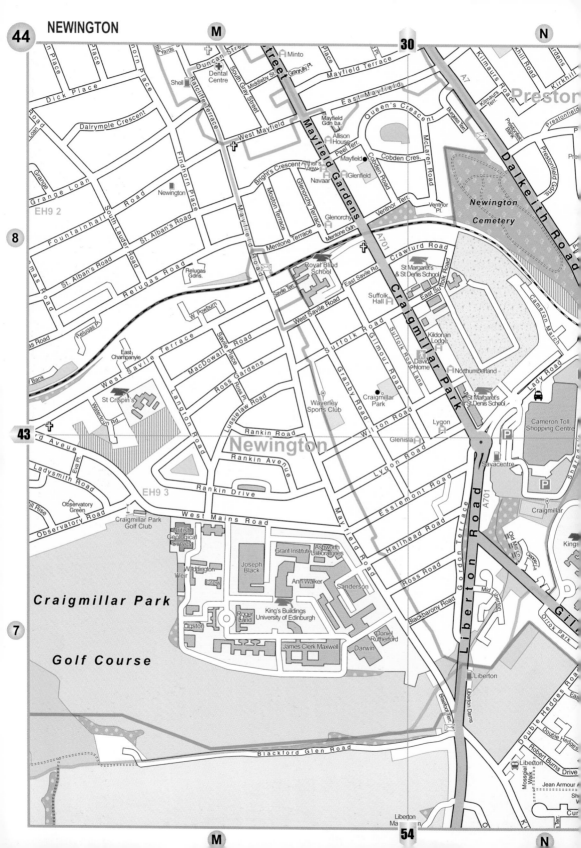

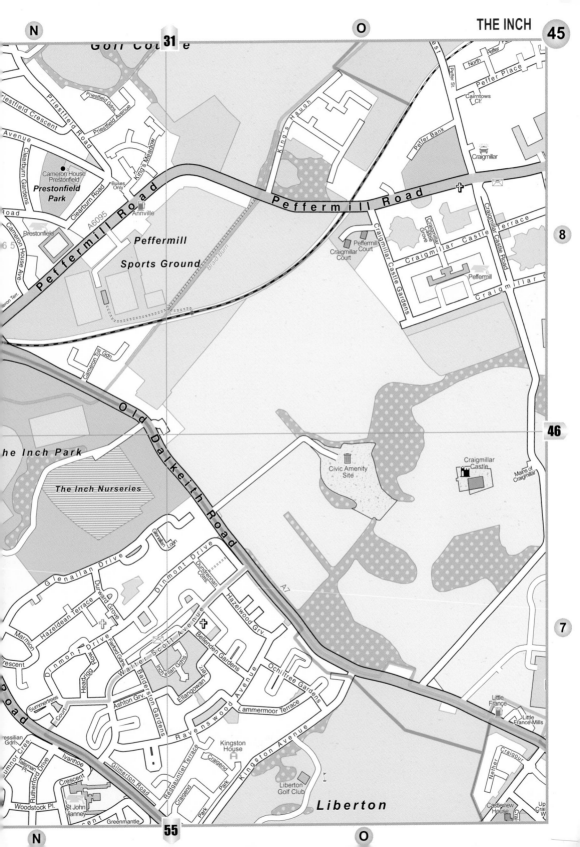

N

O

31

8

46

7

N

O

55

Golf Course

Priestfield Crescent

Priestfield Gdns.

Priestfield Road

Priestfield Avenue

King's Meadow

King's Haugh

Peffer St.

North

Peffer Place

Peffer

Cairntows Cl.

Craigmillar

Peffer Bank

Avenue

Clearburn Gardens

Cameron House
Prestonfield

Prestonfield Park

Clearburn Road

Buses Only

Peffermill Road

Craigmillar Castle Grove

Craigmillar Castle Terrace

Craigmillar Castle Road

Cameron House Ave.

A6095

Peffermill Road

Annville

Prestonfield

Craigmillar Court

Peffermill Court

Craigmillar Castle Gardens

Craigmillar Castle

Peffermill

Craigmillar

Cameron Terr.

Peffermill

Sports Ground

Brae Burn

Cameron Toll Gdn.

Old Dalkeith Road

The Inch Park

The Inch Nurseries

Civic Amenity Site

Craigmillar Castle

Mains of Craigmillar

Glenallan Drive

Glenallan Loan

Dinmont Drive

Dunedin Court

A7

Hazelwood Grv.

Marmion

Hazeldean Terrace

Dunwald Grove

Dinmont Drive

Headrigg Row

Walter Scott Avenue

Parkgrove

Inchlellan Gdns.

Bellenden Gardens

Ellangowan Road

Ochiltree Gardens

Little France

Little France Mills

Crescent

Summertrees

Court

Baldertston Gardens

Ashton Grv.

Ravenswood Avenue

Lammermoor Terrace

Kingston Avenue

Craigour

Netherby

Nether Craig

Cressilian Gdn.

Dunmore Cres.

Ivanhoe Crescent

Rutherford Drive

Telferton

Gilmerton Road

Redgauntlet Terrace

Craigend Park

Kingston House

Kingston Terrace

Liberton Golf Club

Castleview House

Upper Craig W.

Woodstock Pl.

St John Vianney

Greenmantle

Liberton

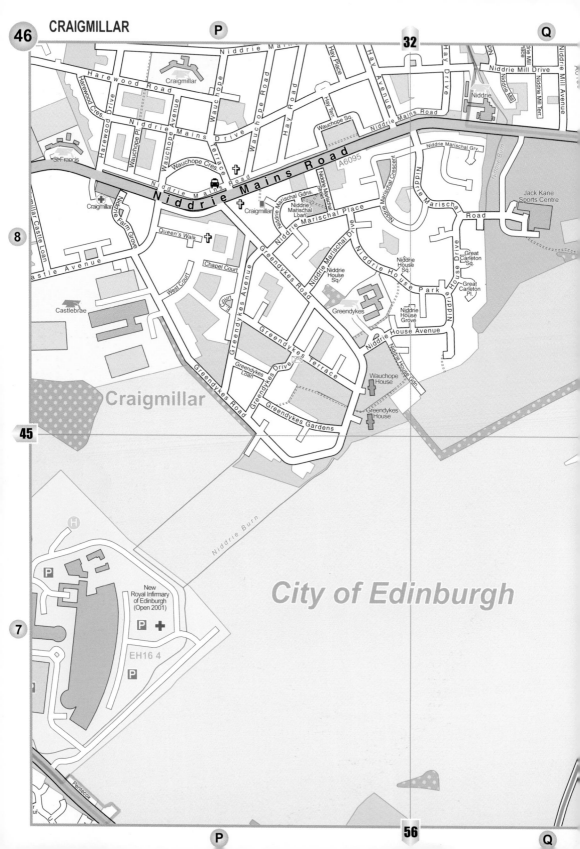

Q
R
33
8
7

Edinburgh Fort Retail Park

Premier Beverages

UCI

Mega Bowl

Toys R Us

McDonald's Restaurant (Drive-Thru)

Petsmart

Kinnaird Park

Sher Discount Warehouse

Wickes

B & Q

Living Well Health Club

A6095

Newcraighall

Whi

Newcraighall Road

Musselburgh Road

Musselburgh By-pass

A6095

Peacocktail Close

Blackchapel Close

Blackchapel Road

Quarry Cotts.

Clerkimfield

Clerkimfield

Wisp Green

A6095

Niddrie Cotts.

Fortview

The Wisp

A6106

Whitehill Road

Whitehill Road

Cauldcoats Farm

Midlothian

Shawfair

Millerhill Road

Hillcrest House

Hilltown Farm Cottages

Hilltown

A6106

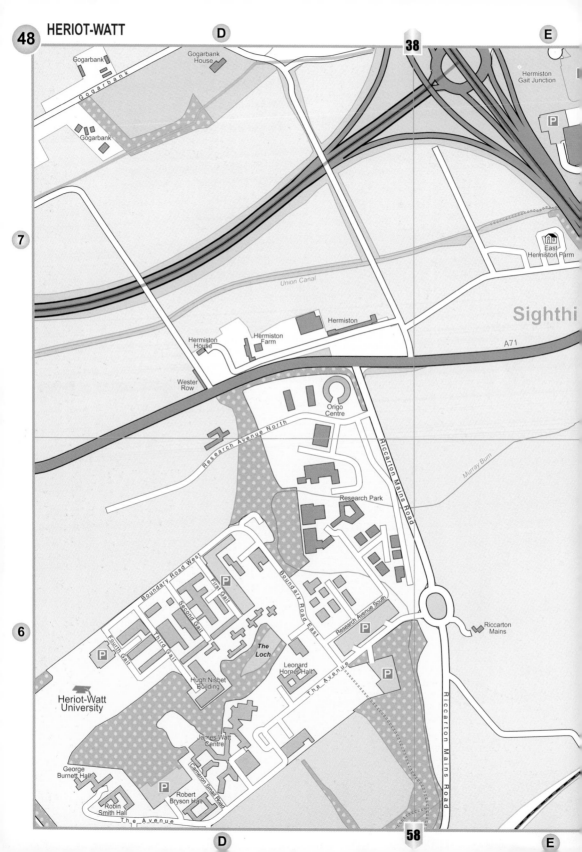

Gogarbank

Gogarbank House

Hermiston Gait Junction

P

Gogarbank

Gogarbank

East Hermiston Farm

Union Canal

Sighthi

Hermiston

A71

Hermiston House

Hermiston Farm

Wester Row

Origo Centre

Research Avenue North

Riccarton Mains Road

Murray Burn

Research Park

Boundary Road West

First Gait

P

Second Gait

Boundary Road East

Research Avenue South

P

Fourth Gait

Third Gait

P

The Loch

Leonard Horner Hall

Riccarton Mains

P

The Avenue

🎓 Heriot-Watt University

Hugh Nisbet Building

James Watt Centre

Riccarton Mains Road

George Burnett Hall

P

Cameron Smail Road

Robert Bryson Hall

Robin Smith Hall

The Avenue

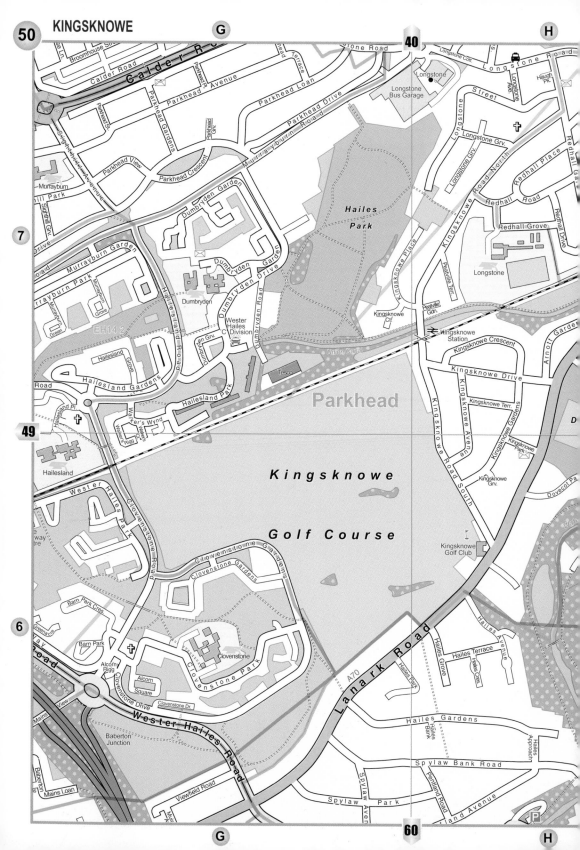

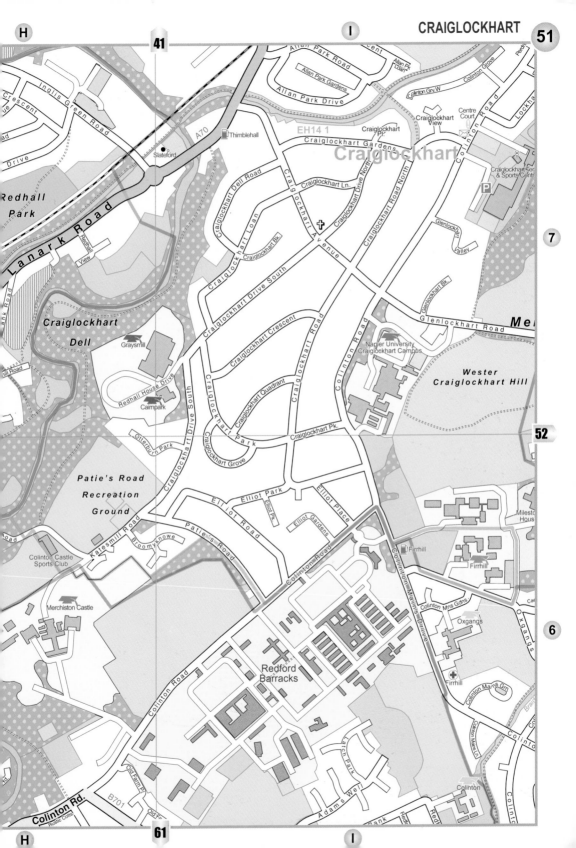

Allan Park Road
Allan Park Gardens
Allan Pk Loan
Allan Park Drive
Colinton Grv.W
Colinton Grove
Perdh
Craiglockhart View
Centre Court
Craiglockhart Road
Lockha
Thimblehall
EH14 1
Craiglockhart
Craiglockhart Gardens
Craiglockhart
Slateford
A70
Craiglockhart Dell Road
Craiglockhart Ln.
Craiglockhart Drive North
Craiglockhart Road North
Craiglockhart Ter & Sports Centr
P
Craiglockhart Loan
Craiglockhart Avenue
Glenlockhart Valley
7
Redhall Park
Redhall
Redhall View
Craiglockhart Bk.
Craiglockhart Drive South
Glenlockhart Bk
Craiglockhart Crescent
Craiglockhart Road
Glenlockhart Road
Me
Craiglockhart Dell
Graysmill
Napier University Craiglockhart Campus
Wester Craiglockhart Hill
Redhall House Drive
Caimpark
Craiglockhart Quadrant
Craiglockhart Park
Colinton Road
Craiglockhart Drive South
Craiglockhart Pk.
52
Otterburn Park
Craiglockhart Grove
Patie's Road Recreation Ground
Elliot Park
Elliot Place
Milesto Hous
Katesmill Road
Broomyknowe
Elliot Road
Elliot Pk.
Elliot Gardens
Firrhill
Firrhill
Patie's Road
Road
Colinton Castle Sports Club
Colinton Road
Colinton Mns Gdns
Oxgangs
Oxgangs
6
Merchiston Castle
Colinton Mains Drive
Firrhill
Firrhill
Colinton Mains Grn
Brai
Redford Barracks
Adam's Well
Colinton
Colinton
Colinton
Colin Mains Ln
Re
Bank

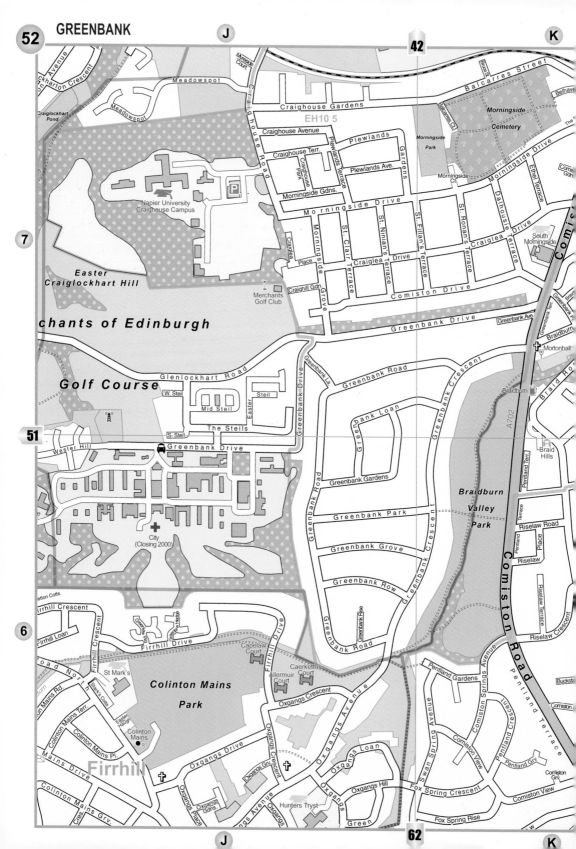

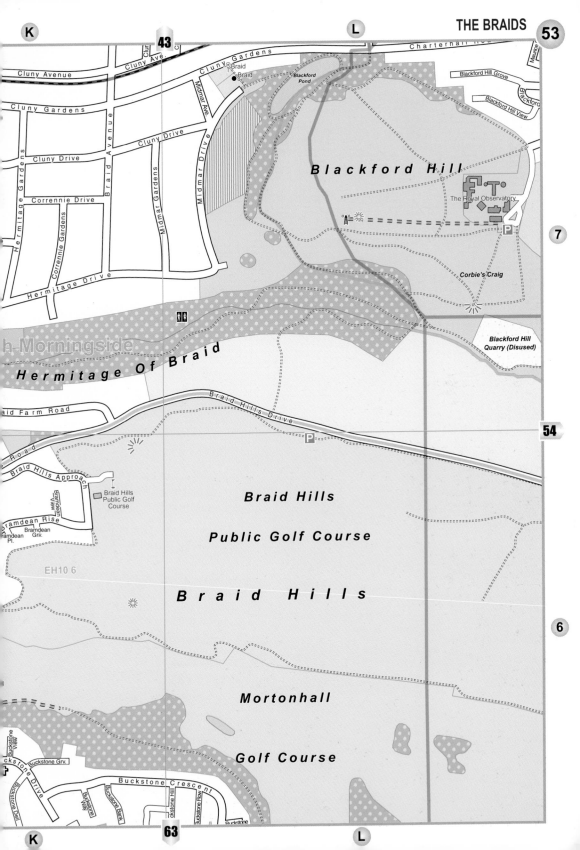

Cluny Avenue
Cluny Ave.
Cluny Gardens
Cluny Gardens
Braid
Braid
Blackford Pond
Charterhall Rd.
Blackford Hill Grove
Blackford Hill View
Blackford

Cluny Gardens
Cluny Drive
Cluny Drive
Hermitage Gardens
Corrennie Drive
Braid Avenue
Midmar Gardens
Midmar Ave.
Midmar Drive

Blackford Hill

The Royal Observatory

P

Corbie's Craig

Corrennie Gardens
Hermitage Drive
Corrennie Drive

h·Morningside

Hermitage Of Braid

Blackford Hill Quarry (Disused)

aid Farm Road

Braid Hills Drive

P

Road
Braid Hills Approach
Branxean View
Braid Hills Public Golf Course

Braid Hills

Public Golf Course

Bramdean Rise
Bramdean Grv.
Bramdean Pl.

EH10 6

Braid   Hills

Mortonhall

Buckstone View
ckstone Drive
Buckstone Grv.
Buckstone Bank
Buckstone Well
Buckstone Hill
Buckstone Row

Golf Course

Buckstone Crescent

Buckstone

Braid Hills Drive

Liberton Tower

Alnwickhill

Leadervale Road

Clackmae Grv.

Clackmae Road

Leadervale Terr.

Beauchamp Grv.

Beauchamp Crescent

Beauchamp Ct.

Liberton Cemetery

Orchardhead Rd.

Orchardhead Loan

A701

Wolrige Road

Liberton Brae

6

Braid Hills Golf Range

Braid Hills

Golf Range

Tower Farm Riding Stables

Liberton Drive

Kedslie Road

Kedslie Pl.

Alnwickhill Road

Hawkhead Road

Hawkhead Grv.

Cadogan Road

Liberton Drive

EH16 6

Liberton

Park

Liberton Gardens

A701

Meadowhead Farm

53

Stanedykehead

Alnwickhill Road

Netherbank

Netherbank View

Alnwickhill Terr.

Alnwickhill Drive

Alnwickhill Gdn.

View

Alnwickhill Grv.

Alnwickhill Pk.

Alnwickhill Loan

Alnwickhill Ct.

Alnwickhill Ct.

Back Row

Howden Hall Loan

Howden Hall Pk.

Cres.

Howden Hall

Howden Hall

St. Katharine's Brae

Liberton

Howdenhall

St. Katharine's

5

Mortonhall Caravan Park

Mortonhall Gate

Howden Hall Court

Howden Hall Drive

Howden Hall Way

The Balm Well

Balm Well

Kaime

Mortonhall Crematorium

Mortonhall

Cemetery

Howden Hall Road

A701

Balmwell

Grace

Pentland

Nurseries

Mortonhall Pk. Way

Mortonhall Pk. Ave.

Mortonhall Pk. Grv.

Mortonhall Park View

Mortonhall Pk. Loan

Mortonhall Pk. Grn.

Mortonhall Park Gardens

Mortonhall Park Drive

Mortonhall Pk. Terr.

Mortonhall Pk. Bank

Mortonhall Pk. Pl.

Mortonhall Park Crescent

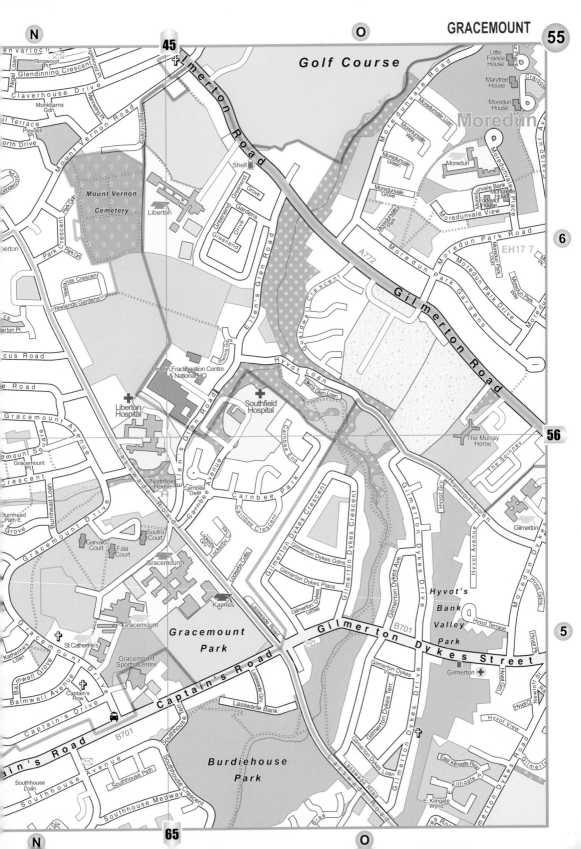

Golf Course

Little France House

Marytree House

Craigo

Moredun House

Moredun

Moredunvale Loan

Moredunvale Way

Moredunvale Green

Moredun

Moredunvale Grove

Moredunvale Bank

Monciclife House

Shelbytield House

Moredunvale Place

Moredunvale Park

Moredunvale View

Moredun Park Court

EH17 7

Whinnie Burn

Gilmerton Road

Neilti field

Shell

Mount Vernon Cemetery

Liberton

Greenend

Greenend Grove

Greenend Gardens

Greenend Drive

A772

Moredun Park Road

Moredun Park Gardens

Moredun Park Drive

Moredun Park

Moredun Park Way

Ringwood Pl.

Glendinning Crescent

Claverhouse Drive

Monkbarns Gdn.

Pleydell Pl.

North Drive

Park Crescent

Park Gro.

Yewlands Crescent

Yewlands Gardens

Gracemount Avenue

Park Gro.

Moredun Park Loan

Guardwell Crescent

Ellens Glen Road

Protein Fractionation Centre & National HQ

Hyvot Loan

Liberton Hospital

Southfield Hospital

Ellen's Glen Loan

Gracemount Square

Gracemount Crescent

Lasswade Road

Carnbee Avenue

Carnbee Park

Carnbee End

Northfield House

Carnbee Dell

Carnbee Crescent

Glynns Gdns.

The Murray Home

The Spinney

Burnhead Path E.

Grove

Burnhead Loan

Soutra Court

Garvald Court

Fala Court

Gilmerton Dykes Crescent

Gilmerton Dykes Crescent

Hyvot Gro.

Hyvot Loan

Gilmerton

Lockerby Grove

Lockerby Cres.

Gilmerton Dykes Gdns.

Gilmerton Dykes Place

Gilmerton Dykes Grove

Gilmerton Dykes Ave.

Gilmerton Dykes Drive

Hyvot Avenue

Gracemount

Kajmes

Lasswade Road

Gracemount Park

Hyvot's Bank Valley Park

Hyvot Terrace

St Catherine's

Katherine's Loan

Gracemount Sports Centre

Gilmerton Dykes Street

B701

Gilmerton

Gilmerton

Bamwell Grove

Balmwell Avenue

Captain's Row

Captain's Drive

Captain's Road

Gilmerton Dykes View

Gilmerton Dykes Terr.

Hyvot Gdns.

Moredun Dykes Road

Hyvot Gro.

Hyvot View

Southhouse Terr.

Lasswade Bank

Gilmerton Dykes Loan

East Kingate Rig

Southhouse Crescent

Lasswade Gro.

Burdiehouse Park

Lasswade Road

Kilngate P.

E. Kilngate Wynd

Southhouse Loan

Southhouse Avenue

Southhouse Path

Southhouse Medway

Brae

P

Q

6

Edmonstone Cottage

Toscana Ct.

Stewart

Three Winsp

Speedwell

Redcroft Street

Backd

Redcrof

Craigour Green

Craigour Drive

Craigour Cres

Craigour Terrace

Craigour Grove

Craigour Loan

Craigour Drive

Craigour Crescent

Craigour Crescent

Craigour Grn

Old Dalkeith Road

A7

Fernieside Drive

Fernieside Avenue

Fernieside

Fernieside Grove

Moredun

Fernieside

Park Street

Moredun Park Road

Fernieside Gardens

Fernieside Crescent

Fernieside

Fernieside Drive

Gilmerton Park

Moredun Park Green

Moredun Park View

Moredun Park Road

Fernieside Crescent

Fernieside Grove

Ferniehill Rd.

Ferniehill Road

Ferniehill Way

Ferniehill Grv.

Ferniehill Drive

Drumbank Farm

55

Ferniehill Road

Ferniehill Street

Ferniehill Gardens

Fernieside Street

B701

Candlemaker's Cres.

Drum

Moredun Park Grove

Ferniehill Road

Fernieside Ave.

Fernieside Place

Fernieside Square

Fernieside Street

Drum Place

Drum Crescent

Drum Avenue

Candlemaker's Park

Drum Riding Centre

Drum Farm

5

Drum St.

Gilmerton Miners Social Club

Pyvot's Bank Avenue

East of Gilmerton

Gilmerton

Newtoft Street

Hawthorn Pl

Drum Street

A772

Gilmerton

Limefield

Gilmerton Cotts

Ravenscroft Street

Ravenscroft

Ravenscroft

Gilmerton

Ravenscroft Pl

Ravenscroft St.

Gilmerton on Road

A772

P

66

Q

47

Danderhall Miners' Welfare and Social Club

Edmonstone Avenue

one Road

Danderhall

oolmet Crescent

Edmonstone Terrace

The Circle

Fornview Avenue Terrace

The Square

Arthur View Avenue

Edmonstone Drive

Edmonstone Road

Angres Ct.

Medic Centre

Danderhall Crescent

Newton Church Road

Danderhall

Danderhall Leisure Centre

Campview

Campview Crescent

Magislord Avenue

Campview Terrace

Campview Ave.

Campview Gdns

Campview Grove

Crescent

Campview

Kaimes View

Danderhall

een Avenue

ld Dalkeith Road

Newton Village

Newton Village

Millerhill Road

Newton Church Road

Scotway Business Cer

P

6

Dalkeith/Newton

A6106

5

Campend Farm

Q 67 R

5

P

Currievale
Cottages

Curriehill Road

Malcolmstone
Farm

Riccarton Mains Road

P

Curriehill
Station

71

Weaver's Knowe Crescent

Corslet Road

Riccarton Drive

Corslet
Place

Riccarton Avenue

E
Br

Bryce Pl.

Bryce Cres

Cur03level Drive

Cur03level Park Grove

Cur03level Park

Cur03level Park

Rowantree Avenue

Rowantree Grove

Cherry Tree Ave

Cherry Tree Loan

Cherry Tree
View

e Crescent

Stewart Avenue

Stewart Cres

Stewart
Pl.

Cherry Tree Pl.

Stewart Pl.

Stewart Rd.

Dolphin Avenue

Dolphin Gardens West

Stewart Gdns

Dolphin Road

Forthview Crescent

Palmer Place

Palmer Road

Curriehill Road

Riccarton Crescent

Riccarton Grove

Riccarton

Currie

Forthview
Ave.

Forthview Road

Pentland Place

Pentland View

Pentland
Ave.

Dolphin Gdns East

Curriehill

Currie

Easter Currie Pl.

Easter Currie Cres.

Easter Currie

Easter
Currie
Ct.

Pentland

P

Currie

A70

Lanark Road West

Kinauld
Tan Works

Kirkgate

Rosebank

EH14 6

4

Waukmill
Loan

Kinnauld
Farm

Lymphoy
House

Baberton

Golf Course

Juniper Green

Baberton
Club House

Woodhall Terrace

Baberton Drive

Woodhall Drive

Woodhall Avenue

Juniper Park Road

Woodhall Terrace

Belmont Road

Juniper Gv.

Baberton Sq.

Baberton Avenue

Lanark

Baberton Park

Juniper La.

A70

Nether Currie Crescent

Muir Wood Place

Muir Wood Road

Muir Wood Crescent

Muir Wood Road

Juniper
Gdn.

Juniper
Terr.

Juniper
Green

Juniper Avenue

Juniper Pl.

5

Muir Wood Road

Nether Currie Road

Woodhall
Mains

W
Ridi

Muir Wood Drive

Muir Wood
Gdns.

Woodhall Road

Nether
Currie

Thomson Grv.

Thomson Drive

Thomson Drive

Nether
Currie

Thomson Road

Thomson Crescent

Lanark Road West

Rosebank

Blinkbonny Rd.

60

Water of Leith

Blinkbonny Road

Moidart
House

Baberton

nny Road

Braeburn Drive

4

Braeburn
Coach House

Easter
Kinleith Farm

Middle
Kinleith Farm

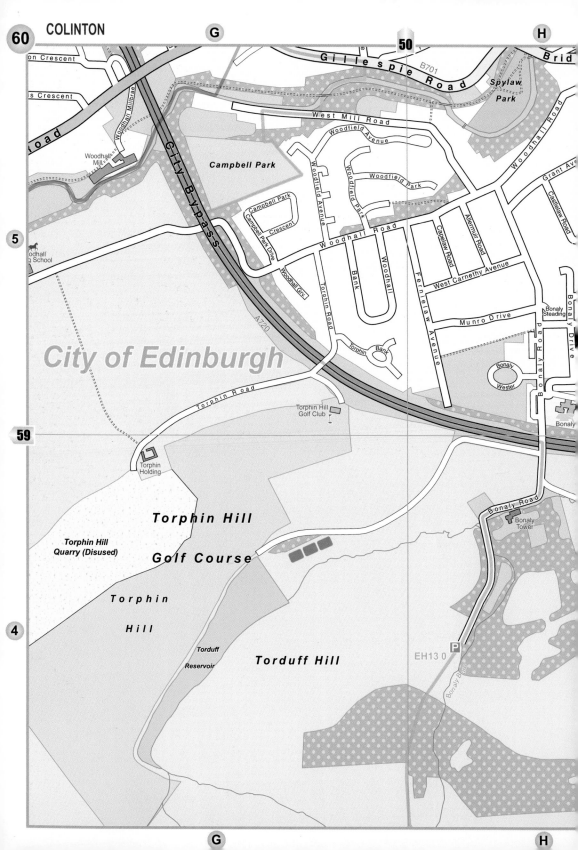

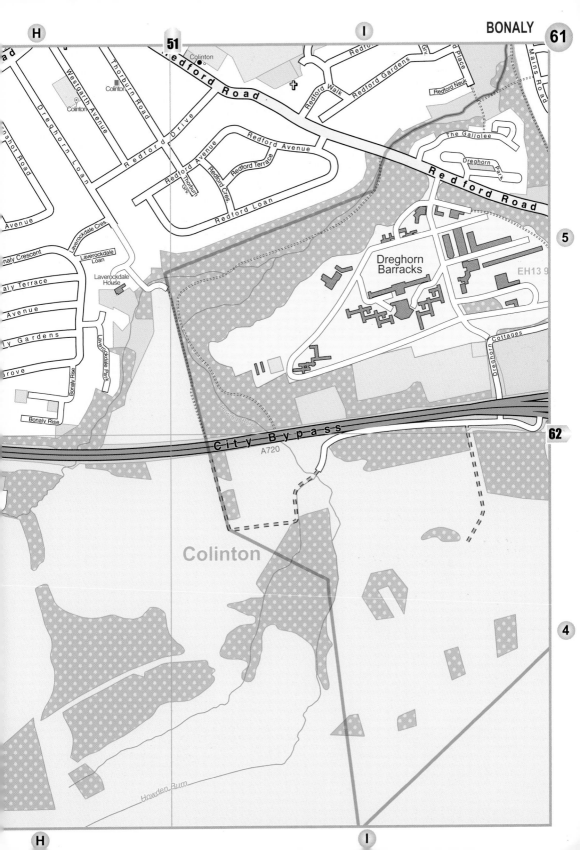

H
I
51
I
61
5
62
4
H
I

Colinton

Redford Road
Redford Road
Redford Walk
Redford Gardens
Redford Neuk
The Gallolee
Dreghorn Park
Redford Avenue
Redford Avenue
Redford Terrace
Redford Cres.
Redford Loan
Redford Drive
Thorburn Rd.
Thorburn Grv.
Thorburn Road
Westgarth Avenue
Dreghorn Loan
Colinton
Colinton

EH13 9

Dreghorn
Barracks

Laverockdale Cres.
Laverockdale Loan
Laverockdale House
Laverockdale Park

Dreghorn Cottages

nshol Road
Avenue
naly Crescent
ly Terrace
Avenue
y Gardens
rove
Bonaly Rise
Bonaly Rise

Mains Road

Howden Burn

City Bypass
A720

Colinton

Howden Burn

5

61

4

J

K

Oxgangs Terrace

Clinton Mall

Oxgangs 'C' Division

Oxgangs Farm Drive

Oxgangs Park

Oxgangs Row

Oxgangs Street

Oxgangs Road North

Oxgangs Farm Grove

Oxgangs Farm Avenue

Oxgangs Farm Gdns.

Oxgangs Farm Loan

Oxgangs Farm Terrace

Comiston

Pentland V

Pentland Drive

Fairmilehead

Park

Oxgangs Bank

Oxgangs View

Oxgangs Broadway

Oxgangs Medway

Oxgangs Path

Oxgangs Brae

Camus Avenue

East Camus Pl.

West Camus Rd.

Camus Park.

Camus Park

Colmestone

East Col

Buses Only

B701

Redford Road

Dreghorn Gardens

Dreghorn Place

Dreghorn Ave.

Dreghorn Grv.

Dreghorn

Drive

Caiystane Gardens

Caiystane Drive

Caiystane Terr.

Caiystane Hill

East Caiystane Pl.

West Caiystane Rd.

Caiystane Aver

Caiystane Avenue

B701

Dreghorn Link

Oxgangs Road

Hunters Tryst

P

P

Safeway

Auchingane

Swanston Muir

Dreghorn

New Swanston

Hailburn Park

Howe Park

Howe Park

Tryst Park

Tryst Park

Tryst Park

Swanston Road

Trench Knowe

Swanston Park

Swanston Green

Swanston Crescent

Swanston Loan

Swanston Way

Swanston Row

Oxgangs Road

Swanston Avenue

Swanston Place

Swanston View

Swa

Sw

Dreghorn Junction

A720

Caiyside

Caiyside

Swanston Burn

Swanston

Golf Course

Swanston Golf Club

Swanston House

Swanston Village

Lothian

EH10 7

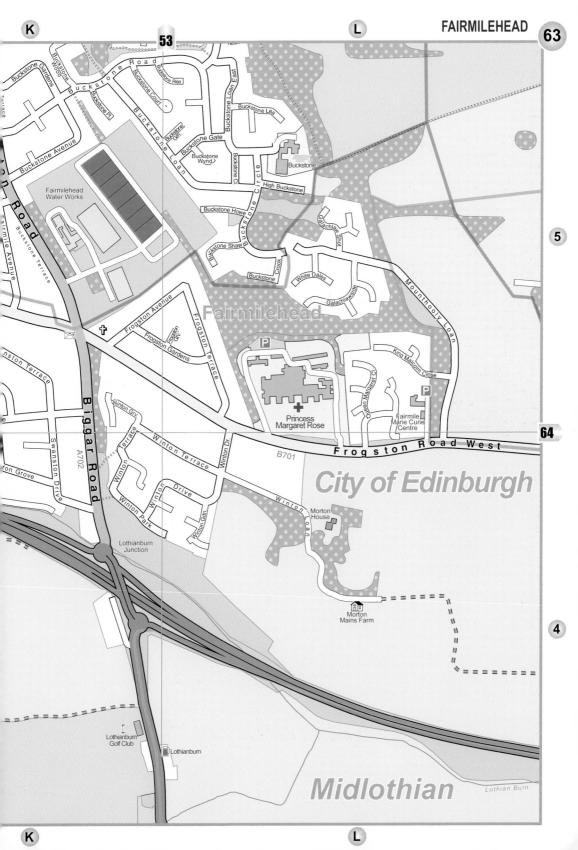

K
L
53
63
5
64
4
K
L

Buckstone Wood
Buckstone Gardens
Buckstone Terrace
Buckstone Road
Buckstone Pl.
Buckstone Court
Buckstone Rise
Buckstone Loan
Buckstone Loan East
Buckstone Lea
Buckstone Gate
Buckstone Grn.
Buckstone Wynd
Buckstone Circle
High Buckstone
Buckstone
Buckstone Howe
Buckstone Shaw
Buckstone Crook
Buckstone Avenue
Fairmilehead Water Works
Fairmile Avenue
Buckstone Terrace
White Dales
Galachlaw Shot
Galachlawside
Mountholly Loan
Fairmilehead
Frogston Avenue
Frogston Gardens
Frogston Grn.
Frogston Terrace
King Malcolm Close
Queen Margaret Ct.
P
P
Princess Margaret Rose
Fairmile Marie Curie Centre
Winton Gro.
Winton Terrace
Winton Dr.
Winton
Terrace
Winton Drive
Winton Park
Winton Gdn.
Winton Loan
B701
Frogston Road West
City of Edinburgh
Swanston Drive
Swanston Grove
Swanston Terrace
Biggar Road
A702
Lothianburn Junction
Morton House
Morton Mains Farm
Lothianburn Golf Club
Lothianburn
Midlothian
Lothian Burn

4

B701

Morton Mains

Old Burdiehouse Road

A701

Burdiehouse
Square

A720

C i t y   B y p a s s

Straiton
Junction

63

Pentland Burn

Straiton Rd

Loa

Straiton
Cottages

Straiton
Farm

3

Straiton Mains

P

Straiton Re

Straiton Road

A701

Burndene
Dr.
Lorne
Grv.

Straiton
Caravan Park
(Residential)

Lomond
Walk

Burndene Drive

P

Sainsbury's

Old Pentland
Sawmill

*Old
Pentland*

Sainsbury's

E

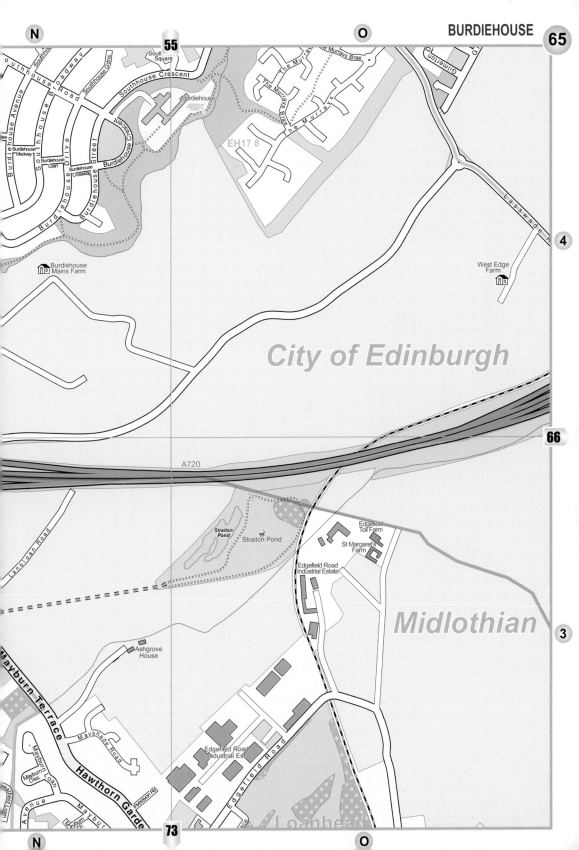

South Square

Southhouse Broadway

Southhouse Road

Southhouse Gdns.

Southhouse Crescent

Burdiehouse

Burdiehouse Avenue

Burdiehouse Drive

Burdiehouse Medway

Southhouse Loan

Burdiehouse Crossway

Burdiehouse Crescent

Burdiehouse Loan

Burdiehouse Street

EH17 8

The Murrays Brae

The Murrays Brae

The Murrays

The Murrays

Gilmerton

Lasswade

4

Burdiehouse Mains Farm

West Edge Farm

City of Edinburgh

66

A720

Langloan Road

Straiton Pond

Straiton Pond

Edgefield Toll Farm

St Margaret's Farm

Edgefield Road Industrial Estate

Midlothian

3

Ashgrove House

Mayburn Terrace

Mayshade Road

Hawthorn Garden

Mayburn Loan

Mayburn Cres.

Avenue

Mayburn

Edgefield Road Industrial Est

Edgefield Road

Loanhead

P

Q

Gilm
Junc

Melville
Grange Farm

Gilmerton Station Road

A720

City Bypass

4

Lasswade
Junction

Kings Acre

Golf Course

Melville
Mains

65

Wester
Melville Farm

Lasswade Road

3

A768

Lasswade Road

High Street

Wadingburn Lane

Glebe Pl.

Church Road

School Green

W. Mill

P

Q

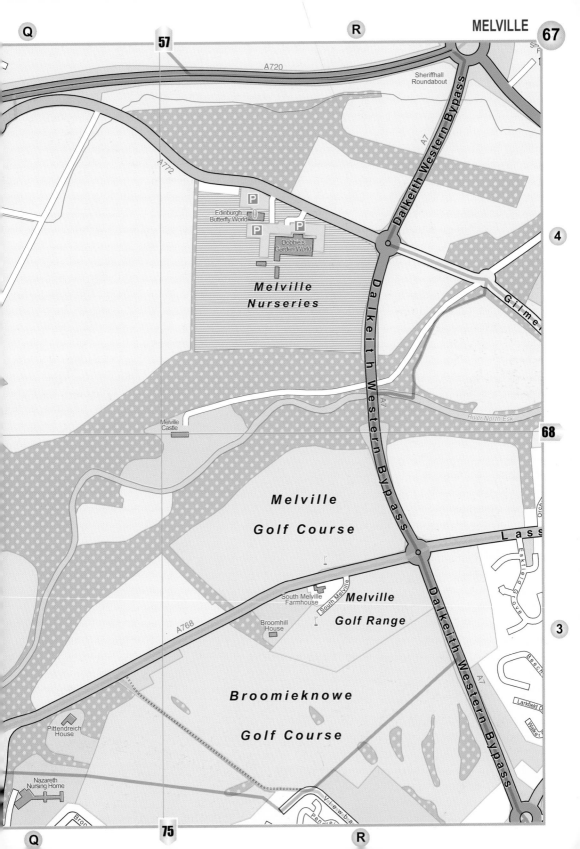

A720

Sheriffhall
Roundabout

A7

Dalkeith Western Bypass

A772

4

P

P

Edinburgh
Butterfly World

P

Dobbie's
Garden World

Melville
Nurseries

Gilme

Dalkeith Western Bypass

A7

River North Esk

Melville
Castle

68

Melville

Golf Course

Lass

Melville

Golf Range

South Melville
Farmhouse

South Melville

Eskfield Grove

Orch

3

Broomhill
House

A768

Beech

A7

Broomieknowe

Larkfield D

Wake

Golf Course

Dalkeith Western Bypass

Pittendreich
House

Nazareth
Nursing Home

View

Pen

Broc

S

T

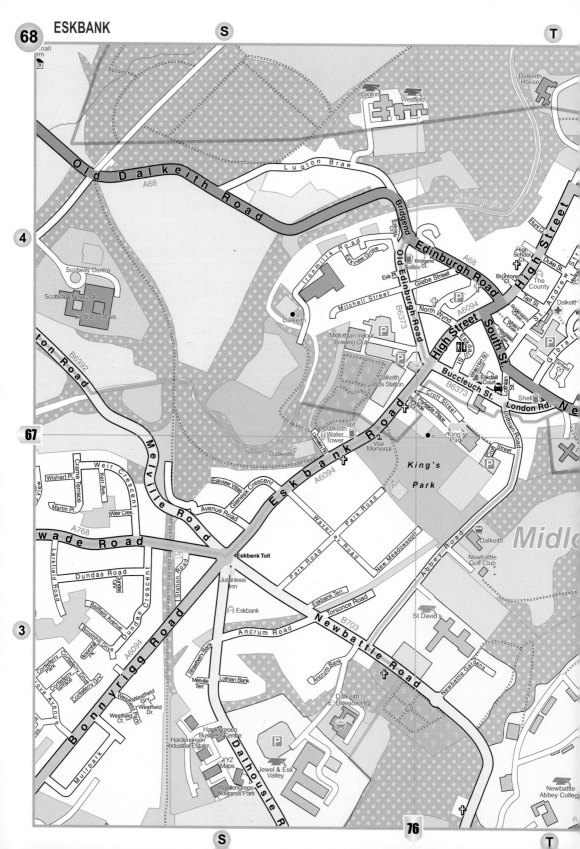

Dalkeith
House

Lugton
Westfield

Old Dalkeith Road
A68

Lugton Brae

River North Esk

Bridgend

Ironmills Road

Eastview Grove

Eskdale Ct.

Edinburgh Road
A68

High Street

Hunt Ct.

High
School
Ch.

Duke St.

The
County

Bruntons
Ct.

Dalkeith

Scotway Centre

Scottish & Newcastle

Scottish Widows

Esk Pl.

Old Edinburgh Road

Bridgend
Saltire Ct.

Glebe Street

North Wynd

A6094

Tait St.

St. Andrew St.

Dalkeith

Mitchell Street

B6373

Dalkeith

High Street

South St.

Elmfield
Ct.

Dalkeith
Bus Station

Midlothian Indoor
Bowling Club

Buccleuch St.

B6373

Eskdaill
Court

Lothian

Shell

London Rd.

New

B6392

ton Road

Melville Road

Dalkeith
Water
Tower

Dalkeith

Carberry Rd.

Eskbank Road

Parkside Place

Croft Street

King's
Park

Croft Street

War
Memorial

King's

Park

Wishart Pl.

Weir Crescent

Kerr Ave.

Crane Terrace

Martin Pl.

Weir Cres.

Eskview Villa

Gleneask Crescent

Avenue Road

A6094

Waverley Road

Park Road

New Meadowspott

Abbey Road

Dalkeith

Newbattle
Golf Club

Midlo

A768

wade Road

Larkfield Road

Dundas Road

Dundas Crescent

Belfield Avenue

Broomhill Drive

Dundas
Gdns.

Station Road

Eskbank Toll

Justinlees
Inn

Eskbank

Park Road

Eskbank Terr.

Torsonce Road

B703

St David's

Newbattle Gardens

Cortleferry
Park

Cortleferry Drive

Cortleferry Terrace

Cortleferry Gro.

Bonnyrigg Road

A6094

Strawberry Bank

Ancrum Road

Ancrum Bank

Newbattle Road

Westfield
Gro.

Westfield
Dr.

Westfield
Park

Westfield
Ct.

Dove Avenue

Dalhousie R.

Multrpark

Melville
Terr.

Lothian Bank

Hardengreen
Business Centre

Hardengreen
Industrial Estate

XYZ Maps

Jewel & Esk
Valley

Hardengreen
Business Park

Dalkeith
'E' Division HQ

Newbattle
Abbey College

S

T

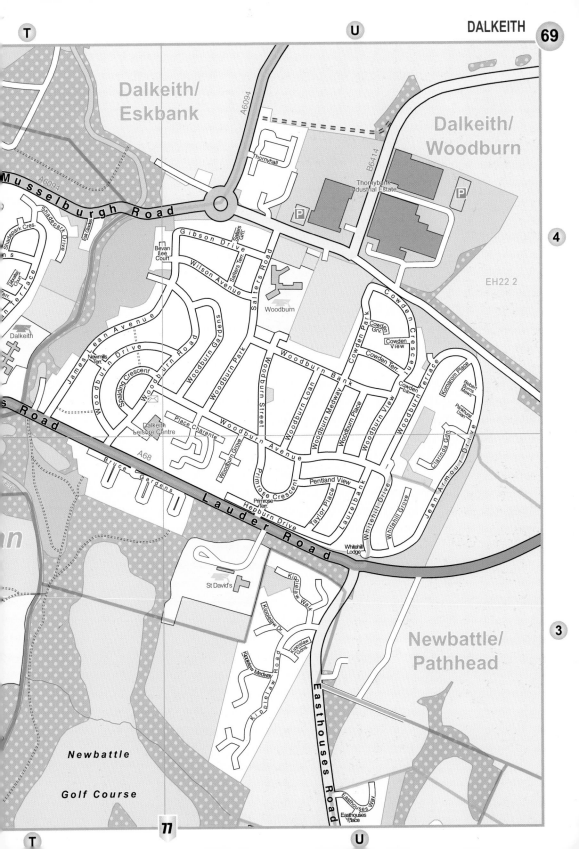

Dalkeith/
Eskbank

Dalkeith/
Woodburn

A6094

Thornyhall

B6414

Thornybank
Industrial Estate

P

P

EH22 2

4

Musselburgh Road

A6094

Shadepark Cres

Shadepark Drive

Esk Glades

Terrace

Gibson Drive

Salters Gait

Salters Terr.

Bevan
Lee Court

Wilson Avenue

Salters Road

Woodburn

James Lean Avenue

Newmills Terr.

Woodburn Drive

Spalding Crescent

Woodburn Road

Woodburn Park

Woodburn Gardens

Woodburn Street

Woodburn Loan

Woodburn Bank

Woodburn Medway

Woodburn Place

Cowden Park

Cowden
Grv.

Cowden
View

Cowden Terr.

Cowden
La.

Woodburn View

Cowden Crescent

Woodburn Terrace

Kongaton Place

Robert Burns
Mews

Parkhead
Loan

Dalkeith

Dalkeith
Leisure Centre

Place Charente

Woodburn Grove

Woodburn Avenue

Pentland View

Laurelbank

Clarinda Gdn

Jean Armour Drive

Bruce Gardens

A68

Primrose Crescent

Hepburn Drive

Primrose
Terr.

Taylor Place

Whitehill Drive

Whitehill Grove

Whitehill
Lodge

Lauder Road

Road

St David's

Kinglelaw Walk

Kinglelaw Dr.

Kinglelaw Road

Kinglelaw
Gdns

Kinglelaw Medway

Newbattle/
Pathhead

3

Easthouses Road

Newbattle

Golf Course

Easthouses Way

Easthouses
Place

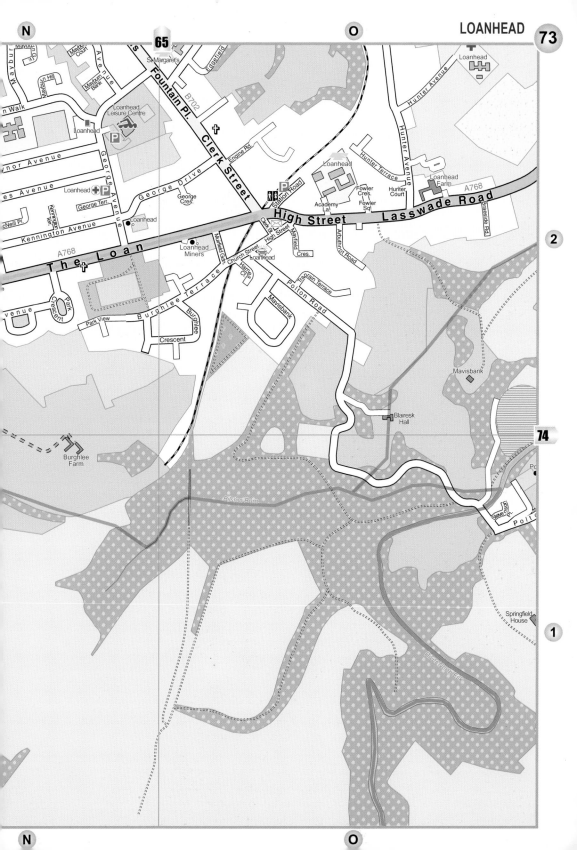

65

St Margaret's

Edgefield

Loanhead

Maybury Court

Maybury Bank

n Hill

Maybur

n Walk

Avenue

Fountain Pl.

B702

Loanhead
Leisure Centre

Loanhead

P

Clerk Street

Engine Rd

Station Road

P

Loanhead

Hunter Terrace

Hunter Avenue

Loanhead
Farm

A768

nor Avenue

George Avenue

George Drive

Loanhead

P

George Terr.

George
Cres.

Academy
La.

Fowler
Cres.

Fowler
Sq.

Hunter
Court

Braeside Rd.

Lasswade Road

s Avenue

Kerryon
Terr.

cNeill Pl.

Kennington Avenue

A768

Loanhead

High Street

Clerk

High Street

Mayfield
Cres.

Arbuthnot Road

2

The Loan

Loanhead
Miners

Muirfield Gdn.

Church Street

Loanhead

Harris
Clo.

Train Terrace

Polton Road

Mavisbank

Mavisbank

Park
Crescent

venue

Park View

Burghlee Terrace

Burghlee
Crescent

Blairesk
Hall

74

Burghlee
Farm

Po

Springfield
House

1

Edston Burn

Saveson

Polt

River North Esk

Wadingburn Road
A768

Kevock Road

Green Lane

Kevock Vale
Caravan Park
(Residential)

W Mill Wynd

West Mill Road

Polton Road

Bonn
No

Edinburgh & Lasswade
Riding Centre

River North Esk

2

EH18 1

Polton
House

Polton Terrace

Polton Gardens

Pryde Terrace

Eskdale Drive

Eskdale Ct.

Eskdale

Do

Lasswade

Pryde Avenu

Polton Road

Pentland Road

73

Polton Bank

Farm Avenue

Mason Pl.

Dalhousie Avenue West

Bank

Mavisbank Pl

Methven Terrace

Ramsay Terr.

Polton Bank Terrace

MacLean Pl.

De Quincey Road

Polton Road West

Seaforth Terrace

Argyll Pl.

Argyll Pl.

Gordon Avenue

Dalhousie Place

Dalhousie Gardens

Dalhousie Ave.

Hopefi

Hawthornden

Polton Avenue Road

Dalhousie Drive

Dalhousie Rd West

Hopefield Terr.

Springfield
Farm

St. Anne's Avenue

Wink's Pl.

Cameron Cres.

Cameron Crescent

Hop

1

Poltonhall/

Rosewell

Lasswade
Rugby Football
Club

Rosewell Road

Cockpen View

Skeltie

Sk

Cockpen Terr.

Cockpen Drive

Cockpen Crescent

Cockpen Ave.

Montrose
Stables

Polton Road West

A6094

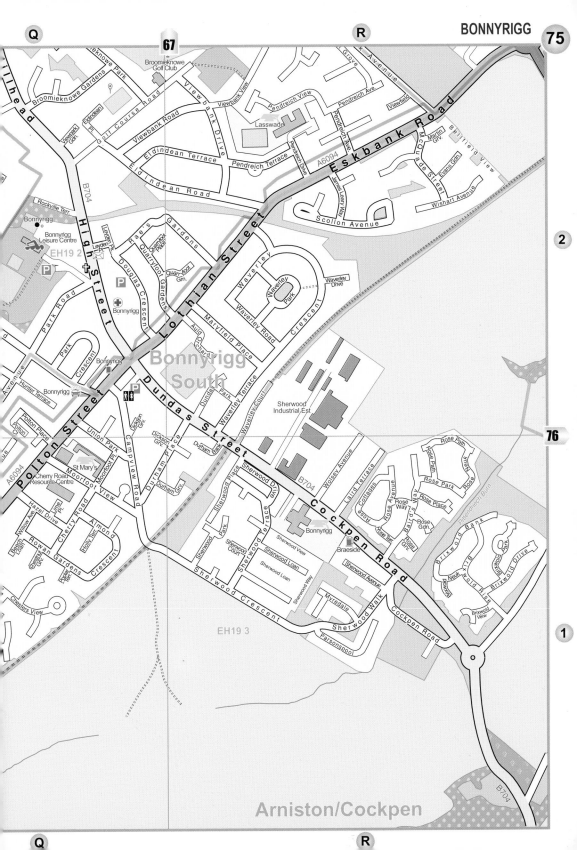

Q
67
R
75

Broomieknowe Park
Broomieknowe Golf Club
Broomieknowe Gardens
Millhead
Eldindean Pl.
Golf Course Road
Viewbank Drive
Viewbank View
Viewbank Road
Pendreich View
Lasswade
Viewfield
Pendreich Ave.
Grove Avenue
Eskbank Road
Bellfield View
Martin Grv.
McQuade Street
Viewpark Gdn.
Eldindean Terrace
Pendreich Terrace
Pendreich Ave.
Evans Gdn.
James Leary Way
B704
Eldindean Road
A6094
Pendreich Drive
Wishart Avenue
Rockville Terr.
High Street
Scollon Avenue

Bonnyrigg
Bonnyrigg Leisure Centre
Park Road
EH19 2
P
Leyden Pl.
Rae's Gardens
Quarryfoot Gardens
Quarryfoot Place
Quarryfoot Grn.
Lothian Street
Waverley Park
Waverley Road
Waverley Drive

2

P
Bonnyrigg
Douglas Crescent
Maryfield Place
Auld Orchard
Crescent

Park Avenue
Hunter Terrace
Park Crescent
Bonnyrigg
Bonnyrigg
Bonnyrigg South
Dundas Street
Dundas Park
Waverley Terrace
Waverley Court
Sherwood Industrial Est.
B704
Polton Street
Polton Place
Polton Ct.
Union Park
P
Campview Road
Durham Place
Dickson Grv.
Durham Bank
Durham Gro.
Moorfoot Pl.
Sherwood Place
Sherwood Drive
Wolsey Avenue
Rose Path
Rose Path
Rose Path
Rose Neuk
76

A6094
St Mary's
Cherry Road Resource Centre
Moorfoot View
Laird Terrace
Cottages
Rose Avenue
Rose Way
Rose Gdn.
Rose Place
Rose Park
Rose
EH19 3

Willow Hazel Drive
Ling Pl.
Almond
Holly Terr.
Sherwood Park
Sherwood Court
Sherwood View
Sherwood Loan
Bonnyrigg
Braeside
Rose Terr.
Millbank
Pitlochrie Burn
Brixwold Bank

Chesters View
Rowan Gardens
Cherry Road
Crescent
Sherwood Crescent
Sherwood Loan
Sherwood Way
Myredale
Sherwood Avenue
Cockpen Road
Brixwold Neuk
Brixwold Rise
Brixwold Drive
Brixwold Park

Sherwood Walk
Parsonspool
Cockpen Road
Brixwold View

1

Arniston/Cockpen

B704

Q
R

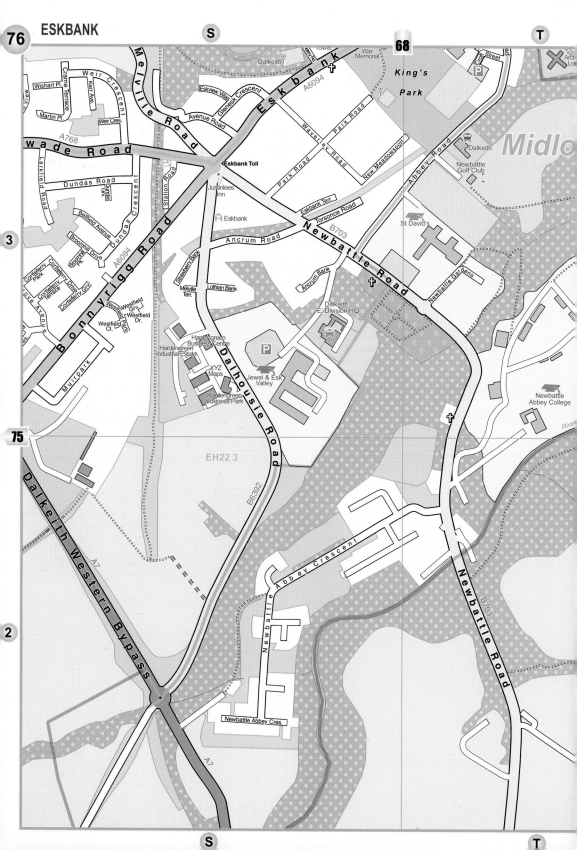

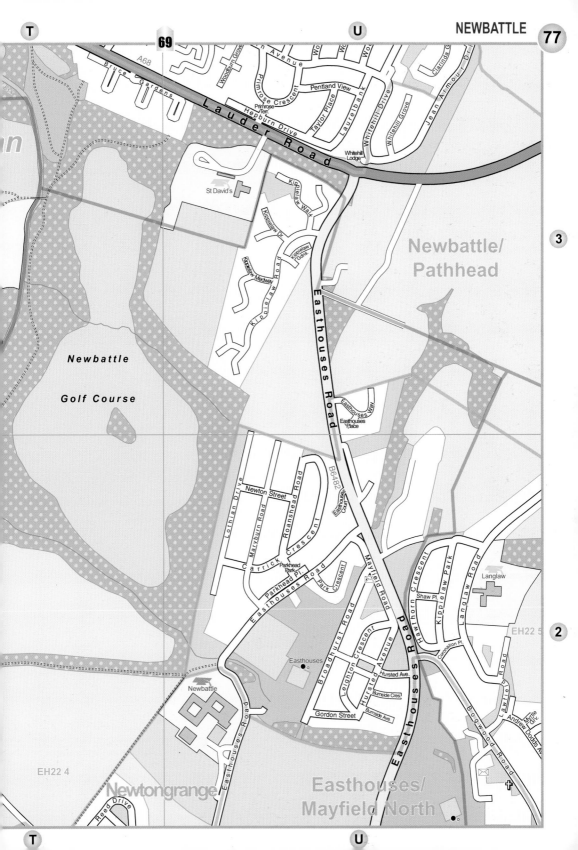

A68

Bruce Gardens

Woodburn Grove

Woodburn Avenue

Primrose Crescent

Pentland View

Taylor Place

Laurelbank

Whitehill Drive

Whitehill Grove

Clarinda G

Jean Armour Dr

Primrose
Terr.

Hepburn Drive

Whitehill
Lodge

Lauder Road

Kippielaw Walk

St David's

Kippielaw Dr

Kippielaw
Gdns

Kippielaw Medway

Kippielaw Road

**Newbattle/
Pathhead**

3

Easthouses Road

Newbattle

Golf Course

Easthouses
View

Easthouses
Place

B6482

Easthouses
Court

Newton Street

Roanshead Road

Lothian Drive

Maryburn Road

Carrick Crescent

Parkhead
Park

Parkhead Pl.

Easthouses Road

Park Crescent

Mayfield Road

Hawthorn Crescent

Kippielaw Park

Langlaw Road

Langlaw

Shaw Pl.

EH22 5

2

Broadhurst Road

Leighton Crescent

Hursted Avenue

Hursted Ave.

Coronation Pl.

Easthouses
●

Newbattle

Burnside Cres.

Burnside Ave.

Gordon Street

Bogwood Road

Lawfield Road

Andrew Dodds Av.

Myrtle
Grv.

EH22 4

Easthouses Road

Reed Drive

Newtongrange

**Easthouses/
Mayfield North**

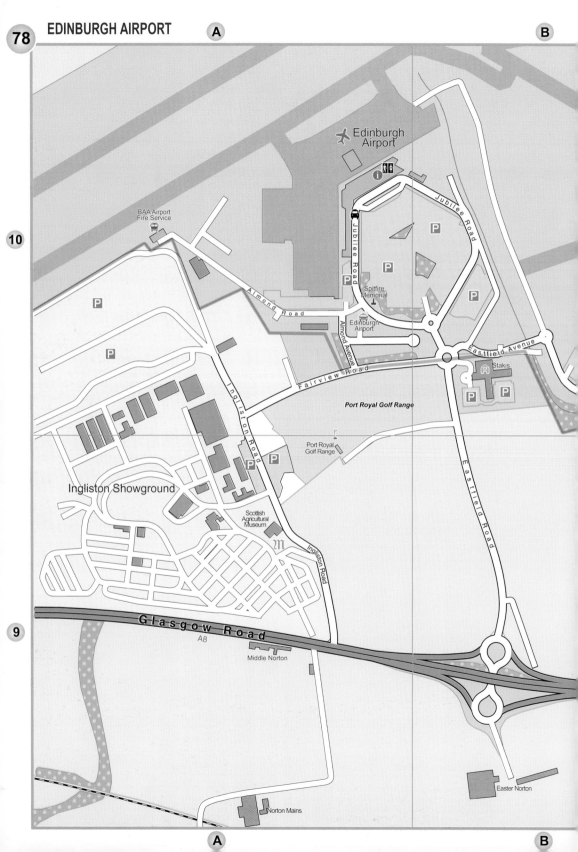

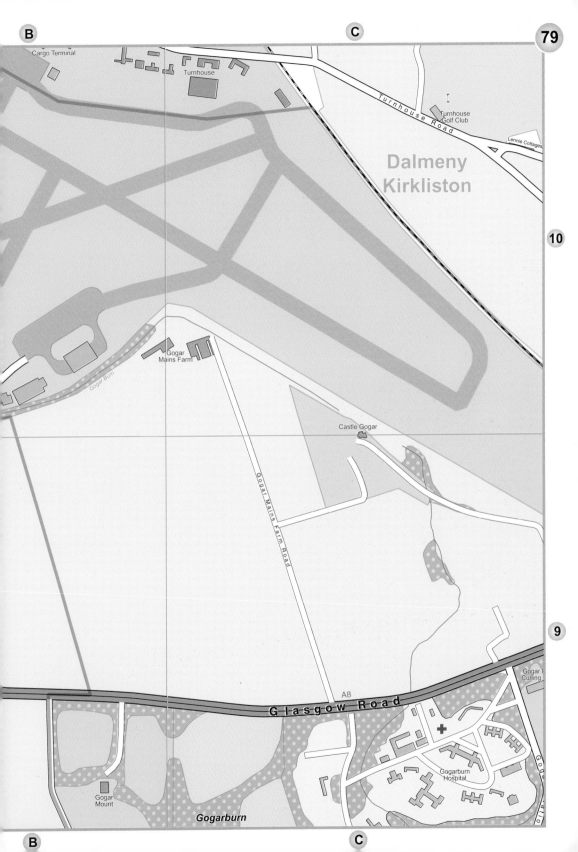

Cargo Terminal

Turnhouse

Turnhouse Road

Turnhouse Golf Club

Lennie Cottages

Dalmeny Kirkliston

Gogar Mains Farm

Gogar Burn

Castle Gogar

Gogar Mains Farm Road

Gogar Curling

A8

G l a s g o w   R o a d

Gogar Hill

Gogar Mount

Gogarburn Hospital

Gogarburn

Street	Page	Grid
Abbey Lane EH8 8	20-21	N11
Abbey Mount EH8 8	20-21	M11
Abbey Strand EH8 8	30-31	M10
Abbey Street EH7 5	20-21	N11
Abbeyhill EH8 8	30-31	M10
Abbeyhill Crescent EH8 8	30-31	M10
Abbotsford Crescent EH10 5	42-43	K8
Abbotsford Park EH10 5	42-43	K8
Abercorn Avenue EH8 7	30-31	O10
Abercorn Cottages EH15 3	30-31	O9
Abercorn Court EH8 7	30-31	O10
Abercorn Crescent EH8 7	30-31	O10
Abercorn Drive EH8 7	30-31	O10
Abercorn Gardens EH8 7	20-21	O11
Abercorn Grove EH8 7	30-31	O10
Abercorn Road EH8 7	30-31	O10
Abercorn Terrace EH15 2	32-33	R10
Abercromby Place EH3 6	28-29	L11
Abinger Gardens EH12 6	26-27	I10
Academy Park EH6 8	20-21	N12
Academy Street EH6 7	20-21	N12
Adams Well EH13 0	50-51	I6
Adelphi Grove EH15 1	32-33	Q10
Adelphi Place EH15 1	32-33	Q10
Admiral Terrace EH10 4	42-43	K9
Admiralty Street EH6 6	12-13	M13
Advocate's Close EH1 1	8-9	
Afton Place EH5 3	10-11	K13
Afton Terrace EH5 3	10-11	K13
Agnew Terrace EH6 4	12-13	L13
Ainslie Place EH3 6	28-29	K10
Airlie Place EH3 0	28-29	L11
Aitchison's Place EH15 1	22-23	Q11
Alan Breck Gardens EH4 7	24-25	F10
Albany Lane EH1 3	28-29	L11
Albany Street EH1 3	28-29	L11
Albany Street Lane EH1 3	28-29	L11
Albert Place EH7 5	20-21	M11
Albert Street EH7 5	20-21	M12
Albert Terrace EH10 5	42-43	K8
Albion Place EH7 5	20-21	N11
Albion Road EH7 5	20-21	N11
Albion Terrace EH7 5	20-21	N11
Albyn Place EH2 4	28-29	K11
Alcorn Rigg EH14 3	50-51	G6
Alcorn Square EH14 3	50-51	G6
Alderbank Gardens EH11 1	42-43	J8
Alderbank Place EH11 1	42-43	J8
Alderbank Terrace EH11 1	42-43	J8
Alemoor Crescent EH7 6	20-21	N12
Alemoor Park EH7 6	20-21	N12
Alexander Drive EH11 2	40-41	I9
Alfred Place EH9 1	30-31	M9
Allan Park Crescent EH14 1	40-41	I8
Allan Park Drive EH14 1	50-51	I7
Allan Park Gardens EH14 1	50-51	I7
Allan Park Loan EH14 1	50-51	I7
Allan Park Road EH14 1	50-51	I7
Allan Street EH4 1	28-29	K11
Allanfield EH7 5	20-21	M11
Allendale EH13 0	50-51	H6
Allendale EH13 0	50-51	H6
Allermuir Road EH13 0	60-61	H5
Almond Avenue EH12 9	78-79	A10
Almond Green EH12 8	24-25	E10
Almond Road EH12 9	78-79	A10
Almond Square EH12 8	24-25	E10
Almondbank Terrace EH11 1	42-43	J8
Alnwickhill Court EH16 6	54-55	M5
Alnwickhill Crescent EH16 6	54-55	M5
Alnwickhill Drive EH16 6	54-55	M5
Alnwickhill Gardens EH16 6	54-55	M5
Alnwickhill Grove EH16 6	54-55	M5
Alnwickhill Loan EH16 6	54-55	M5
Alnwickhill Park EH16 6	54-55	N5
Alnwickhill Road EH16 6	54-55	N6
Alnwickhill Terrace EH16 6	54-55	M5
Alnwickhill View EH16 6	54-55	M5
Alva Place EH7 5	20-21	N11
Alva Street EH2 4	28-29	K11
Alvanley Terrace EH9 1	42-43	K9
Anchor Close EH1 1	8-9	
Anchorfield EH6 4	12-13	M13
Anderson Place EH6 5	12-13	M13
Anderson's Close EH1 2	8-9	
Andrew Wood Court EH6 4	12-13	M13
Angle Park Terrace EH11 2	42-43	J9
Ann Street EH4 1	28-29	K11
Annandale Street EH7 4	28-29	L11
Annandale Street Lane EH7 4	20-21	M11
Annfield EH6 4	12-13	L14
Annfield Street EH6 4	12-13	L13
Antigua Street EH1 3	20-21	M11
Appin Terrace EH14 1	40-41	I8
Arboretum Avenue EH4 1	28-29	K11
Arboretum Place EH3 5	18-19	K12
Arboretum Road EH3 5	18-19	K12
Archibald Place EH3 9	28-29	L10
Arden Street EH9 1	42-43	L9
Ardmillan Place EH11 2	42-43	J9
Ardmillan Terrace EH11 2	42-43	J9
Ardmillan Terrace Lane EH11 2	42-43	J9
Ardshiel Avenue EH4 7	24-25	F11
Argyle Crescent EH15 2	32-33	Q10
Argyle Park Terrace EH9 1	42-43	L9
Argyle Place EH9 1	42-43	L9
Argyle Street EH6 4	12-13	M13
Argyll Terrace EH11 2	28-29	K10
Arnott Gardens EH14 2	50-51	H7
Arran Place EH15 2	32-33	R10
Arthur Street EH6 5	20-21	M12
Arthur Street Lane EH6 5	20-21	M12
Ashley Drive EH11 1	42-43	J8
Ashley Gardens EH11 1	42-43	J8
Ashley Grove EH11 1	42-43	J8
Ashley Place EH6 5	20-21	M12
Ashley Terrace EH11 1	42-43	J8
Ashton Grove EH16 5	44-45	N7
Ashton Villas EH15 2	32-33	R10
Ashville Terrace EH6 8	20-21	N12
Assembly Street EH6 7	12-13	N13
Atholl Crescent EH3 8	28-29	K10
Atholl Crescent Lane EH3 8	28-29	K10
Atholl Place EH3 8	28-29	K10
Atholl Terrace EH11 2	28-29	K10
Auchingane EH10 7	62-63	J5
Auchinleck's Brae EH6 4	12-13	L13
Avenue Villas EH4 2	28-29	J11
Avenue, The EH14 4	48-49	D6
Avon Grove EH4 6	14-15	E12
Avon Place EH4 6	14-15	E12
Avon Road EH4 6	14-15	E12
Avondale Place EH3 5	28-29	K11
Baberton Avenue EH14 5	58-59	F5
Baberton Crescent EH14 5	58-59	F5
Baberton Mains Avenue EH14 3	48-49	F6
Baberton Mains Bank EH14 3	48-49	F6
Baberton Mains Brae EH14 3	48-49	F6
Baberton Mains Court EH14 3	48-49	F6
Baberton Mains Crescent EH14 3	48-49	F6
Baberton Mains Dell EH14 3	48-49	F6
Baberton Mains Drive EH14 3	48-49	F6
Baberton Mains Gardens EH14 3	48-49	F6
Baberton Mains Green EH14 3	48-49	F6
Baberton Mains Grove EH14 3	48-49	F6
Baberton Mains Hill EH14 3	48-49	F6
Baberton Mains Lea EH14 3	48-49	F6
Baberton Mains Loan EH14 3	50-51	G6
Baberton Mains Park EH14 3	48-49	F6
Baberton Mains Place EH14 3	48-49	F6
Baberton Mains Rise EH14 3	48-49	F6
Baberton Mains Row EH14 3	48-49	F6
Baberton Mains Terrace EH14 3	48-49	F6
Baberton Mains View EH14 3	48-49	F6
Baberton Mains Way EH14 3	48-49	F6
Baberton Mains Wood EH14 3	48-49	F6
Baberton Mains Wynd EH14 3	48-49	F6
Baberton Park EH14 5	58-59	F5
Baberton Square EH14 5	58-59	F5
Back Dean EH4 3	28-29	J10
Backlee EH15 3	54-55	N5
Baileyfield Crescent EH15 1	32-33	Q10
Baileyfield Road EH15 1	22-23	P11
Bailie Fyfe's Close EH1 1	8-9	
Bailie Grove EH15 3	32-33	Q9
Bailie Path EH15 3	32-33	Q9
Bailie Terrace EH15 3	32-33	Q9
Baird Avenue EH12 5	40-41	I9
Baird Drive EH12 5	40-41	I9
Baird Gardens EH12 5	40-41	H9
Baird Grove EH12 5	40-41	I9
Baird Terrace EH12 5	40-41	I9
Bakehouse Close EH8 8	8-9	
Baker's Place EH3 5	28-29	K11
Balbirnie Place EH12 5	28-29	J10
Balcarres Court EH10 5	52-53	K7
Balcarres Street EH10 5	52-53	K7
Balderston Gardens EH16 5	44-45	N7
Balfour Place EH6 5	20-21	M12
Balfour Street EH6 5	20-21	M12
Balfron Loan EH4 7	24-25	F11
Balgreen Avenue EH12 5	40-41	H9
Balgreen Gardens EH12 5	40-41	H9
Balgreen Park EH12 5	40-41	H9
Balgreen Road EH12 5	40-41	H9
Ballantyne Lane EH6 5	12-13	M13
Ballantyne Road EH6 5	12-13	M13
Balmoral Place EH3 5	28-29	K11
Balmwell Avenue EH16 6	54-55	N5
Balmwell Grove EH16 6	54-55	N5
Balmwell Terrace EH16 6	54-55	N5
Baltic Street EH6 7	12-13	N13
Bangholm Avenue EH5 3	10-11	K13
Bangholm Bower Avenue EH5 3	10-11	K13
Bangholm Grove EH5 3	12-13	L13
Bangholm Loan EH5 3	12-13	L13
Bangholm Park EH5 3	10-11	K13
Bangholm Place EH5 3	10-11	K13
Bangholm Road EH5 3	10-11	K13
Bangholm Terrace EH3 5	18-19	K12
Bangholm View EH5 3	12-13	L13
Bangholm Villas EH5 3	12-13	L13
Bangor Road EH6 5	12-13	M13
Bank Street EH1 2	28-29	L10
Bankhead Loan EH11 4	48-49	F7
Bankhead Avenue EH11 4	38-39	F8
Bankhead Broadway EH11 4	38-39	E8
Bankhead Crossway North EH11 4	38-39	E8
Bankhead Crossway South EH11 4	48-49	E7
Bankhead Drive EH11 4	48-49	
Bankhead Medway EH11 4	38-39	
Bankhead Place EH11 4	48-49	
Bankhead Terrace EH11 4	48-49	
Bankhead Way EH11 4	48-49	
Barclay Place EH10 4	42-43	
Barclay Terrace EH10 4	42-43	
Barn Park EH14 3	50-51	
Barn Park Crescent EH14 3	50-51	
Barnshot Road EH13 0	60-61	
Barnton Avenue EH4 6	16-17	
Barnton Avenue West EH4 6	14-15	
Barnton Brae EH4 6	14-15	
Barnton Court EH4 6	14-15	
Barnton Gardens EH4 6	16-17	
Barnton Grove EH4 6	14-15	
Barnton Loan EH4 6	14-15	
Barnton Park EH4 6	16-17	
Barnton Park Avenue EH4 6	14-15	
Barnton Park Crescent EH4 6	14-15	
Barnton Park Dell EH4 6	14-15	
Barnton Park Drive EH4 6	14-15	
Barnton Park Gardens EH4 6	14-15	
Barnton Park Grove EH4 6	14-15	
Barnton Park Place EH4 6	14-15	
Barnton Park View EH4 6	14-15	
Barnton Park Wood EH4 6	24-25	
Barnton Roundabout EH4 6	24-25	
Barntongate Avenue EH4 8	24-25	
Barntongate Drive EH4 8	24-25	
Barntongate Terrace EH4 8	24-25	
Baron Maule's Close EH1 1	8-9	
Baronscourt Road EH8 7	20-21	
Baronscourt Terrace EH8 7	20-21	
Barony Place EH3 6	28-29	
Barony Street EH3 6	28-29	
Barony Terrace EH12 8	24-25	
Barrie's Close EH1 1	8-9	
Bath Place EH15 1	22-23	
Bath Road EH6 7	12-13	
Bath Street EH15 1	32-33	
Bath Street Lane EH15 1	32-33	
Bathfield EH6 4	12-13	
Baxters Place EH1 3	20-21	
Beach Lane EH15 1	22-23	
Beauchamp Grove EH16 6	54-55	
Beauchamp Road EH16 6	54-55	
Beaufort Road EH9 1	42-43	
Beaverbank Place EH7 4	18-19	
Beaverhall Road EH7 4	18-19	
Bedford Court EH12 5	40-41	
Bedford Street EH4 1	28-29	
Bedford Terrace EH15 2	32-33	
Beechmount Crescent EH12 5	26-27	
Beechmount Park EH12 5	40-41	
Beechwood Mains EH12 6	26-27	
Beechwood Terrace EH6 8	20-21	
Belford Avenue EH4 3	28-29	
Belford Gardens EH4 3	28-29	
Belford Mews EH4 3	28-29	
Belford Park EH4 3	28-29	
Belford Place EH4 3	28-29	
Belford Road EH4 3	28-29	
Belford Terrace EH4 3	28-29	
Belgrave Crescent EH4 3	28-29	
Belgrave Crescent Lane EH4 3	28-29	
Belgrave Gardens EH12 6	26-27	
Belgrave Mews EH4 3	28-29	
Belgrave Place EH4 3	28-29	
Belgrave Road EH12 6	40-41	
Belgrave Terrace EH12 6	40-41	
Belhaven Place EH10 5	52-53	
Belhaven Terrace EH10 5	52-53	
Bell Place EH3 5	28-29	
Bell's Brae EH4 3	28-29	
Bell's Mills EH4 3	28-29	
Bell's Wynd EH1 1	8-9	
Bellenden Gardens EH16 5	44-45	
Bellevue EH7 4	28-29	
Bellevue Crescent EH3 6	28-29	
Bellevue Gardens EH7 4	18-19	
Bellevue Grove EH7 4	28-29	
Bellevue Lane EH7 4	28-29	
Bellevue Place EH7 4	28-29	
Bellevue Road EH7 4	18-19	
Bellevue Street EH7 4	28-29	
Bellevue Terrace EH7 4	28-29	
Bellfield Lane EH15 2	32-33	
Bellfield Street EH15 2	32-33	
Bellfield Terrace EH15 2	32-33	
Belmont Avenue EH12 6	26-27	
Belmont Crescent EH12 6	26-27	
Belmont Gardens EH12 6	26-27	
Belmont Park EH12 6	26-27	
Belmont Road EH14 5	58-59	
Belmont Terrace EH12 6	26-27	
Belmont View EH12 6	26-27	
Belvedere Park EH6 4	12-13	
Beresford Avenue EH5 3	12-13	
Beresford Gardens EH5 3	12-13	
Beresford Place EH5 3	10-11	
Beresford Terrace EH5 3	12-13	
Bernard Street EH6 6	12-13	
Bernard Terrace EH8 9	30-31	
Biggar Road EH10 7	62-63	
Bingham Avenue EH15 3	32-33	

Street	Page	Grid
ham Broadway EH15 3	32-33	P9
ham Crescent EH15 3	32-33	Q9
ham Crossway EH15 3	32-33	P9
ham Drive EH15 3	32-33	Q9
ham Medway EH15 3	32-33	P9
ham Place EH15 3	32-33	P9
ham Way EH15 3	32-33	P9
h Court EH4 8	24-25	E11
ie's Court EH4 4	16-17	H13
kadder Place EH5 2	10-11	J13
kbarony Road EH9 3	44-45	N7
kchapel Close EH15 3	46-47	Q8
kchapel Road EH15 3	46-47	Q8
ket Avenue EH9 1	30-31	M9
ket Place EH9 1	30-31	M9
kford Avenue EH9 3	42-43	L8
kford Bank EH9 2	42-43	L8
kford Glen Road EH16 6	44-45	M7
kford Hill Grove EH9 3	52-53	L7
kford Hill Rise EH9 3	52-53	L7
kford Hill View EH9 3	52-53	L7
kford Road EH9 2	42-43	L8
kfriars Street EH1 1	30-31	M10
kie Road EH6 7	20-21	N12
kthorn Court EH4 8	24-25	E11
kwood Crescent EH9 1	30-31	M9
eberry Gardens EH4 8	24-25	E11
Street EH1 1	28-29	L10
ntyre Terrace EH10 5	42-43	K8
chfield EH6 5	18-19	L12
nheim Place EH7 5	20-21	M11
kbonny Avenue EH4 3	26-27	I11
kbonny Crescent EH4 3	26-27	I11
kbonny Gardens EH4 3	26-27	I11
kbonny Grove EH4 3	26-27	I11
kbonny Grove West EH4 3	26-27	I11
kbonny Road EH14 6	58-59	E4
kbonny Road EH4 3	26-27	I11
kbonny Terrace EH4 3	26-27	I11
t Green EH3 5	18-19	L12
smill Road EH14 2	50-51	H7
aly Avenue EH13 0	60-61	H5
aly Brae EH13 0	60-61	H5
aly Crescent EH13 0	60-61	H5
aly Drive EH13 0	60-61	H5
aly Gardens EH13 0	60-61	H5
aly Grove EH13 0	60-61	H5
aly Rise EH13 0	60-61	H5
aly Road EH13 0	60-61	H5
aly Steading EH13 0	60-61	H5
aly Terrace EH13 0	60-61	H5
aly Wester EH13 0	60-61	H5
ar Place EH6 4	12-13	L13
ngton Avenue EH6 5	12-13	L13
ngton Grove EH6 4	12-13	L13
ngton Road EH6 5	20-21	M12
ngton Road Lane EH6 5	20-21	M12
ngton Terrace EH6 4	12-13	L13
nyhaugh Lane EH6 5	18-19	L12
hacre Cottages EH6 7	20-21	O12
hacre Lane EH6 7	20-21	O12
ughloch Loan EH8 9	30-31	M9
ughloch Square EH8 9	30-31	M9
nwick Place EH12 5	28-29	J10
nwick's Close EH1 1	8-9	
wall Avenue EH5 2	10-11	J13
wall Crescent EH5 2	10-11	J13
wall Drive EH5 2	10-11	J13
wall Gardens EH5 2	10-11	J13
wall Green EH5 2	10-11	K13
wall Grove EH5 2	10-11	J13
wall Loan EH5 1	10-11	J13
wall Parkway EH5 2	10-11	J13
wall Place EH5 2	10-11	J13
wall Quadrant EH5 2	10-11	J13
wall Road EH5 3	10-11	K13
wall Square EH5 2	10-11	J13
wall Terrace EH5 2	10-11	J13
well Street EH6 7	20-21	M11
ndary Road East EH14 4	48-49	D6
ndary Road West EH14 4	48-49	D6
hill Terrace EH3 5	18-19	K12
ling Green, The EH6 5	12-13	M13
ling Lane EH6 6	12-13	M13
mont Place EH8 9	30-31	M9
d's Entry EH1 1	30-31	M10
Park EH4 6	14-15	E12
Park EH4 6	14-15	E12
burn Drive EH14 6	58-59	E4
foot Terrace EH9 3	44-45	N7
head Avenue EH4 6	14-15	E12
head Bank EH4 6	14-15	E12
head Crescent EH4 6	14-15	E12
head Drive EH4 6	14-15	E12
head Grove EH4 6	14-15	E12
head Loan EH4 6	14-15	E12
head Park EH4 6	14-15	E12
head Road EH4 6	14-15	E12
head Row EH4 6	14-15	E12
head View EH4 6	14-15	E12
d Avenue EH10 6	52-53	K7
d Crescent EH10 6	52-53	K7
d Farm Road EH10 6	52-53	K7
d Hills Approach EH10 6	52-53	K6
d Hills Avenue EH10 6	52-53	K7
d Hills EH10 6	52-53	K6
Braid Hills Drive EH16 6	52-53	L6
Braid Hills Road EH10 6	52-53	K6
Braid Mount EH10 6	52-53	K6
Braid Mount Crest EH10 6	52-53	K6
Braid Mount Rise EH10 6	52-53	K6
Braid Mount View EH10 6	52-53	K6
Braid Road EH10 6	52-53	K7
Braidburn Crescent EH10 6	52-53	K7
Braidburn Terrace EH10 6	52-53	K7
Bramble Drive EH4 8	24-25	E11
Bramdean Grove EH10 6	52-53	K6
Bramdean Place EH10 6	52-53	K6
Bramdean Rise EH10 6	52-53	K6
Bramdean View EH10 6	52-53	K6
Brand Drive EH15 3	32-33	Q10
Brand Gardens EH15 3	32-33	Q10
Brand Place EH6 8	20-21	N11
Brandfield Street EH3 8	42-43	K9
Brandon Street EH3 5	28-29	L11
Brandon Terrace EH3 5	28-29	L11
Bread Street EH3 9	28-29	K10
Bread Street South Lane EH3 9	28-29	K10
Breadalbane Street EH6 5	12-13	M13
Breadalbane Terrace EH11 2	28-29	K10
Briarbank Terrace EH11 1	42-43	J8
Brickfield EH15 1	22-23	Q11
Bridge Place EH4 1	28-29	K11
Bridge Road EH13 0	60-61	H5
Bridge Street EH15 1	22-23	Q11
Bridge Street Lane EH15 1	22-23	Q11
Briery Bauks EH8 9	30-31	M10
Bright Terrace EH11 2	28-29	K10
Bright's Crescent EH9 2	44-45	M8
Brighton Crescent East EH15 1	32-33	Q10
Brighton Crescent West EH15 1	32-33	Q10
Brighton Place EH15 1	32-33	Q10
Brighton Street EH1 1	28-29	L10
Bristo Place EH1 1	28-29	L10
Bristo Port EH1 1	28-29	L10
Britannia Way EH6 6	12-13	M13
Britwell Crescent EH7 6	20-21	O11
Broad Wynd EH6 6	12-13	N13
Broombank Terrace EH12 7	38-39	F8
Broomburn Grove EH12 7	40-41	G9
Broomfield Crescent EH12 7	40-41	G9
Broomhall Avenue EH12 7	38-39	F9
Broomhall Bank EH12 7	38-39	F9
Broomhall Crescent EH12 7	38-39	F9
Broomhall Drive EH12 7	38-39	F9
Broomhall Gardens EH12 7	38-39	F9
Broomhall Loan EH12 7	38-39	F9
Broomhall Park EH12 7	38-39	F9
Broomhall Place EH12 7	38-39	F9
Broomhall Road EH12 7	38-39	F9
Broomhall Terrace EH12 7	38-39	F9
Broomhouse Avenue EH11 3	40-41	G8
Broomhouse Bank EH11 3	40-41	G8
Broomhouse Cottages EH11 3	38-39	F8
Broomhouse Cottages EH11 3	40-41	G8
Broomhouse Court EH11 3	40-41	G8
Broomhouse Crescent EH11 3	40-41	G8
Broomhouse Drive EH11 3	40-41	G8
Broomhouse Gardens EH11 3	38-39	F8
Broomhouse Gardens East EH11 3	40-41	G8
Broomhouse Gardens West EH11 3	38-39	F8
Broomhouse Grove EH11 3	40-41	G8
Broomhouse Loan EH11 3	40-41	G8
Broomhouse Market EH11 3	40-41	G8
Broomhouse Medway EH11 3	40-41	G8
Broomhouse Park EH11 3	38-39	F8
Broomhouse Place North EH11 3	38-39	F8
Broomhouse Place South EH11 3	40-41	G8
Broomhouse Road EH12 9	38-39	F8
Broomhouse Row EH11 3	40-41	G8
Broomhouse Square EH11 3	40-41	G8
Broomhouse Street North EH11 3	38-39	F8
Broomhouse Street South EH11 3	50-51	G7
Broomhouse Terrace EH11 3	40-41	G8
Broomhouse Walk EH11 3	40-41	G8
Broomlea Crescent EH12 7	38-39	F9
Broompark Road EH12 7	38-39	F9
Broomside Terrace EH12 7	40-41	G9
Broomyknowe EH14 1	50-51	H6
Brougham Place EH3 9	42-43	L9
Brougham Street EH3 9	42-43	K9
Broughton Market EH3 6	28-29	L11
Broughton Place EH1 3	28-29	L11
Broughton Place East EH1 3	28-29	L11
Broughton Place Lane EH1 3	28-29	L11
Broughton Road EH7 4	18-19	L12
Broughton Street EH1 3	28-29	L11
Broughton Street Lane EH1 3	28-29	L11
Brown Street EH8 9	30-31	M10
Brown's Close EH8 8	30-31	M10
Brown's Place EH1 2	28-29	L10
Bruce Street EH10 5	52-53	K7
Brunstane Bank EH15 2	32-33	R9
Brunstane Crescent EH15 2	32-33	R9
Brunstane Drive EH15 2	32-33	R9
Brunstane Gardens EH15 2	32-33	R10
Brunstane Gardens Mews EH15 2	32-33	R10
Brunstane Road EH15 2	32-33	R10
Brunstane Road North EH15 2	32-33	R10
Brunstane Road South EH15 2	32-33	R9
Brunswick Place EH7 5	20-21	M11
Brunswick Road EH7 5	20-21	M11
Brunswick Street EH7 5	20-21	M11
Brunswick Street Lane EH7 5	20-21	M11
Brunswick Terrace EH7 5	20-21	M11
Brunton Gardens EH7 5	20-21	M11
Brunton Place EH7 5	20-21	M11
Brunton Terrace EH7 5	20-21	M11
Bruntsfield Avenue EH10 4	42-43	K9
Bruntsfield Crescent EH10 4	42-43	K9
Bruntsfield Gardens EH10 4	42-43	K9
Bruntsfield Place EH10 4	42-43	K9
Bruntsfield Terrace EH10 4	42-43	K9
Bryce Avenue EH7 6	22-23	P11
Bryce Crescent EH14 5	58-59	E5
Bryce Grove EH7 6	22-23	P11
Bryce Place EH14 5	58-59	E5
Bryce Road EH14 5	58-59	E5
Bryson Road EH11 1	42-43	J9
Buccleuch Place EH8 9	42-43	L9
Buccleuch Street EH8 9	30-31	M9
Buccleuch Terrace EH8 9	30-31	M9
Buchanan Street EH6 8	20-21	M12
Buckingham Terrace EH4 3	28-29	J11
Buckstane Park EH10 6	52-53	K5
Buckstone Avenue EH10 6	62-63	K5
Buckstone Bank EH10 6	52-53	K6
Buckstone Circle EH10 6	62-63	L5
Buckstone Close EH10 6	62-63	L5
Buckstone Court EH10 6	62-63	L5
Buckstone Crescent EH10 6	52-53	K6
Buckstone Crook EH10 6	62-63	L5
Buckstone Dell EH10 6	52-53	K6
Buckstone Drive EH10 6	52-53	K6
Buckstone Gardens EH10 6	62-63	K5
Buckstone Gate EH10 6	62-63	L5
Buckstone Green EH10 6	62-63	L5
Buckstone Grove EH10 6	52-53	K6
Buckstone Hill EH10 6	52-53	L6
Buckstone Howe EH10 6	62-63	L5
Buckstone Lea EH10 6	62-63	L5
Buckstone Loan EH10 6	62-63	K5
Buckstone Loan East EH10 6	62-63	L5
Buckstone Neuk EH10 6	52-53	L6
Buckstone Place EH10 6	62-63	K5
Buckstone Rise EH10 6	62-63	K5
Buckstone Road EH10 6	62-63	K5
Buckstone Row EH10 6	62-63	L5
Buckstone Shaw EH10 6	62-63	L5
Buckstone Terrace EH10 6	62-63	K5
Buckstone View EH10 6	52-53	K6
Buckstone Way EH10 6	52-53	K6
Buckstone Wood EH10 6	62-63	K5
Buckstone Wynd EH10 6	62-63	L5
Bughtlin Drive EH12 8	24-25	E11
Bughtlin Gardens EH12 8	24-25	E10
Bughtlin Green EH12 8	24-25	E11
Bughtlin Loan EH12 8	24-25	E10
Bughtlin Market EH12 8	24-25	E10
Bughtlin Park EH12 8	24-25	E10
Bughtlin Place EH12 8	24-25	E11
Bull's Close EH8 8	8-9	
Burdiehouse Avenue EH17 8	64-65	N4
Burdiehouse Crescent EH17 8	64-65	N4
Burdiehouse Crossway EH17 8	64-65	N4
Burdiehouse Drive EH17 8	64-65	N4
Burdiehouse Loan EH17 8	64-65	N4
Burdiehouse Medway EH17 8	64-65	N4
Burdiehouse Place EH17 8	64-65	N4
Burdiehouse Road EH17 8	64-65	N4
Burdiehouse Square EH17 8	64-65	N4
Burdiehouse Street EH17 8	64-65	N4
Burdiehouse Terrace EH17 8	64-65	N4
Burgess Street EH6 6	12-13	N13
Burgess Terrace EH9 2	44-45	N8
Burghtoft EH17 8	56-57	P5
Burlington Street EH6 5	12-13	M13
Burnbrae EH12 8	24-25	E10
Burnet's Close EH1 1	8-9	
Burnhead Crescent EH16 6	54-55	N5
Burnhead Grove EH16 6	54-55	N5
Burnhead Loan EH16 6	54-55	N5
Burnhead Path East EH16 6	54-55	N5
Burnhead Path West EH16 6	54-55	N5
Burns Place EH16 5	18-19	L12
Burns Street EH6 8	20-21	N12
Burnside EH12 8	24-25	E10
Cables Wynd EH6 5	12-13	M13
Caddell's Row EH4 5	14-15	E13
Cadiz Street EH6 7	12-13	N13
Cadogan Road EH16 6	54-55	N6
Caerketton Cottages EH13 9	50-51	I6
Cairnmuir Road EH12 6	26-27	G10
Cairntows Close EH16 4	44-45	O8
Caithness Place EH5 3	10-11	K13
Caiyside EH10 7	62-63	K4
Caiystane Avenue EH10 6	62-63	K5
Caiystane Crescent EH10 6	62-63	J5
Caiystane Drive EH10 6	62-63	J5
Caiystane Gardens EH10 6	62-63	J5
Caiystane Hill EH10 6	62-63	K5
Caiystane Terrace EH10 6	62-63	J5
Caiystane View EH10 7	62-63	K5
Calder Court EH11 4	48-49	F7
Calder Crescent EH11 4	48-49	E7
Calder Drive EH11 4	48-49	F7
Calder Gardens EH11 4	48-49	F7

Street	Pages	Grid
Calder Grove EH11 4	48-49	F7
Calder Park EH11 4	48-49	F7
Calder Place EH11 4	48-49	F7
Calder Road EH11 3	40-41	G8
Calder Road Gardens EH11 3	40-41	H8
Calder View EH11 4	48-49	E7
Caledonian Crescent EH11 2	42-43	J9
Caledonian Place EH11 2	42-43	J9
Caledonian Road EH11 2	28-29	K10
Calton Hill EH1 3	28-29	L11
Calton Road EH8 8	30-31	M10
Cambridge Avenue EH6 5	20-21	M12
Cambridge Gardens EH6 5	20-21	M12
Cambridge Street EH1 2	28-29	K10
Cambusnethan Street EH7 5	20-21	N11
Cameron Crescent EH16 5	44-45	N8
Cameron House Avenue EH16 5	44-45	N8
Cameron March EH16 5	44-45	N8
Cameron Park EH16 5	44-45	N8
Cameron Smail Road EH14 4	48-49	D6
Cameron Terrace EH16 5	44-45	N8
Cameron Toll EH16 5	44-45	N8
Cameron Toll Gardens EH16 4	44-45	N8
Cammo Bank EH4 8	24-25	E11
Cammo Brae EH4 8	24-25	E11
Cammo Crescent EH4 8	24-25	E11
Cammo Gardens EH4 8	24-25	E11
Cammo Grove EH4 8	24-25	D11
Cammo Hill EH4 8	24-25	D11
Cammo Parkway EH4 8	24-25	E11
Cammo Place EH4 8	24-25	E11
Cammo Road EH4 8	24-25	D11
Cammo Walk EH12 0	24-25	D11
Campbell Avenue EH12 6	26-27	I10
Campbell Park Crescent EH13 0	60-61	G5
Campbell Park Drive EH13 0	60-61	G5
Campbell Road EH12 6	26-27	I10
Campbell's Close EH8 8	8-9	
Camus Avenue EH10 6	62-63	K5
Camus Park EH10 6	62-63	K5
Canaan Lane EH10 4	42-43	K8
Candlemaker Row EH1 2	28-29	L10
Candlemaker's Crescent EH17 8	56-57	P5
Candlemaker's Park EH17 8	56-57	P5
Canning Street EH3 8	28-29	K10
Canning Street Lane EH3 8	28-29	K10
Cannon Wynd EH6 4	12-13	M13
Canon Lane EH3 5	28-29	L11
Canon Street EH3 5	18-19	L12
Canongate EH8 8	30-31	M10
Canonmills EH3 5	18-19	L12
Capelaw Road EH13 0	60-61	H5
Captain's Drive EH16 6	54-55	N5
Captain's Road EH17 8	54-55	N5
Captain's Row EH16 6	54-55	N5
Carberry Place EH12 5	28-29	J10
Carfrae Gardens EH4 3	26-27	H11
Carfrae Grove EH4 3	26-27	H11
Carfrae Park EH4 3	26-27	H11
Carfrae Road EH4 3	26-27	H11
Cargil Court EH5 3	10-11	K13
Cargil Terrace EH5 3	10-11	K13
Carlton Street EH4 1	28-29	K11
Carlton Terrace EH7 5	20-21	M11
Carlton Terrace Brae EH7 5	20-21	M11
Carlton Terrace Mews EH7 5	20-21	M11
Carlyle Place EH7 5	20-21	N11
Carnbee Avenue EH16 6	54-55	O5
Carnbee Crescent EH16 6	54-55	O5
Carnbee Dell EH16 6	54-55	O5
Carnbee End EH16 6	54-55	O6
Carnbee Park EH16 6	54-55	O5
Carnegie Street EH8 9	30-31	M10
Carnethy Avenue EH13 0	60-61	H5
Caroline Gardens EH12 6	26-27	G10
Caroline Park Grove EH5 1	10-11	I13
Caroline Place EH12 6	26-27	G10
Caroline Terrace EH12 8	24-25	F10
Carrick Knowe Avenue EH12 7	40-41	G9
Carrick Knowe Drive EH12 7	40-41	G9
Carrick Knowe Gardens EH12 7	40-41	G9
Carrick Knowe Grove EH12 7	40-41	G9
Carrick Knowe Hill EH12 7	40-41	G9
Carrick Knowe Loan EH12 7	40-41	G9
Carrick Knowe Parkway EH12 7	40-41	G9
Carrick Knowe Place EH12 7	40-41	G9
Carrick Knowe Road EH12 7	40-41	G8
Carrick Knowe Terrace EH12 7	40-41	G9
Carrington Road EH4 1	28-29	J11
Carron Place EH6 7	12-13	N13
Carrubber's Close EH1 1	8-9	
Casselbank Street EH6 5	20-21	M12
Cassels Lane EH6 5	20-21	M12
Castle Avenue EH12 7	38-39	F9
Castle Street EH2 3	28-29	K10
Castle Terrace EH1 2	28-29	K10
Castlehill EH1 2	28-29	L10
Castlelaw Road EH13 0	60-61	H5
Cathcart Place EH11 2	42-43	J9
Cathedral Lane EH1 3	28-29	L11
Causeway, The EH15 3	30-31	O9
Causewayside EH9 1	30-31	M9
Cavalry Park Drive EH15 3	30-31	O9
Chalmer's Buildings EH3 8	28-29	K10
Chalmer's Close EH1 1	8-9	
Chalmers Crescent EH9 1	42-43	L9
Chalmers Street EH3 9	28-29	L10
Chamberlain Road EH10 4	42-43	K8
Chambers Street EH1 1	28-29	L10
Chancelot Crescent EH6 4	12-13	L13
Chancelot Grove EH5 3	12-13	L13
Chancelot Terrace EH6 4	12-13	L13
Chapel Court EH16 4	46-47	P8
Chapel Lane EH6 6	12-13	N13
Chapel Street EH8 9	30-31	M9
Charles Street EH8 9	28-29	L10
Charles Street Lane EH8 9	28-29	L10
Charlesfield EH8 9	28-29	L10
Charlotte Lane EH2 4	28-29	K10
Charlotte Square EH2 4	28-29	K10
Charterhall Grove EH9 3	42-43	L8
Charterhall Road EH9 3	52-53	L7
Cherry Tree Avenue EH14 5	70-71	C4
Cherry Tree Crescent EH14 5	70-71	C4
Cherry Tree Gardens EH14 5	70-71	C4
Cherry Tree Grove EH14 5	70-71	C4
Cherry Tree Loan EH14 5	58-59	D4
Cherry Tree Park EH14 5	70-71	C4
Cherry Tree Place EH14 5	58-59	D4
Cherry Tree View EH14 5	58-59	D4
Chessel's Court EH8 8	8-9	
Chesser Avenue EH14 1	40-41	H8
Chesser Cottages EH11 3	40-41	I8
Chesser Crescent EH14 1	40-41	I8
Chesser Gardens EH14 1	40-41	H8
Chesser Grove EH14 1	40-41	H8
Chesser Loan EH14 1	40-41	H8
Chester Street EH3 7	28-29	K10
Chestnut Street EH5 1	10-11	J14
Cheyne Street EH4 1	28-29	K11
Christian Crescent EH15 3	32-33	Q10
Christian Grove EH15 3	32-33	Q10
Christie Miller Avenue EH7 6	22-23	P11
Christie Miller Grove EH7 6	22-23	P11
Christie Miller Place EH7 6	22-23	P11
Chuckie Pend EH3 9	28-29	K10
Church Hill EH10 4	42-43	K8
Church Hill Drive EH10 4	42-43	K8
Church Hill Place EH10 4	42-43	K8
Circus Gardens EH3 6	28-29	K11
Circus Lane EH3 6	28-29	K11
Circus Place EH3 6	28-29	K11
Citadel Place EH6 6	12-13	M13
City Bypass EH12 9	38-39	D9
Clackmae Grove EH16 6	54-55	M6
Clackmae Road EH16 6	54-55	M6
Clapper Lane EH16 5	44-45	N7
Clarebank Crescent EH6 7	20-21	N12
Claremont Bank EH7 4	28-29	L11
Claremont Court EH7 4	18-19	L12
Claremont Crescent EH7 4	18-19	L12
Claremont Gardens EH6 7	20-21	N12
Claremont Grove EH7 4	18-19	L12
Claremont Park EH6 7	20-21	N12
Claremont Road EH6 7	20-21	N12
Clarence Street EH3 5	28-29	K11
Clarendon Crescent EH4 1	28-29	K11
Clarinda Terrace EH16 6	54-55	N6
Clark Avenue EH5 3	12-13	L13
Clark Place EH5 3	10-11	K13
Clark Road EH5 3	10-11	K13
Claverhouse Drive EH16 6	54-55	N6
Clearburn Crescent EH15 5	44-45	N8
Clearburn Gardens EH16 5	44-45	N8
Clearburn Road EH16 5	44-45	N8
Cleekim Drive EH15 3	46-47	Q8
Cleikiminfield EH15 3	46-47	Q8
Cleikiminrig EH15 3	46-47	Q8
Clerk Street EH8 9	30-31	M9
Clermiston Avenue EH4 7	24-25	F11
Clermiston Crescent EH4 7	24-25	F11
Clermiston Drive EH4 7	24-25	F11
Clermiston Gardens EH4 7	24-25	F11
Clermiston Green EH4 7	24-25	F11
Clermiston Grove EH4 7	24-25	F11
Clermiston Hill EH4 7	24-25	F11
Clermiston Loan EH4 7	24-25	F11
Clermiston Medway EH4 7	24-25	F11
Clermiston Park EH4 7	24-25	F11
Clermiston Place EH4 7	24-25	F11
Clermiston Road EH12 6	26-27	G10
Clermiston Road North EH4 7	26-27	G11
Clermiston Terrace EH12 6	26-27	G10
Clermiston View EH4 7	26-27	G10
Clerwood Bank EH12 8	24-25	F10
Clerwood Gardens EH12 8	24-25	F10
Clerwood Gardens EH12 8	24-25	F10
Clerwood Grove EH12 8	26-27	G10
Clerwood Loan EH12 8	24-25	F10
Clerwood Park EH12 8	24-25	F10
Clerwood Place EH12 8	26-27	G10
Clerwood Row EH12 8	24-25	F10
Clerwood Terrace EH12 8	26-27	G10
Clerwood View EH12 8	26-27	G10
Clerwood Way EH12 8	24-25	F10
Clifton Terrace EH12 5	28-29	K10
Clinton Road EH9 2	42-43	K8
Clockmill Lane EH8 8	20-21	N11
Clovenstone Drive EH14 3	50-51	G6
Clovenstone Gardens EH14 3	50-51	G6
Clovenstone Park EH14 3	50-51	G6
Clovenstone Road EH14 3	50-51	G6
Cluny Avenue EH10 4	52-53	
Cluny Drive EH10 6	52-53	
Cluny Gardens EH10 6	52-53	
Cluny Place EH10 4	52-53	
Cluny Terrace EH10 4	52-53	
Clyde Street EH1 3	28-29	
Coates Crescent EH3 7	28-29	
Coates Gardens EH12 5	28-29	
Coates Place EH12 5	28-29	
Coatfield Lane EH6 6	12-13	
Cobden Crescent EH9 2	44-45	
Cobden Road EH9 2	44-45	
Cobden Terrace EH11 2	28-29	
Coburg Street EH6 6	12-13	
Cochran Terrace EH7 4	28-29	
Cochrane Place EH6 8	20-21	
Cockburn Street EH1 1	28-29	
Coillesdene Avenue EH15 2	34-35	
Coillesdene Crescent EH15 2	32-33	
Coillesdene Drive EH15 2	32-33	
Coillesdene Gardens EH15 2	32-33	
Coillesdene Grove EH15 2	32-33	
Coillesdene Loan EH15 2	34-35	
Coillesdene Terrace EH15 2	32-33	
Colinton Grove EH14 1	50-51	
Colinton Grove West EH14 1	50-51	
Colinton Mains Crescent EH13 9	60-61	
Colinton Mains Drive EH13 9	50-51	
Colinton Mains Gardens EH13 9	50-51	
Colinton Mains Green EH13 9	50-51	
Colinton Mains Grove EH13 9	52-53	
Colinton Mains Loan EH13 9	50-51	
Colinton Mains Place EH13 9	52-53	
Colinton Mains Road EH13 9	50-51	
Colinton Mains Terrace EH13 9	52-53	
Colinton Road EH14 1	50-51	
College Court EH7 6	22-23	
Collins Place EH3 5	28-29	
Colmestone Gate EH10 6	62-63	
Coltbridge Avenue EH12 6	26-27	
Coltbridge Gardens EH12 6	28-29	
Coltbridge Millside EH12 6	26-27	
Coltbridge Terrace EH12 6	26-27	
Coltbridge Vale EH12 6	28-29	
Columba Avenue EH4 3	26-27	
Columba Road EH4 3	26-27	
Colville Place EH3 5	28-29	
Comely Bank Road EH4 1	28-29	
Comely Bank EH4 1	28-29	
Comely Bank Avenue EH4 1	28-29	
Comely Bank Grove EH4 1	28-29	
Comely Bank Place EH4 1	28-29	
Comely Bank Place Mews EH4 1	28-29	
Comely Bank Row EH4 1	28-29	
Comely Bank Street EH4 1	28-29	
Comely Bank Terrace EH4 1	28-29	
Comely Green Crescent EH7 5	20-21	
Comely Green Place EH7 5	20-21	
Comiston Drive EH10 5	52-53	
Comiston Gardens EH10 5	52-53	
Comiston Grove EH10 6	52-53	
Comiston Place EH10 6	52-53	
Comiston Rise EH10 6	52-53	
Comiston Road EH10 6	62-63	
Comiston Springs Avenue EH10 6	52-53	
Comiston Terrace EH10 6	52-53	
Comiston View EH10 6	52-53	
Comley Bank Road EH4 1	28-29	
Commercial Street EH6 6	12-13	
Commercial Wharf EH6 6	12-13	
Connaught Place EH6 4	12-13	
Considine Gardens EH8 7	20-21	
Considine Terrace EH8 7	20-21	
Constitution Street EH6 7	12-13	
Corbiehill Avenue EH4 5	16-17	
Corbiehill Crescent EH4 5	16-17	
Corbiehill Gardens EH4 5	16-17	
Corbiehill Grove EH4 5	16-17	
Corbiehill Park EH4 5	16-17	
Corbiehill Place EH4 5	16-17	
Corbiehill Road EH4 5	16-17	
Corbieshot EH15 3	32-33	
Cornhill Terrace EH6 8	20-21	
Cornwall Street EH3 9	28-29	
Cornwallis Place EH7 4	28-29	
Corrennie Drive EH10 6	52-53	
Corrennie Gardens EH10 6	52-53	
Corslet Crescent EH14 5	58-59	
Corslet Place EH14 5	58-59	
Corslet Road EH14 5	58-59	
Corstorphine Bank Avenue EH12 8	24-25	
Corstorphine Bank Drive EH12 8	24-25	
Corstorphine Bank Terrace EH12 8	24-25	
Corstorphine High Street EH12 7	38-39	
Corstorphine Hill Avenue EH12 6	26-27	
Corstorphine Hill Crescent EH12 6	26-27	
Corstorphine Hill Gardens EH12 6	26-27	
Corstorphine Hill Road EH12 6	26-27	
Corstorphine House Avenue EH12 7	40-41	
Corstorphine House Terrace EH12 7	40-41	
Corstorphine Park Gardens EH12 7	40-41	
Corstorphine Road EH12 6	40-41	
Corunna Place EH6 5	12-13	
Cottage Green EH4 6	14-15	
Cottage Park EH4 6	26-27	

Street	Page	Grid
...per Street EH6 6	12-13	M13
...enant Close EH1 1	8-9	
...an Road EH11 1	42-43	J8
...an's Close EH8 9	30-31	M9
...gate EH1 1	30-31	M10
...gatehead EH1 2	28-29	L10
...field EH11 2	40-41	I9
...g's Close EH1 1	8-9	
gcrook Avenue EH4 3	26-27	G11
gcrook Gardens EH4 3	26-27	H11
gcrook Grove EH4 3	26-27	H11
gcrook Park EH4 3	26-27	H11
gcrook Place EH4 3	26-27	I11
gcrook Road EH4 7	26-27	G11
gcrook Square EH4 3	26-27	H11
gcrook Terrace EH4 3	26-27	H11
gend EH16 5	44-45	O7
gentinny Avenue EH7 6	22-23	P11
gentinny Avenue North EH7 7	20-21	O12
gentinny Crescent EH7 6	22-23	P11
gentinny Grove EH7 6	22-23	P11
gentinny Place EH7 6	22-23	P11
gentinny Road EH7 6	22-23	P11
ghall Avenue EH6 4	12-13	L13
ghall Bank EH6 4	12-13	L13
ghall Crescent EH6 4	12-13	L13
ghall Gardens EH6 4	12-13	L13
ghall Road EH5 3	12-13	L13
ghall Terrace EH6 4	12-13	L13
ghill Gardens EH10 5	52-53	J7
ghouse Avenue EH10 5	52-53	J7
ghouse Gardens EH10 5	52-53	J7
ghouse Park EH10 5	52-53	J7
ghouse Road EH10 5	52-53	J7
ghouse Terrace EH10 5	52-53	J7
gievar Square EH12 8	24-25	E10
gievar Wynd EH12 8	24-25	E10
glea Drive EH10 5	52-53	K7
glea Place EH10 5	52-53	J7
gleith Avenue North EH4 3	26-27	I10
gleith Avenue South EH4 3	26-27	I10
gleith Bank EH4 3	26-27	I11
gleith Crescent EH4 3	26-27	I11
gleith Drive EH4 3	26-27	I11
gleith Gardens EH4 3	26-27	I11
gleith Grove EH4 3	26-27	I11
gleith Hill EH4 2	26-27	I11
gleith Hill Avenue EH4 2	28-29	J11
gleith Hill Crescent EH4 2	26-27	I11
gleith Hill Gardens EH4 2	28-29	J11
gleith Hill Green EH4 2	26-27	I11
gleith Hill Grove EH4 2	26-27	I11
gleith Hill Loan EH4 2	26-27	I11
gleith Hill Park EH4 2	26-27	I11
gleith Hill Row EH4 2	26-27	I11
gleith Rise EH4 2	26-27	I10
gleith Road EH4 2	26-27	I11
gleith View EH4 3	26-27	I10
glockhart Avenue EH14 1	50-51	I7
glockhart Bank EH14 1	50-51	I7
glockhart Crescent EH14 1	50-51	I7
glockhart Dell Road EH14 1	50-51	I7
glockhart Drive North EH14 1	50-51	I7
glockhart Drive South EH14 1	50-51	I7
glockhart Gardens EH14 1	50-51	I7
glockhart Grove EH14 1	50-51	I7
glockhart Loan EH14 1	50-51	I6
glockhart Park EH14 1	50-51	I7
glockhart Place EH14 1	50-51	I7
glockhart Quadrant EH14 1	50-51	I7
glockhart Road EH14 1	50-51	I7
glockhart Road North EH14 1	50-51	I7
glockhart Terrace EH14 1	42-43	J8
glockhart View EH14 1	50-51	I7
igmillar Castle Avenue EH16 4	44-45	O8
igmillar Castle Gardens EH16 4	44-45	O8
igmillar Castle Grove EH16 4	44-45	O8
igmillar Castle Loan EH16 4	44-45	O8
igmillar Castle Road EH16 4	44-45	O8
igmillar Castle Terrace EH16 4	44-45	O8
igmillar Park EH16 5	44-45	M8
igmount Avenue EH12 8	24-25	F10
igmount Avenue North EH12 8	24-25	F11
igmount Bank EH4 8	24-25	E11
igmount Bank West EH4 8	24-25	E11
igmount Brae EH12 8	24-25	E11
igmount Court EH4 8	24-25	E11
igmount Crescent EH12 8	24-25	E10
igmount Drive EH12 8	24-25	E10
igmount Gardens EH12 8	24-25	E10
igmount Grove EH12 8	24-25	E10
igmount Grove North EH12 8	24-25	E10
igmount Hill EH4 8	24-25	E11
igmount Loan EH12 8	24-25	E10
igmount Park EH12 8	24-25	E10
igmount Place EH12 8	24-25	E10
igmount Terrace EH12 8	24-25	E10
igmount View EH12 8	24-25	E10
igmount Way EH12 8	24-25	F11
igour Avenue EH17 7	54-55	O6
igour Crescent EH17 7	56-57	P6
igour Drive EH17 7	56-57	P6
igour Gardens EH17 7	54-55	O6
igour Green EH17 7	54-55	O6
igour Grove EH17 7	56-57	P6
igour Loan EH17 7	56-57	P6
Craigour Place EH17 7	56-57	P6
Craigour Terrace EH17 7	56-57	P6
Craigs Avenue EH12 8	38-39	F9
Craigs Bank EH12 8	24-25	E10
Craigs Crescent EH12 8	24-25	F10
Craigs Drive EH12 8	24-25	E10
Craigs Gardens EH12 8	24-25	E10
Craigs Grove EH12 8	38-39	F9
Craigs Loan EH12 8	24-25	F10
Craigs Park EH12 8	24-25	E10
Craigs Road EH12 8	24-25	E10
Cramond Avenue EH4 6	14-15	E13
Cramond Bank EH4 6	14-15	E13
Cramond Bridge Cottages EH4 6	14-15	D12
Cramond Brig Toll EH4 6	14-15	D12
Cramond Crescent EH4 6	14-15	E13
Cramond Gardens EH4 6	14-15	E13
Cramond Glebe Gardens EH4 6	14-15	E13
Cramond Glebe Road EH4 6	14-15	F13
Cramond Glebe Terrace EH4 6	14-15	E13
Cramond Green EH4 6	14-15	E13
Cramond Grove EH4 6	14-15	E13
Cramond Park EH4 6	14-15	E13
Cramond Place EH4 6	14-15	F13
Cramond Regis EH4 6	14-15	E12
Cramond Road North EH4 6	14-15	F13
Cramond Road South EH4 5	16-17	G13
Cramond Terrace EH4 6	14-15	E13
Cramond Vale EH4 6	14-15	E13
Cramond Village EH4 6	14-15	E13
Cranston Street EH1 1	30-31	M10
Crarae Avenue EH4 3	26-27	I10
Craufurdland EH4 6	14-15	E12
Crawford Road EH16 5	44-45	M8
Crewe Bank EH5 2	10-11	J13
Crewe Crescent EH5 2	10-11	I13
Crewe Grove EH5 2	10-11	J13
Crewe Loan EH5 2	10-11	I13
Crewe Place EH5 2	10-11	I13
Crewe Road Gardens EH5 2	10-11	I13
Crewe Road North EH5 2	10-11	I13
Crewe Road South EH4 2	16-17	I12
Crewe Road West EH5 2	10-11	I13
Crewe Terrace EH5 2	10-11	J13
Crewe Toll EH4 2	16-17	I12
Crichton Street EH8 9	28-29	L10
Crighton Place EH7 4	20-21	M12
Crighton's Close EH8 8	8-9	
Croall Place EH7 4	20-21	M11
Croft-an-Righ EH8 8	20-21	M11
Cromwell Place EH6 6	12-13	M13
Crown Street EH6 8	20-21	M12
Cuddy Lane EH10 4	42-43	K8
Cuddy Lane EH10 4	42-43	K8
Cultins Road EH11 4	48-49	E7
Cumberland Street EH3 6	28-29	L11
Cumberland Street; NE. Lane EH3 6	28-29	L11
Cumberland Street; NW. Lane EH3 6	28-29	L11
Cumberland Street; SE. Lane EH3 6	28-29	L11
Cumberland Street; SW. Lane EH3 6	28-29	L11
Cumin Place EH9 2	30-31	M9
Cumlodden Avenue EH12 6	26-27	I10
Cumnor Crescent EH16 6	44-45	N7
Curriehill Castle Drive EH14 5	70-71	C4
Curriehill Road EH14 4	58-59	D5
Currievale Drive EH14 5	58-59	D4
Currievale Park EH14 5	58-59	D4
Currievale Park Grove EH14 5	58-59	D4
Daiches Braes EH15 2	32-33	R9
Daisy Terrace EH11 1	42-43	J8
Dalgety Avenue EH7 5	20-21	N11
Dalgety Road EH7 5	20-21	N11
Dalgety Street EH7 5	20-21	N11
Dalhousie Terrace EH10 5	52-53	K7
Dalkeith Road EH16 5	44-45	N8
Dalkeith Road EH16 5	30-31	M9
Dalkeith Street EH15 2	32-33	R10
Dalmeny Road EH6 4	12-13	L13
Dalmeny Street EH6 8	20-21	M12
Dalry Place EH11 2	28-29	K10
Dalry Road EH11 2	42-43	J9
Dalrymple Crescent EH9 2	44-45	M8
Dalziel Place EH7 5	20-21	N11
Damside EH4 3	28-29	J10
Dania Court EH11 3	40-41	G8
Danube Street EH4 1	28-29	K11
Darnaway Street EH3 6	28-29	K11
Darnell Road EH5 3	10-11	K13
Davidson Gardens EH4 5	16-17	H12
Davidson Park EH4 2	18-19	J12
Davidson Road EH4 2	16-17	I12
Davie Street EH8 9	30-31	M10
Dean Bank Lane EH3 5	28-29	K11
Dean Bridge EH3 7	28-29	K10
Dean Park Crescent EH4 1	28-29	K11
Dean Park Mews EH4 1	28-29	K11
Dean Park Street EH4 1	28-29	K11
Dean Path EH4 3	28-29	J11
Dean Street EH4 1	28-29	K11
Dean Terrace EH4 1	28-29	K11
Deanery Close EH7 6	20-21	O11
Deanhaugh Street EH4 1	28-29	K11
Dechmont Road EH12 8	24-25	E10
Delhaig EH11 3	40-41	H8
Dell Road EH13 0	50-51	H6
Denham Green Avenue EH5 3	10-11	K13
Denham Green Place EH5 3	10-11	K13
Denham Green Terrace EH5 3	10-11	K13
Derby Street EH6 4	12-13	L13
Devon Place EH12 5	28-29	J10
Dewar Place EH3 8	28-29	K10
Dewar Place Lane EH3 8	28-29	K10
Dick Place EH9 2	44-45	M8
Dickson Street EH6 8	20-21	M12
Dickson's Close EH1 1	30-31	M10
Dinmont Drive EH16 5	44-45	N7
Distillery Lane EH11 2	28-29	J10
Dochart Drive EH4 7	24-25	F11
Dock Place EH6 6	12-13	M13
Dock Street EH6 6	12-13	M13
Dolphin Avenue EH14 5	58-59	D4
Dolphin Gardens East EH14 5	58-59	D4
Dolphin Gardens West EH14 5	58-59	D4
Dolphin Road EH14 5	58-59	D4
Dorset Place EH11 1	42-43	K9
Double Hedges Park EH16 6	44-45	N7
Double Hedges Road EH16 6	44-45	N7
Douglas Crescent EH12 5	28-29	J10
Douglas Gardens EH4 3	28-29	J10
Douglas Gardens Mews EH4 3	28-29	J10
Douglas Terrace EH11 2	28-29	K10
Doune Terrace EH3 6	28-29	K11
Dovecot Grove EH14 2	50-51	H7
Dovecot Loan EH14 2	50-51	H7
Dovecot Park EH14 2	50-51	H6
Dovecot Road EH12 7	38-39	F9
Dowies Mill Lane EH4 6	14-15	D12
Downfield Place EH11 2	42-43	J9
Downie Grove EH12 7	40-41	G9
Downie Terrace EH12 7	40-41	G9
Dreghorn Avenue EH13 9	62-63	J5
Dreghorn Cottages EH13 9	60-61	I5
Dreghorn Drive EH13 9	62-63	J5
Dreghorn Gardens EH13 9	62-63	J5
Dreghorn Grove EH13 9	62-63	J5
Dreghorn Link EH13 9	62-63	J5
Dreghorn Loan EH13 9	60-61	I5
Dreghorn Park EH13 9	60-61	I5
Dreghorn Place EH13 9	62-63	J5
Drum Avenue EH17 7	56-57	P5
Drum Brae Avenue EH12 8	24-25	F10
Drum Brae Crescent EH4 7	24-25	F11
Drum Brae Drive EH4 7	24-25	F11
Drum Brae Gardens EH12 8	24-25	F10
Drum Brae Grove EH4 7	24-25	F11
Drum Brae Neuk EH4 7	24-25	E11
Drum Brae North EH4 8	24-25	E11
Drum Brae Park EH12 8	24-25	F10
Drum Brae Park Approach EH12 8	24-25	F10
Drum Brae Place EH12 8	24-25	F10
Drum Brae South EH12 8	24-25	F10
Drum Brae Terrace EH4 7	24-25	F11
Drum Brae Walk EH4 8	24-25	E11
Drum Cottages EH17 7	56-57	P5
Drum Crescent EH17 7	56-57	P5
Drum Place EH17 7	56-57	P5
Drum Street EH17 8	56-57	P5
Drum Terrace EH7 5	20-21	N12
Drumdryan Street EH3 9	42-43	K9
Drummond Place EH3 6	28-29	L11
Drummond Street EH8 9	30-31	M10
Drumsheugh Gardens EH3 7	28-29	K10
Drumsheugh Place EH3 7	28-29	K10
Dryden Gardens EH7 4	20-21	M12
Dryden Place EH9 1	30-31	M9
Dryden Street EH7 4	20-21	M12
Dryden Terrace EH7 4	20-21	M12
Drylaw Avenue EH4 2	26-27	I11
Drylaw Crescent EH4 2	16-17	H12
Drylaw Gardens EH4 2	16-17	H12
Drylaw Green EH4 2	26-27	H11
Drylaw Grove EH4 2	26-27	H11
Drylaw House Gardens EH4 2	16-17	H12
Drylaw House Paddock EH4 2	16-17	H12
Duart Crescent EH4 7	24-25	F11
Dublin Meuse EH3 6	28-29	L11
Dublin Street EH3 6	28-29	L11
Dublin Street Lane North EH3 6	28-29	L11
Dublin Street Lane South EH1 3	28-29	L11
Duddingston Avenue EH15 1	32-33	Q9
Duddingston Crescent EH15 3	32-33	Q9
Duddingston Gardens North EH15 1	32-33	P10
Duddingston Gardens South EH15 1	32-33	P10
Duddingston Grove East EH15 1	32-33	P10
Duddingston Grove West EH15 1	32-33	P10
Duddingston Loan EH15 3	32-33	Q9
Duddingston Mains Cotts EH15 3	32-33	Q9
Duddingston Mills EH8 7	32-33	P10
Duddingston Park EH15 1	32-33	Q10
Duddingston Park South EH15 3	32-33	Q9
Duddingston Rise EH15 3	32-33	Q9
Duddingston Road EH16 5	30-31	N9
Duddingston Road EH15 1	32-33	P10
Duddingston Road West EH15 3	30-31	O9
Duddingston Row EH15 3	32-33	P10
Duddingston Square East EH15 1	32-33	P10
Duddingston Square West EH15 1	32-33	P10
Duddingston View EH15 3	32-33	Q9
Duddingston Yards EH15 3	32-33	Q9
Dudley Avenue EH6 4	12-13	L13
Dudley Avenue South EH6 4	12-13	M13

Dudley Bank EH6 4	12-13	L13	Easter Steil EH10 5	52-53	J7	Fettes Square EH3 5	28-29	
Dudley Crescent EH6 4	12-13	L13	Easter Warriston EH7 4	18-19	L12	Figgate Bank EH15 1	22-23	
Dudley Gardens EH6 4	12-13	L13	Eastfield EH15 2	34-35	S10	Figgate Court EH15 1	22-23	
Dudley Grove EH6 4	12-13	L13	Eastfield Avenue EH12 9	78-79	B10	Figgate Lane EH15 1	22-23	
Dudley Terrace EH6 4	12-13	L13	Eastfield Gardens EH15 2	34-35	S10	Figgate Street EH15 1	22-23	
Duff Street EH11 2	42-43	J9	Eastfield Place EH15 2	34-35	S10	Fillyside Avenue EH7 6	22-23	
Duff Street Lane EH11 2	42-43	J9	Eastfield Road EH28 8	78-79	B9	Fillyside Road EH7 6	22-23	
Duke Place EH6 7	20-21	N12	Eden Lane EH10 4	42-43	K8	Fillyside Terrace EH7 6	22-23	
Duke Street EH6 8	20-21	N12	Eden Terrace EH10 4	42-43	K8	Findhorn Place EH9 2	30-31	
Duke's Walk EH8 8	20-21	N11	Edina Place EH7 5	20-21	M11	Findlay Avenue EH7 6	20-21	
Dumbeg Park EH14 3	48-49	F6	Edina Street EH7 5	20-21	M11	Findlay Cottages EH7 6	20-21	
Dumbiedykes Road EH8 9	30-31	M10	Eglinton Crescent EH12 5	28-29	J10	Findlay Gardens EH7 6	20-21	
Dumbryden Drive EH14 2	50-51	G7	Egypt Mews EH10 4	42-43	L8	Findlay Grove EH7 6	20-21	
Dumbryden Gardens EH14 2	50-51	G7	Eildon Street EH3 5	18-19	L12	Findlay Medway EH7 6	20-21	
Dumbryden Grove EH14 2	50-51	G7	Eildon Terrace EH3 5	18-19	K12	Fingal Place EH9 1	42-43	
Dumbryden Road EH14 2	50-51	G7	Elbe Street EH6 7	12-13	N13	Fingzies Place EH6 8	20-21	
Dun-Ard Garden EH9 2	42-43	L8	Elcho Terrace EH15 2	32-33	R10	Firrhill Crescent EH13 9	52-53	
Dunbar Street EH3 9	28-29	K10	Elder Street EH1 3	28-29	L11	Firrhill Drive EH13 9	52-53	
Dunbar's Close EH8 8	8-9		Elder Street East EH1 3	28-29	L11	Firrhill Loan EH13 9	52-53	
Duncan Place EH6 7	20-21	N12	Electra Place EH15 1	22-23	Q11	First Gait EH14 4	48-49	
Duncan Street EH9 1	44-45	M8	Elgin Terrace EH7 5	20-21	M11	Fishmarket Square EH6 4	12-13	
Dundas Street EH3 5	28-29	L11	Ellangowan Terrace EH16 5	44-45	O7	Fishwives' Causeway EH7 6	22-23	
Dundee Street EH11 1	42-43	K9	Ellen's Glen Loan EH17 7	54-55	O6	Fleshmarket Close EH1 1	8-9	
Dundee Terrace EH11 1	42-43	J9	Ellen's Glen Road EH16 6	54-55	O5	Forbes Road EH10 4	42-43	
Dundonald Street EH3 6	28-29	L11	Ellersly Road EH12 6	26-27	H10	Forbes Street EH8 9	30-31	
Dundrennan Cottages EH16 5	44-45	O7	Elliot Gardens EH14 1	50-51	I6	Ford's Road EH11 3	40-41	
Dunedin Street EH7 4	18-19	L12	Elliot Park EH14 1	50-51	I6	Forres Street EH3 6	28-29	
Dunrobin Place EH3 5	28-29	K11	Elliot Place EH14 1	50-51	I6	Forrest Hill EH1 2	28-29	
Dunsmuir Court EH12 7	38-39	F9	Elliot Road EH14 1	50-51	I6	Forrest Road EH1 2	28-29	
Dunvegan Court EH4 6	14-15	E12	Elliot Street EH7 5	20-21	M11	Forrester Park Avenue EH12 9	38-39	
Durar Drive EH4 7	24-25	F11	Elm Place EH6 8	20-21	N12	Forrester Park Drive EH12 9	38-39	
Durham Avenue EH15 1	32-33	P10	Elm Row EH7 4	20-21	M11	Forrester Park Gardens EH12 9	38-39	
Durham Drive EH15 1	32-33	Q9	Elm Row EH7 4	20-21	M11	Forrester Park Green EH12 9	40-41	
Durham Gardens North EH15 1	32-33	Q10	Elmwood Terrace EH6 8	20-21	N12	Forrester Park Grove EH12 9	38-39	
Durham Gardens South EH15 1	32-33	Q9	Eltringham Gardens EH14 1	40-41	I8	Forrester Park Loan EH12 9	38-39	
Durham Grove EH15 1	32-33	Q10	Eltringham Grove EH14 1	40-41	I8	Forrester Road EH12 8	24-25	
Durham Place East EH15 1	32-33	Q10	Eltringham Terrace EH14 1	40-41	I8	Forth Street EH1 3	28-29	
Durham Place West EH15 1	32-33	P9	Esplanade Terrace EH15 2	32-33	R10	Forthview EH13 3	46-47	
Durham Road EH15 1	32-33	Q10	Essendean Place EH4 7	24-25	F11	Forthview Avenue EH14 5	58-59	
Durham Road South EH15 3	32-33	Q9	Essendean Terrace EH4 7	24-25	F11	Forthview Crescent EH14 5	58-59	
Durham Square EH15 1	32-33	P10	Essex Brae EH4 6	14-15	E12	Forthview Road EH14 5	58-59	
Durham Terrace EH15 1	32-33	P10	Essex Park EH4 6	14-15	E12	Forthview Road EH4 2	26-27	
Durward Grove EH16 5	44-45	N7	Essex Road EH4 6	14-15	E12	Forthview Terrace EH4 2	26-27	
Durward Grove EH16 5	44-45	N7	Esslemont Road EH16 5	44-45	M7	Foulis Crescent EH14 5	58-59	
			Ethel Terrace EH10 5	52-53	K7	Fountain Close EH1 1	8-9	
Earl Grey Street EH3 9	28-29	K10	Eton Terrace EH4 1	28-29	K11	Fountainbridge EH3 9	42-43	
Earl Haig Gardens EH5 3	10-11	K13	Ettrick Grove EH10 5	42-43	K9	Fountainhall Road EH9 2	44-45	
Earlston Place EH7 5	20-21	N11	Ettrick Road EH10 5	42-43	J8	Fourth Gait EH14 4	48-49	
East Adam Street EH8 9	30-31	M10	Ettrickdale Place EH3 5	18-19	K12	Fowler Terrace EH11 1	42-43	
East Barnton Avenue EH4 6	16-17	G12	Eva Place EH9 3	44-45	M7	Fox Covert Avenue EH12 6	26-27	
East Barnton Gardens EH4 6	16-17	G12	Ewerland EH4 6	14-15	E12	Fox Covert Grove EH12 6	26-27	
East Caiystane Place EH10 6	62-63	K5	Eyre Crescent EH3 5	28-29	L11	Fox Spring Crescent EH10 6	52-53	
East Caiystane Road EH10 6	62-63	K5	Eyre Place EH3 5	28-29	L11	Fox Spring Rise EH10 6	52-53	
East Camus Place EH10 6	62-63	K5	Eyre Terrace EH3 5	28-29	L11	Fraser Avenue EH5 2	10-11	
East Camus Road EH10 6	62-63	K5				Fraser Crescent EH5 2	10-11	
East Castle Road EH11 1	42-43	K9	Fair-a-Far EH4 6	14-15	E13	Fraser Gardens EH5 2	10-11	
East Champanyie EH9 3	44-45	M8	Fair-a-Far Cottages EH4 6	14-15	E13	Fraser Grove EH5 2	10-11	
East Clapperfield EH16 5	44-45	N7	Fair-a-Far Shot EH4 6	14-15	E13	Frederick Street EH2 1	28-29	
East Claremont Street EH7 4	28-29	L11	Fairbrae EH11 3	40-41	G8	Frogston Avenue EH10 7	62-63	
East Comiston EH10 6	62-63	K5	Fairford Gardens EH16 5	44-45	N7	Frogston Gardens EH10 7	62-63	
East Court EH4 3	26-27	I11	Fairmile Avenue EH10 6	62-63	K5	Frogston Grove EH10 7	62-63	
East Court EH16 4	46-47	P8	Fairview Road EH28 8	78-79	A10	Frogston Road East EH28 8	54-55	
East Cromwell Street EH6 6	12-13	M13	Falcon Avenue EH10 4	42-43	K8	Frogston Road West EH10 7	62-63	
East Crosscauseway EH8 9	30-31	M9	Falcon Court EH10 4	42-43	K8	Frogston Terrace EH10 7	62-63	
East Farm of Gilmerton EH17 8	56-57	P5	Falcon Gardens EH10 4	42-43	K8	Furcheons Park EH8 7	32-33	
East Fettes Avenue EH3 5	18-19	J12	Falcon Road EH10 4	42-43	K8			
East Fountainbridge EH3 9	28-29	K10	Falcon Road West EH10 4	42-43	K8	Galachlaw Shot EH10 7	62-63	
East Hermitage Place EH6 7	20-21	N12	Falkland Gardens EH12 6	26-27	G11	Galachlawside EH10 7	62-63	
East Kilngate Place EH17 8	54-55	O5	Farrer Grove EH7 6	22-23	P11	Gallolee, The EH13 9	60-61	
East Kilngate Rigg EH17 8	54-55	O5	Farrer Terrace EH7 6	22-23	P11	Galloway's Entry EH8 8	30-31	
East Kilngate Wynd EH17 8	54-55	O5	Fauldburn EH12 8	24-25	E11	Gamekeeper's Loan EH4 6	14-15	
East Lillypot EH5 3	10-11	K13	Fauldburn Park EH12 8	24-25	E11	Gamekeeper's Park EH4 6	14-15	
East London Street EH7 4	28-29	L11	Featherhall Avenue EH12 7	38-39	F9	Gamekeeper's Road EH4 6	14-15	
East Market Street EH1 1	28-29	L10	Featherhall Crescent North EH12 7	38-39	F9	Garden Terrace EH4 6	14-15	
East Mayfield EH9 1	44-45	M8	Featherhall Crescent South EH12 7	38-39	F9	Gardiner Grove EH4 3	26-27	
East Montgomery Place EH7 5	20-21	M11	Featherhall Grove EH12 7	38-39	F9	Gardiner Road EH4 3	26-27	
East Newington Place EH9 1	30-31	M9	Featherhall Place EH12 7	38-39	F9	Gardiner Terrace EH4 3	26-27	
East Norton Place EH7 5	20-21	M11	Featherhall Road EH12 7	38-39	F9	Gardner's Crescent EH3 8	28-29	
East Parkside EH16 5	30-31	M9	Featherhall Terrace EH12 7	38-39	F9	Garscube Terrace EH12 6	26-27	
East Preston Street EH8 9	30-31	M9	Ferniehill Avenue EH17 7	56-57	P5	Gayfield Close EH1 3	20-21	
East Restalrig Terrace EH6 8	20-21	N12	Ferniehill Drive EH17 7	56-57	P5	Gayfield Lane EH7 4	28-29	
East Savile Road EH16 5	44-45	M8	Ferniehill Gardens EH17 7	56-57	P6	Gayfield Place EH7 4	20-21	
East Sciennes Street EH9 1	30-31	M9	Ferniehill Grove EH17 7	56-57	P6	Gayfield Place Lane EH1 3	20-21	
East Silvermills Lane EH3 5	28-29	K11	Ferniehill Road EH17 7	56-57	P5	Gayfield Square EH1 3	20-21	
East Suffolk Road EH16 5	44-45	N8	Ferniehill Square EH17 7	56-57	P5	Gayfield Street EH1 3	28-29	
East Telferton EH7 6	22-23	P11	Ferniehill Street EH17 7	56-57	P6	George IV Bridge EH1 1	28-29	
East Trinity Road EH5 3	12-13	L13	Ferniehill Terrace EH17 7	56-57	P5	George Square EH8 9	42-43	
East Werberside EH4 1	18-19	J12	Ferniehill Way EH17 7	56-57	P6	George Square Lane EH8 9	42-43	
Easter Belmont Road EH12 6	26-27	H10	Ferielaw Avenue EH13 0	60-61	H5	George Street EH2 3	28-29	
Easter Currie Court EH14 5	58-59	E4	Fernieside Avenue EH17 7	56-57	P6	Gibson Street EH7 4	20-21	
Easter Currie Crescent EH14 5	58-59	E5	Fernieside Crescent EH17 7	56-57	P6	Gibson Terrace EH11 1	42-43	
Easter Currie Place EH14 5	58-59	E5	Fernieside Drive EH17 7	56-57	P6	Gifford Park EH8 9	30-31	
Easter Currie Terrace EH14 5	58-59	E4	Fernieside Gardens EH17 7	56-57	P6	Gilberstoun EH15 2	32-33	
Easter Drylaw Avenue EH4 2	16-17	I12	Fernieside Grove EH17 7	56-57	P6	Gilberstoun Brig EH15 2	32-33	
Easter Drylaw Bank EH4 2	16-17	I12	Ferry Road EH4 2	16-17	H12	Gilberstoun Loan EH15 2	32-33	
Easter Drylaw Drive EH4 2	16-17	I12	Ferry Road Avenue EH4 4	16-17	I12	Gilberstoun Place EH15 2	32-33	
Easter Drylaw Gardens EH4 2	16-17	I12	Ferry Road Drive EH4 4	16-17	I12	Gilberstoun Wynd EH15 2	32-33	
Easter Drylaw Grove EH4 2	16-17	I12	Ferry Road Gardens EH4 4	16-17	I12	Giles Street EH6 6	12-13	
Easter Drylaw Loan EH4 2	16-17	I12	Ferry Road Grove EH4 4	16-17	I12	Gillespie Crescent EH10 4	42-43	
Easter Drylaw Place EH4 2	16-17	I12	Ferry Road Place EH4 4	16-17	I12	Gillespie Place EH10 4	42-43	
Easter Drylaw View EH4 2	16-17	I12	Ferryfield EH5 2	10-11	J13	Gillespie Road EH13 0	60-61	
Easter Drylaw Way EH4 2	16-17	I12	Fettes Avenue EH4 1	28-29	J11	Gillespie Street EH3 9	42-43	
Easter Haugh EH13 9	52-53	J6	Fettes Rise EH4 1	18-19	J12	Gillsland Park EH10 5	42-43	
Easter Hermitage EH6 8	20-21	N12	Fettes Row EH3 5	28-29	L11	Gillsland Road EH10 5	42-43	
Easter Park Drive EH4 6	16-17	G12				Gilmerton Dykes Avenue EH17 8	54-55	
Easter Road EH7 5	20-21	M11				Gilmerton Dykes Crescent EH17 8	54-55	

erton Dykes Drive EH17 8	54-55	O5	Granton Square EH5 1	10-11	J14	Hamilton Grove EH15 1	32-33	P10
erton Dykes Gardens EH17 8	54-55	O5	Granton Terrace EH5 1	10-11	J13	Hamilton Park EH15 1	32-33	P10
erton Dykes Grove EH17 8	54-55	O5	Granton View EH5 1	10-11	J14	Hamilton Place EH3 5	28-29	K11
erton Dykes Loan EH17 8	54-55	O5	Grantully Place EH9 1	44-45	M8	Hamilton Terrace EH15 1	32-33	Q10
erton Dykes Place EH17 8	54-55	O5	Granville Terrace EH10 4	42-43	K9	Hamilton Wynd EH6 4	12-13	M13
erton Dykes Road EH17 8	64-65	O4	Grassmarket EH1 2	28-29	L10	Hammermen's Entry EH8 8		8-9
erton Dykes Street EH17 8	54-55	O5	Gray's Court EH8 9	30-31	M10	Hampton Place EH12 5	28-29	J10
erton Dykes Terrace EH17 8	54-55	O5	Gray's Loan EH10 5	42-43	J8	Hampton Terrace EH12 5	28-29	J10
erton Dykes View EH17 8	54-55	O5	Great Cannon Bank EH15 1	22-23	Q11	Hampton Terrace EH12 5	28-29	J10
erton Place EH17 8	54-55	O5	Great Carleton Place EH16 4	46-47	Q8	Hanover Street EH2 1	28-29	L11
erton Road EH16 5	44-45	N7	Great Carleton Square EH16 4	46-47	Q8	Harbour Place EH15 1	22-23	Q11
erton Station Road EH17 8	66-67	P4	Great Junction Street EH6 5	12-13	M13	Harden Place EH11 1	42-43	J9
ore Park EH3 9	42-43	K9	Great King Street EH3 6	28-29	L11	Hardwell Close EH8 9	30-31	M9
ore Place EH3 9	42-43	K9	Great Michael Rise EH6 4	12-13	L13	Harelaw Road EH13 0	60-61	H5
ore Place Lane EH3 9	42-43	K9	Great Stuart Street EH3 7	28-29	K10	Harewood Crescent EH16 4	46-47	P8
our Road EH16 5	44-45	M8	Green Street EH7 4	28-29	L11	Harewood Drive EH16 4	46-47	P8
our Street EH8 9	30-31	M10	Green, The EH4 5	16-17	G12	Harewood Road EH16 4	46-47	P8
lstone Court EH8 8	8-9		Greenacre EH14 3	50-51	G6	Harrismith Place EH7 5	20-21	N11
lstone Place EH6 7	20-21	N12	Greenbank Avenue EH10 5	52-53	K7	Harrison Gardens EH11 1	42-43	J8
lstone Terrace EH9 1	30-31	M9	Greenbank Crescent EH10 5	52-53	K6	Harrison Lane EH11 1	42-43	J9
ville Place EH3 5	28-29	K11	Greenbank Drive EH10 5	52-53	J7	Harrison Place EH11 1	42-43	J8
gow Road EH12 8	38-39	E9	Greenbank Gardens EH10 5	52-53	J6	Harrison Road EH11 1	42-43	J9
e Gardens EH12 7	38-39	F9	Greenbank Grove EH10 5	52-53	J6	Hart Street EH1 3	28-29	L11
e Grove EH12 7	38-39	F9	Greenbank Lane EH10 5	52-53	J7	Hart Street Lane EH1 3	28-29	L11
e Road EH12 7	38-39	F9	Greenbank Loan EH10 5	52-53	J6	Hartington Gardens EH10 4	42-43	K9
e Terrace EH12 7	38-39	F9	Greenbank Park EH10 5	52-53	J6	Hartington Place EH10 4	42-43	K9
n Street EH3 9	28-29	L10	Greenbank Place EH10 6	52-53	K7	Harvesters Way EH14 3	48-49	F6
allan Drive EH16 5	44-45	N7	Greenbank Rise EH10 5	52-53	J6	Hastie's Close EH1 1	8-9	
allan Loan EH16 5	44-45	N7	Greenbank Road EH10 5	52-53	J6	Hatton Place EH9 1	42-43	L9
isla Gardens EH9 2	42-43	L8	Greenbank Row EH10 5	52-53	J6	Haugh Park EH14 1	50-51	H7
isla Gardens Lane EH9 2	42-43	L8	Greenbank Terrace EH10 6	52-53	K7	Haugh Street EH4 1	28-29	K11
cairn Crescent EH12 5	28-29	J10	Greendale Park EH16 4	16-17	H12	Hawkhead Crescent EH16 6	54-55	N6
devon Avenue EH12 5	40-41	H9	Greendykes Avenue EH16 4	46-47	P8	Hawkhead Grove EH16 6	54-55	N6
devon Gardens EH12 5	40-41	H9	Greendykes Drive EH16 4	46-47	P8	Hawkhill EH7 6	20-21	N12
devon Grove EH12 5	40-41	H9	Greendykes Gardens EH16 4	46-47	P8	Hawkhill Avenue EH7 6	20-21	N12
devon Park EH12 5	40-41	H9	Greendykes Loan EH16 4	46-47	P8	Hawthorn Place EH17 8	56-57	P5
devon Place EH12 5	40-41	H9	Greendykes Road EH16 4	46-47	P8	Hawthornbank Lane EH4 3	28-29	J10
devon Road EH12 5	40-41	H9	Greendykes Terrace EH16 4	46-47	P8	Hawthornbank Place EH6 4	12-13	L13
devon Terrace EH12 5	40-41	H9	Greenend Drive EH17 7	54-55	O6	Hawthornbank Terrace EH6 4	12-13	L13
dinning Crescent EH16 6	54-55	N6	Greenend Gardens EH17 7	54-55	O6	Hawthornden Place EH7 4	20-21	M12
finlas Street EH3 6	28-29	K10	Greenend Grove EH17 7	54-55	O6	Hawthornvale EH6 4	12-13	L13
gyle Terrace EH3 9	42-43	K9	Greenhill Court EH9 1	42-43	K9	Hay Avenue EH16 4	46-47	P8
isla Gardens EH9 2	42-43	L8	Greenhill Gardens EH10 4	42-43	K9	Hay Drive EH16 4	46-47	Q8
isla Gardens Lane EH9 2	42-43	L8	Greenhill Park EH10 4	42-43	K8	Hay Place EH16 4	46-47	P8
lee Avenue EH8 7	30-31	O10	Greenhill Place EH10 4	42-43	K8	Hay Road EH16 4	46-47	P8
lee Gardens EH8 7	30-31	O10	Greenhill Terrace EH10 4	42-43	K9	Hay Terrace EH16 4	46-47	P8
lockhart Bank EH14 1	50-51	I7	Greenlaw Hedge EH13 9	52-53	J6	Hayfield EH12 8	24-25	E10
lockhart Road EH14 1	50-51	I7	Greenlaw Rig EH13 9	52-53	J6	Haymarket EH3 8	28-29	K10
lockhart Valley EH14 1	50-51	I7	Greenmantle Loan EH16 6	44-45	N7	Haymarket Terrace EH12 5	28-29	J10
ogle House EH3 5	28-29	K11	Greenside End EH7 5	20-21	M11	Hazelbank Terrace EH11 1	42-43	J8
ogle Place EH3 5	28-29	K11	Greenside Lane EH1 3	20-21	M11	Hazeldean Terrace EH16 5	44-45	N7
ogle Road EH3 5	28-29	K11	Greenside Place EH1 3	20-21	M11	Hazelwood Grove EH16 5	44-45	O7
ogle Terrace EH3 5	18-19	K12	Greenside Row EH1 3	20-21	M11	Headrig Row EH16 5	44-45	N7
orchy Terrace EH9 2	44-45	M8	Greyfriars Place EH1 2	28-29	L10	Henderland Road EH12 6	26-27	I10
ure Loan EH4 7	24-25	F11	Grierson Avenue EH5 2	10-11	K13	Henderson Gardens EH6 6	12-13	M13
varloch Crescent EH16 6	54-55	N6	Grierson Crescent EH5 2	10-11	K13	Henderson Place EH3 5	28-29	L11
cester Lane EH3 6	28-29	K11	Grierson Gardens EH5 2	10-11	K13	Henderson Place Lane EH3 5	28-29	K11
cester Place EH3 6	28-29	K11	Grierson Road EH5 2	10-11	J13	Henderson Row EH3 5	28-29	K11
cester Square EH3 6	28-29	K11	Grierson Square EH5 2	10-11	K13	Henderson Street EH6 6	12-13	M13
cester Street EH3 6	28-29	K11	Grierson Villas EH5 2	10-11	K13	Henderson Terrace EH11 2	42-43	J9
Avenue EH7 6	22-23	P11	Grigor Avenue EH4 2	16-17	I12	Heriot Bridge EH1 2	28-29	L10
ar Mains Farm Road EH12 9	78-79	C9	Grigor Drive EH4 2	16-17	I12	Heriot Place EH3 9	28-29	L10
ar Roundabout EH12 9	38-39	D9	Grigor Gardens EH4 2	16-17	I12	Heriot Row EH3 6	28-29	K11
ar Station Road EH12 9	38-39	D8	Grigor Terrace EH4 2	16-17	I12	Heriothill Terrace EH7 4	18-19	L12
arbank EH12 9	48-49	D7	Grindlay Street EH1 2	28-29	K10	Hermand Crescent EH11 1	42-43	J8
arloch Haugh EH12 9	38-39	E9	Grindlay Street Court EH3 9	28-29	K10	Hermand Street EH11 1	40-41	I8
arloch Muir EH12 9	38-39	E9	Groathill Avenue EH4 2	26-27	I11	Hermand Terrace EH11 1	40-41	I8
arloch Road EH12 9	38-39	E9	Groathill Gardens East EH4 2	26-27	I11	Hermit's Croft EH8 9	30-31	M9
arloch Syke EH12 9	38-39	E9	Groathill Gardens West EH4 2	26-27	I11	Hermitage Courts EH6 8	20-21	N12
enacre Terrace EH3 5	18-19	K12	Groathill Road North EH4 2	16-17	I12	Hermitage Drive EH10 6	52-53	K7
lon Loan EH4 2	26-27	G10	Groathill Road South EH4 2	26-27	I11	Hermitage Gardens EH10 6	52-53	K7
lon Road EH12 6	26-27	G10	Grosvenor Crescent EH12 5	28-29	J10	Hermitage Park EH6 8	20-21	N12
lon Street EH6 8	20-21	N12	Grosvenor Gardens EH12 5	28-29	J10	Hermitage Park Grove EH6 8	20-21	N12
lon Terrace EH16 5	44-45	N7	Grosvenor Street EH12 5	28-29	K10	Hermitage Park South EH6 8	20-21	N12
ie Park Close EH14 1	40-41	I8	Grove Street EH3 8	28-29	K10	Hermitage Place EH6 8	20-21	N12
ie Park Road EH14 1	40-41	I8	Grundie's Well Road EH17 8	56-57	P5	Hermitage Terrace EH10 4	42-43	K8
ie Road EH11 3	40-41	H8	Guardianswood EH12 6	26-27	I10	High Buckstone EH10 6	62-63	L5
ord Place EH6 4	12-13	L13	Guardwell Crescent EH17 7	54-55	O6	High Riggs EH3 9	28-29	K10
cemount Avenue EH16 6	54-55	N6	Gullan's Close EH8 8	30-31	M10	High School Yards EH1 1	30-31	M10
cemount Drive EH16 6	54-55	N5	Gunnet Court EH4 4	16-17	H13	High Street EH1 1	30-31	M10
cemount Place EH16 6	54-55	N5	Guthrie Street EH1 1	28-29	L10	Hill Place EH8 9	30-31	M10
cemount Road EH16 6	54-55	N5	Gyle Park Gardens EH12 8	38-39	E9	Hill Square EH8 9	30-31	M10
cemount Square EH16 6	54-55	N6	Gylemuir Road EH12 7	38-39	F9	Hill Street EH2 3	28-29	K11
ham Street EH6 5	12-13	M13				Hill Street Lane North EH2 3	28-29	K11
by Road EH16 5	44-45	M8	Haddington Place EH7 4	20-21	M11	Hill Street Lane South EH2 3	28-29	K10
dfield EH6 4	12-13	L13	Haddon's Court EH8 9	30-31	M10	Hillcoat Loan EH15 1	22-23	Q11
dville EH6 4	12-13	L13	Hailes Approach EH13 0	50-51	H6	Hillcoat Place EH15 1	22-23	Q11
ge Crescent EH9 2	44-45	M8	Hailes Avenue EH13 0	50-51	H6	Hillend Place EH8 7	20-21	O11
ge Loan EH9 2	44-45	M8	Hailes Bank EH13 0	50-51	H6	Hillhouse Road EH4 5	16-17	G12
ge Loan Gardens EH9 2	42-43	L8	Hailes Crescent EH13 0	50-51	H6	Hillpark Avenue EH4 7	16-17	G12
ge Road EH9 1	42-43	L9	Hailes Gardens EH13 0	50-51	G6	Hillpark Brae EH4 7	26-27	G11
ge Terrace EH9 2	42-43	L8	Hailes Grove EH13 0	50-51	H6	Hillpark Court EH4 7	26-27	G11
nt Avenue EH13 0	60-61	H5	Hailes Park EH13 0	50-51	G6	Hillpark Crescent EH4 7	26-27	G11
nton Crescent EH5 1	10-11	J13	Hailes Street EH3 9	42-43	K9	Hillpark Drive EH4 7	16-17	G12
nton Gardens EH5 1	10-11	J13	Hailes Terrace EH13 0	50-51	H6	Hillpark Gardens EH4 7	26-27	G11
nton Grove EH5 1	10-11	J13	Hailesland Gardens EH14 2	50-51	G7	Hillpark Green EH4 7	26-27	G11
nton Mains Avenue EH4 4	10-11	I13	Hailesland Grove EH14 2	50-51	G7	Hillpark Grove EH4 7	26-27	G11
nton Mains Bank EH4 4	10-11	I13	Hailesland Park EH14 2	50-51	G7	Hillpark Loan EH4 7	26-27	H11
nton Mains Brae EH4 4	10-11	I13	Hailesland Place EH14 2	50-51	G7	Hillpark Road EH4 7	26-27	G11
nton Mains Court EH4 4	10-11	I13	Hailesland Road EH14 2	50-51	G7	Hillpark Terrace EH4 7	26-27	G11
nton Mains East EH4 4	10-11	I13	Hainburn Park EH10 7	62-63	J5	Hillpark Way EH4 7	26-27	H11
nton Mains Gait EH4 4	10-11	I13	Hallhead Road EH16 5	44-45	M7	Hillpark Wood EH4 7	26-27	H11
nton Mains Vale EH4 4	10-11	I13	Halmyre Street EH6 8	20-21	M12	Hillside Crescent EH7 5	20-21	M11
nton Mains Wynd EH4 4	10-11	I13	Hamilton Drive EH15 1	32-33	P10	Hillside Street EH7 5	20-21	M11
nton Medway EH5 1	10-11	J13	Hamilton Drive West EH15 1	32-33	P10	Hillview EH4 2	26-27	H11
nton Place EH5 1	10-11	J13	Hamilton Gardens EH15 1			Hillview Crescent EH12 8	24-25	F10
nton Road EH5 1	10-11	J14	Hamilton Gardens EH15 1					

Street	Page	Grid
Hillview Drive EH12 8	24-25	F10
Hillview Road EH12 8	24-25	F10
Hillview Terrace EH12 8	24-25	F10
Hollybank Terrace EH11 1	42-43	J8
Holyrood Park Road EH16 5	30-31	M9
Holyrood Road EH8 9	30-31	M10
Home Street EH3 9	42-43	K9
Hope Lane EH15 2	32-33	Q10
Hope Lane North EH15 2	32-33	Q10
Hope Park Crescent EH8 9	30-31	M9
Hope Park Terrace EH8 9	30-31	M9
Hope Street EH2 4	28-29	K10
Hope Street Lane EH2 4	28-29	K10
Hope Terrace EH9 2	42-43	L8
Hopefield Terrace EH6 4	12-13	M13
Hopetoun Crescent EH7 4	20-21	M11
Hopetoun Street EH7 4	20-21	M11
Horne Terrace EH11 1	42-43	K9
Horse Wynd EH8 8	30-31	M10
Hoseason Gardens EH4 7	24-25	F11
Hosie Rigg EH15 3	32-33	Q9
House o' Hill Avenue EH4 5	16-17	H12
House o' Hill Brae EH4 5	16-17	H12
House o' Hill Crescent EH4 5	16-17	H12
House o' Hill Gardens EH4 2	16-17	H12
House o' Hill Green EH4 5	16-17	H12
House o' Hill Grove EH4 5	16-17	H12
House o' Hill Place EH4 5	16-17	H12
House o' Hill Road EH4 2	16-17	H12
House o' Hill Row EH4 2	16-17	H12
House o' Hill Terrace EH4 2	26-27	H11
Howard Place EH3 5	18-19	L12
Howard Street EH3 5	18-19	L12
Howden Hall Court EH16 6	54-55	M5
Howden Hall Crescent EH16 6	54-55	M5
Howden Hall Drive EH16 6	54-55	M5
Howden Hall Gardens EH16 6	54-55	M5
Howden Hall Loan EH16 6	54-55	N5
Howden Hall Park EH16 6	54-55	M5
Howden Hall Road EH16 6	54-55	M5
Howden Hall Way EH16 6	54-55	N5
Howden Street EH8 9	30-31	M9
Howe Park EH10 7	62-63	J5
Howe Street EH3 6	28-29	L11
Hugh Miller Place EH3 5	28-29	K11
Hunter Square EH1 1	28-29	L10
Huntingdon Place EH7 4	20-21	M11
Huntly Street EH3 5	18-19	L12
Hutchison Avenue EH14 1	40-41	I8
Hutchison Cottages EH14 1	40-41	I8
Hutchison Crossway EH14 1	40-41	I8
Hutchison Gardens EH14 1	40-41	I8
Hutchison Grove EH14 1	40-41	I8
Hutchison Loan EH14 1	40-41	I8
Hutchison Medway EH14 1	40-41	I8
Hutchison Park EH14 1	40-41	I8
Hutchison Place EH14 1	40-41	I8
Hutchison Road EH14 1	40-41	I8
Hutchison Terrace EH14 1	40-41	I8
Hutchison View EH14 1	40-41	I8
Hyndford's Close EH1 1	8-9	
Hyvot Avenue EH17 8	54-55	O5
Hyvot Court EH17 8	54-55	O5
Hyvot Gardens EH17 8	54-55	O5
Hyvot Green EH17 8	54-55	O5
Hyvot Grove EH17 8	54-55	O5
Hyvot Loan EH17 7	54-55	O5
Hyvot Park EH17 8	54-55	O5
Hyvot Terrace EH17 8	54-55	O5
Hyvot View EH17 8	54-55	O5
Hyvot's Bank Avenue EH17 8	54-55	O5
Inchcolm Court EH4 4	10-11	I13
Inchellan Gardens EH16 5	44-45	N7
Inchmickery Court EH4 4	16-17	H13
Inchview Terrace EH7 6	22-23	P11
India Place EH3 6	28-29	K11
India Street EH3 6	28-29	K11
Industrial Road EH6 8	20-21	N12
Industry Lane EH6 4	12-13	M13
Infirmary Street EH1 1	30-31	M10
Inglewood Place EH16 6	54-55	N6
Inglis Green Road EH14 2	50-51	H7
Ingliston Road EH28 8	78-79	A9
Inveralmond Drive EH4 6	14-15	E13
Inveralmond Gardens EH4 6	14-15	E13
Inveralmond Grove EH4 6	14-15	E13
Inverleith Avenue EH3 5	18-19	K12
Inverleith Avenue South EH3 5	18-19	K12
Inverleith Gardens EH3 5	18-19	K12
Inverleith Grove EH3 5	18-19	J12
Inverleith Place EH3 5	18-19	K12
Inverleith Place Lane EH3 5	18-19	K12
Inverleith Row EH3 5	18-19	K12
Inverleith Terrace EH3 5	18-19	K12
Inverleith Terrace Lane EH3 5	18-19	K12
Iona Street EH6 8	20-21	M12
Ivanhoe Crescent EH16 6	44-45	N7
Ivy Terrace EH11 1	42-43	J9
Jackson's Close EH1 1	8-9	
Jamaica Mews EH3 6	28-29	K11
Jamaica Street EH3 6	28-29	K11
Jamaica Street; North Lane EH3 6	28-29	K11
Jamaica Street; South Lane EH3 6	28-29	K11
James Street EH15 2	32-33	R10
James Street Lane EH15 2	32-33	R10
James' Court EH1 2	8-9	
Jameson Place EH6 8	20-21	M12
Jane Street EH6 5	20-21	M12
Janefield EH17 8	64-65	N4
Jeffrey Avenue EH4 3	26-27	H11
Jeffrey Street EH1 1	30-31	M10
Jessfield Terrace EH6 4	12-13	L13
Jewel, The EH15 3	32-33	Q9
Jock's Lodge EH8 7	20-21	O11
John Street EH15 2	32-33	R10
John Street Lane East EH15 2	32-33	R10
John Street Lane West EH15 2	32-33	R10
John's Lane EH6 7	12-13	N13
John's Place EH6 7	12-13	N13
Johnston Terrace EH1 2	28-29	L10
Joppa Gardens EH15 2	32-33	R10
Joppa Grove EH15 2	32-33	R10
Joppa Pans EH15 2	34-35	S10
Joppa Park EH15 2	32-33	R10
Joppa Road EH15 2	32-33	R10
Joppa Terrace EH15 2	32-33	R10
Jordan Lane EH10 4	42-43	K8
Jubilee Road EH12 9	78-79	B10
Junction Place EH6 5	20-21	M12
Juniper Avenue EH14 5	58-59	F5
Juniper Gardens EH14 5	58-59	F5
Juniper Grove EH14 5	58-59	F5
Juniper Lane EH14 5	58-59	F5
Juniper Park Road EH14 5	58-59	F5
Juniper Place EH14 5	58-59	F5
Juniper Terrace EH14 5	58-59	F5
Juniperlee EH14 5	58-59	F5
Kaimes Road EH12 6	26-27	G10
Katesmill Road EH14 1	50-51	H6
Kedslie Road EH16 6	54-55	M6
Keir Street EH3 9	28-29	L10
Keith Crescent EH4 3	26-27	H11
Keith Row EH4 3	26-27	I11
Keith Terrace EH4 3	26-27	H11
Kekewich Avenue EH7 6	22-23	P11
Kemp Place EH3 5	28-29	K11
Kenilworth Drive EH16 6	54-55	N6
Kenmure Avenue EH8 7	20-21	O11
Kerr Street EH3 6	28-29	K11
Kew Terrace EH12 5	28-29	J10
Kilgraston Road EH9 2	42-43	L8
Kilmaurs Road EH16 5	44-45	N8
Kilmaurs Terrace EH16 5	44-45	N8
Kincaid's Court EH1 1	28-29	L10
Kinellan Gardens EH12 6	26-27	I10
Kinellan Road EH12 6	26-27	I10
King Malcolm Close EH10 7	62-63	L5
King's Bridge EH1 2	28-29	L10
King's Cramond EH4 6	14-15	E12
King's Haugh EH16 5	44-45	O8
King's Meadow EH16 5	44-45	N8
King's Place EH15 1	22-23	Q11
King's Road EH15 1	22-23	Q11
King's Stables Lane EH1 2	28-29	L10
King's Stables Road EH1 2	28-29	L10
Kinghorn Place EH6 4	12-13	L13
Kingsburgh Road EH12 6	26-27	I10
Kingsknowe Avenue EH14 2	50-51	H7
Kingsknowe Court EH14 2	50-51	G7
Kingsknowe Crescent EH14 2	50-51	H7
Kingsknowe Drive EH14 2	50-51	H7
Kingsknowe Gardens EH14 2	50-51	H6
Kingsknowe Grove EH14 2	50-51	H6
Kingsknowe Park EH14 2	50-51	H6
Kingsknowe Place EH14 2	50-51	G7
Kingsknowe Road North EH14 2	50-51	H7
Kingsknowe Road South EH14 2	50-51	H7
Kingsknowe Terrace EH14 2	50-51	H7
Kingston Avenue EH16 5	44-45	O7
Kinnaird Park EH15 3	46-47	R8
Kinnear Road EH3 5	18-19	K12
Kirk Brae EH16 6	44-45	N7
Kirk Cramond EH4 6	14-15	E13
Kirk Loan EH12 7	40-41	G9
Kirk Park EH16 6	54-55	N6
Kirk Street EH6 5	20-21	M12
Kirkgate EH14 6	58-59	E4
Kirkgate EH16 6	54-55	N6
Kirkhill Drive EH16 5	44-45	N8
Kirkhill Gardens EH16 5	30-31	N9
Kirkhill Road EH16 5	30-31	N9
Kirkhill Terrace EH16 5	30-31	N9
Kirklands EH12 9	38-39	F8
Kirkwood Place EH7 5	20-21	N11
Kittle Yards EH9 1	30-31	M9
Ladehead EH6 5	18-19	L12
Ladiemeadow EH12 7	40-41	G9
Lady Lawson Street EH3 9	28-29	L10
Lady Menzies Place EH7 5	20-21	N11
Lady Nairne Crescent EH8 7	30-31	O10
Lady Nairne Grove EH8 7	30-31	O10
Lady Nairne Loan EH8 7	30-31	O10
Lady Nairne Place EH8 7	30-31	O10
Lady Road EH16 5	44-45	N8
Lady Stair's Close EH1 2	8-9	
Lady Wynd EH1 2	28-29	L10
Ladysmith Road EH9 3	44-45	M7
Ladywell Avenue EH12 7	38-39	F9
Ladywell Gardens EH12 7	38-39	
Ladywell Road EH12 7	38-39	
Laichfield EH14 1	40-41	
Laichpark Loan EH14 1	40-41	
Laichpark Place EH14 1	40-41	
Laichpark Road EH14 1	40-41	
Laing Terrace EH15 2	32-33	
Lammermoor Terrace EH16 5	44-45	
Lampacre Road EH12 7	40-41	
Lanark Road EH13 0	50-51	
Lanark Road EH14 5	58-59	
Lanark Road West EH14 5	58-59	
Langton Road EH9 3	44-45	
Lansdowne Crescent EH12 5	28-29	
Lapicide Place EH6 4	12-13	
Larbourfield EH11 4	48-49	
Largo Place EH6 4	12-13	
Lasswade Bank EH17 8	54-55	
Lasswade Grove EH17 8	54-55	
Lasswade Road EH17 8	54-55	
Latch Park EH13 0	50-51	
Lauder Loan EH9 2	42-43	
Lauder Road EH9 1	42-43	
Lauderdale Street EH9 1	42-43	
Laurel Terrace EH11 1	42-43	
Laurie Street EH6 7	20-21	
Lauriston Farm Road EH4 5	16-17	
Lauriston Gardens EH3 9	28-29	
Lauriston Park EH3 9	28-29	
Lauriston Place EH3 9	28-29	
Lauriston Street EH3 9	28-29	
Lauriston Terrace EH3 9	28-29	
Laverockbank Avenue EH5 3	12-13	
Laverockbank Avenue South EH5 3	12-13	
Laverockbank Crescent EH5 3	12-13	
Laverockbank Gardens EH5 3	12-13	
Laverockbank Grove EH5 3	12-13	
Laverockbank Road EH5 3	12-13	
Laverockbank Terrace EH5 3	12-13	
Laverockdale Crescent EH13 0	60-61	
Laverockdale Loan EH13 0	60-61	
Laverockdale Park EH13 0	60-61	
Law Place EH15 1	22-23	
Lawhouse Toll EH15 3	46-47	
Lawnmarket EH1 2	28-29	
Leadervale Road EH16 6	54-55	
Leadervale Terrace EH16 6	54-55	
Leamington Place EH10 4	42-43	
Leamington Road EH3 9	42-43	
Leamington Terrace EH10 4	42-43	
Learmonth Avenue EH4 1	28-29	
Learmonth Court EH4 1	28-29	
Learmonth Crescent EH4 1	28-29	
Learmonth Gardens EH4 1	28-29	
Learmonth Gardens Lane EH4 1	28-29	
Learmonth Gardens Mews EH4 1	28-29	
Learmonth Grove EH4 1	28-29	
Learmonth Park EH4 1	28-29	
Learmonth Place EH4 1	28-29	
Learmonth Terrace EH4 1	28-29	
Learmonth Terrace Lane EH4 1	28-29	
Learmonth View EH4 1	28-29	
Lee Crescent EH15 1	32-33	
Leith Street EH1 3	20-21	
Leith Walk EH7 4	20-21	
Leith Walk EH6 8	20-21	
Leith Walk EH1 3	20-21	
Lennel Avenue EH12 6	26-27	
Lennie Cottages EH12 0	78-79	
Lennox Row EH5 3	10-11	
Lennox Street EH4 1	28-29	
Lennox Street Lane EH4 1	28-29	
Leopold Place EH7 5	20-21	
Leslie Place EH4 1	28-29	
Leven Street EH10 4	42-43	
Leven Terrace EH3 9	42-43	
Lewis Terrace EH11 2	28-29	
Liberton Brae EH16 6	54-55	
Liberton Dams EH16 6	44-45	
Liberton Drive EH16 6	54-55	
Liberton Gardens EH16 6	54-55	
Liberton Place EH16 6	54-55	
Liberton Road EH16 5	44-45	
Liddesdale Place EH3 5	18-19	
Lily Terrace EH11 1	42-43	
Lilyhill Terrace EH8 7	20-21	
Limefield EH17 8	56-57	
Lindean Place EH6 8	20-21	
Lindsay Place EH6 4	12-13	
Lindsay Road EH6 4	12-13	
Lindsay Street EH6 4	12-13	
Links Gardens EH6 7	20-21	
Links Gardens Lane EH6 7	12-13	
Links Lane EH6 7	12-13	
Links Place EH6 7	12-13	
Lismore Avenue EH8 7	20-21	
Lismore Crescent EH8 7	20-21	
Little France Mills EH16 4	44-45	
Little King Street EH1 3	28-29	
Little Lochend Close EH8 8	8-9	
Little Road EH16 6	54-55	
Livingstone Place EH9 1	42-43	
Lixmount Avenue EH5 3	12-13	
Lixmount Gardens EH5 3	12-13	
Loaning Crescent EH7 6	20-21	
Loaning Road EH7 6	20-21	

Street	Pages	Grid
Road EH4 7	26-27	H11
end Avenue EH7 6	20-21	N12
end Castle Barns EH7 6	20-21	N11
end Close EH8 8	8-9	
end Crescent EH7 6	20-21	O11
end Drive EH7 6	20-21	N11
end Gardens EH7 6	20-21	N11
end Grove EH7 6	20-21	O11
end Park EH7 6	20-21	N11
end Quadrant EH7 6	20-21	O11
end Road EH6 8	20-21	N12
end Road South EH7 6	20-21	N11
end Square EH7 6	20-21	N11
in Buildings EH3 9	42-43	K9
in Place EH3 9	42-43	K9
in Terrace EH3 9	42-43	K9
side Avenue EH12 9	38-39	D8
side Crescent EH12 9	38-39	D9
side Place EH12 9	38-39	D8
side Place EH12 9	38-39	D8
erby Cottages EH16 6	54-55	O5
erby Crescent EH16 6	54-55	O5
erby Grove EH16 6	54-55	O5
harton Avenue EH14 1	50-51	I7
harton Crescent EH14 1	50-51	I7
harton Gardens EH14 1	42-43	J8
in Street EH3 5	28-29	L11
nlea Avenue EH7 6	20-21	O11
nlea Drive EH7 6	20-21	O11
nlea Gardens EH7 6	20-21	O11
nlea Loan EH7 6	20-21	O11
nlea Place EH7 6	20-21	O11
nlea Road EH7 6	20-21	O11
nlea Terrace EH7 6	20-21	O11
e Green Gardens EH7 4	18-19	L12
e Green Loan EH7 4	18-19	L12
e Green Road EH7 4	18-19	L12
e Mill EH7 4	18-19	L12
ond Road EH5 3	10-11	K13
on Road EH7 5	20-21	N11
on Street EH3 6	28-29	L11
formacus Road EH16 6	54-55	N6
stone Avenue EH14 2	50-51	H7
stone Cottages EH14 2	50-51	H7
stone Crescent EH14 2	40-41	H8
stone Gardens EH14 2	40-41	G8
stone Grove EH14 2	50-51	H7
stone Park EH14 2	50-51	H7
stone Road EH14 2	50-51	H7
stone Street EH14 2	50-51	H7
stone Terrace EH14 2	40-41	G8
stone View EH14 2	40-41	G8
dale Terrace EH3 9	42-43	L9
Russel Place EH9 1	30-31	M9
e Place EH6 8	20-21	M12
e Place South EH6 8	20-21	M12
e Square EH6 8	20-21	M12
e Street EH6 8	20-21	M12
an Road EH3 9	28-29	K10
an Street EH8 9	28-29	L10
er Gilmore Place EH3 9	42-43	K9
er Granton Road EH5 1	10-11	K14
er Joppa EH15 2	32-33	R10
er London Road EH8 8	20-21	N11
Bank EH5 1	10-11	K13
ielaw Road EH9 3	44-45	M8
an Place EH8 9	30-31	M9
n Road EH16 5	44-45	M7
Street EH7 5	20-21	M11
doch Place EH3 7	28-29	K10
doch Place Lane EH3 7	28-29	K10
's Close EH1 1	8-9	
Dowall Road EH9 3	44-45	M8
kenzie Place EH3 6	28-29	K11
eira Place EH6 4	12-13	M13
eira Street EH6 4	12-13	M13
dala Crescent EH12 5	28-29	J10
dala Mews EH12 5	28-29	J10
dalene Avenue EH15 3	32-33	Q9
dalene Court EH15 3	32-33	Q9
dalene Drive EH15 3	32-33	Q9
dalene Gardens EH15 3	32-33	Q9
dalene Loan EH15 3	32-33	Q9
dalene Medway EH15 3	32-33	Q9
dalene Place EH15 3	32-33	Q9
encraig Crescent EH4 2	26-27	I11
encraig Grove EH4 2	26-27	I11
Point EH3 9	28-29	L10
ns of Craigmillar EH16 4	44-45	O7
a Green EH4 1	28-29	K11
a Terrace EH4 1	28-29	K11
derston Street EH6 8	20-21	M12
nering Place EH16 6	54-55	N6
or Place EH3 7	28-29	K10
se Road EH12 7	38-39	F9
se Street EH12 7	38-39	F9
sfield Place EH7 4	28-29	L11
sionhouse Road EH9 1	42-43	L9
ch Grove EH4 3	26-27	H11
ch Pines EH4 3	26-27	G11
ch Road EH4 3	26-27	H11
chfield Grove EH4 5	16-17	H11
chfield Park EH4 5	16-17	G12
chfield Terrace EH4 7	26-27	H11
chhall Crescent EH16 5	30-31	N9

Street	Pages	Grid
Marchhall Place EH16 5	30-31	N9
Marchhall Road EH16 5	30-31	N9
Marchmont Crescent EH9 1	42-43	L9
Marchmont Road EH9 1	42-43	L9
Marchmont Street EH9 1	42-43	L9
Mardale Crescent EH10 5	42-43	K8
Marine Drive EH4 5	16-17	H13
Marine Esplanade EH6 7	20-21	O13
Marionville Avenue EH7 6	20-21	N11
Marionville Crescent EH7 6	20-21	O11
Marionville Drive EH7 6	20-21	O11
Marionville Grove EH7 6	20-21	O11
Marionville Medway EH7 6	20-21	N11
Marionville Park EH7 6	20-21	N11
Marionville Road EH7 6	20-21	N11
Marischal Place EH4 3	26-27	I11
Maritime Lane EH6 6	12-13	N13
Maritime Street EH6 6	12-13	N13
Market Street EH1 1	28-29	L10
Marlborough Street EH15 2	32-33	Q10
Marmion Crescent EH16 5	44-45	N7
Marshall Street EH8 9	28-29	L10
Marshall's Court EH1 3	20-21	M11
Mary's Place EH4 1	28-29	K11
Maryfield EH7 5	20-21	M11
Maryfield EH15 1	22-23	Q11
Maryfield Place EH7 5	20-21	N11
Maurice Place EH9 3	44-45	M8
Maxwell Street EH10 5	42-43	K8
May Court EH4 4	16-17	H13
Maybury Drive EH12 8	24-25	E10
Maybury Road EH12 8	24-25	E10
Mayfield Gardens EH9 2	44-45	M8
Mayfield Gardens Lane EH9 1	44-45	M8
Mayfield Place EH12 7	38-39	F9
Mayfield Road EH9 3	44-45	M7
Mayfield Terrace EH9 1	44-45	M8
Mayville Gardens EH5 3	12-13	L13
Mayville Gardens East EH5 3	12-13	L13
McDonald Place EH7 4	18-19	L12
McDonald Road EH7 4	20-21	M12
McDonald Street EH7 4	20-21	M12
McLaren Road EH9 2	44-45	N8
McLaren Terrace EH11 2	28-29	K10
McLeod Street EH11 2	42-43	J9
McNeill Street EH11 1	42-43	K9
Meadow Lane EH8 9	42-43	L9
Meadow Place EH9 1	42-43	L9
Meadow Place Road EH12 7	38-39	F9
Meadowbank EH8 8	20-21	N11
Meadowbank Avenue EH8 7	20-21	N11
Meadowbank Crescent EH8 7	20-21	N11
Meadowbank Place EH8 7	20-21	O11
Meadowbank Terrace EH8 7	20-21	N11
Meadowfield Avenue EH8 7	30-31	O10
Meadowfield Court EH8 7	30-31	O10
Meadowfield Drive EH8 7	30-31	O9
Meadowfield Gardens EH8 7	30-31	O9
Meadowfield Terrace EH8 7	30-31	O9
Meadowhouse Road EH12 7	40-41	G9
Meadowspot EH10 5	52-53	J7
Mearenside EH12 8	24-25	E10
Meggetland Terrace EH14 1	42-43	J8
Melbourne Place EH1 1	28-29	L10
Melgund Terrace EH7 4	28-29	L11
Melville Crescent EH3 7	28-29	K10
Melville Drive EH9 1	42-43	L9
Melville Place EH3 7	28-29	K10
Melville Street EH3 7	28-29	K10
Melville Street Lane EH3 7	28-29	K10
Melville Terrace EH9 1	42-43	L9
Mentone Avenue EH15 1	22-23	Q11
Mentone Gardens EH9 2	44-45	M8
Mentone Terrace EH9 2	44-45	M8
Merchant Street EH1 1	28-29	L10
Merchiston Avenue EH10 4	42-43	K9
Merchiston Bank Avenue EH10 5	42-43	K8
Merchiston Bank Gardens EH10 5	42-43	K8
Merchiston Crescent EH10 5	42-43	K8
Merchiston Gardens EH10 5	42-43	J8
Merchiston Grove EH11 1	42-43	J9
Merchiston Mews EH10 4	42-43	K9
Merchiston Park EH10 4	42-43	K9
Merchiston Place EH10 4	42-43	K8
Mertoun Place EH11 1	42-43	J9
Meuse Lane EH2 2	28-29	L10
Mid Gillsland Road EH10 5	42-43	J8
Mid Gogarloch Syke EH12 9	38-39	E9
Mid Liberton EH16 5	44-45	N7
Mid New Cultins EH11 4	48-49	E7
Mid Steil EH10 5	52-53	J7
Middle Pier EH5 1	10-11	J14
Middleby Street EH9 1	44-45	M8
Middlefield EH7 4	20-21	M12
Middleknowe EH14 2	48-49	F6
Middlepark EH14 2	48-49	F6
Middleshot EH14 2	48-49	F6
Midmar Avenue EH10 6	52-53	L7
Midmar Drive EH10 6	52-53	L7
Midmar Gardens EH10 6	52-53	L7
Mill Lane EH6 6	12-13	M13
Millar Crescent EH10 5	42-43	K8
Millar Place EH10 5	42-43	K8
Millar Place Lane EH10 5	42-43	K8
Miller Row EH4 3	28-29	K10
Millerfield Place EH9 1	42-43	L9

Street	Pages	Grid
Milnacre EH6 5	12-13	L13
Milton Crescent EH15 3	32-33	Q9
Milton Drive EH15 2	32-33	R10
Milton Gardens North EH15 3	32-33	Q9
Milton Gardens South EH15 3	32-33	Q9
Milton Grove EH15 2	34-35	S10
Milton Link EH15 3	32-33	R9
Milton Road EH15 3	32-33	Q9
Milton Road East EH15 2	32-33	R10
Milton Road West EH15 3	32-33	P10
Milton Street EH8 8	20-21	N11
Milton Terrace EH15 2	34-35	S10
Minto Street EH9 1	30-31	M9
Mitchell Street EH6 7	12-13	N13
Moat Drive EH14 1	40-41	I8
Moat Place EH14 1	40-41	I8
Moat Street EH14 1	40-41	I8
Moat Terrace EH14 1	40-41	I8
Moira Park EH7 6	22-23	P11
Moira Terrace EH7 6	22-23	P11
Moncrieff Terrace EH9 1	30-31	M9
Monkbarns Gardens EH16 6	54-55	N6
Monmouth Terrace EH3 5	18-19	K12
Montagu Terrace EH3 5	18-19	K12
Montague Street EH8 9	30-31	M9
Montgomery Street EH7 5	20-21	M11
Montgomery Street Lane EH7 5	20-21	M11
Montpelier EH10 4	42-43	K9
Montpelier Terrace EH10 4	42-43	K9
Montrose Terrace EH7 5	20-21	M11
Moray Park EH7 5	20-21	N11
Moray Park Terrace EH7 5	20-21	N11
Moray Place EH3 6	28-29	K11
Moredun Dykes Road EH17 8	54-55	O5
Moredun Park Court EH17 7	54-55	O6
Moredun Park Drive EH17 7	54-55	O6
Moredun Park Gardens EH17 7	54-55	O6
Moredun Park Green EH17 7	56-57	P6
Moredun Park Grove EH17 7	56-57	P5
Moredun Park Loan EH17 7	54-55	O6
Moredun Park Road EH17 7	56-57	P6
Moredun Park Street EH17 7	54-55	O6
Moredun Park View EH17 7	56-57	P6
Moredun Park Way EH17 7	54-55	O6
Moredunvale Bank EH17 7	54-55	O6
Moredunvale Green EH17 7	54-55	O6
Moredunvale Grove EH17 7	54-55	O6
Moredunvale Loan EH17 7	54-55	O6
Moredunvale Park EH17 7	54-55	O6
Moredunvale Place EH17 7	54-55	O6
Moredunvale Road EH17 7	54-55	O6
Moredunvale View EH17 7	54-55	O6
Moredunvale Way EH17 7	54-55	O6
Morningside Court EH10 5	52-53	K7
Morningside Drive EH10 5	52-53	K7
Morningside Gardens EH10 5	52-53	J7
Morningside Grove EH10 5	52-53	J7
Morningside Park EH10 5	42-43	K8
Morningside Place EH10 5	42-43	K8
Morningside Road EH10 4	42-43	K8
Morningside Terrace EH10 5	42-43	K8
Morrison Circus EH3 8	28-29	K10
Morrison Crescent EH3 8	28-29	K10
Morrison Link EH3 8	28-29	K10
Morrison Street EH3 8	28-29	K10
Morrison's Close EH1 1	8-9	
Morton Street EH15 2	32-33	R10
Morton Street South EH15 2	32-33	R10
Mortonhall Gate EH16 6	54-55	M5
Mortonhall Park Avenue EH17 8	54-55	M5
Mortonhall Park Bank EH17 8	54-55	N5
Mortonhall Park Crescent EH17 8	54-55	N5
Mortonhall Park Drive EH17 8	54-55	N5
Mortonhall Park Gardens EH17 8	54-55	M5
Mortonhall Park Green EH17 8	54-55	N5
Mortonhall Park Grove EH17 8	54-55	M5
Mortonhall Park Loan EH17 8	54-55	N5
Mortonhall Park Place EH17 8	54-55	N5
Mortonhall Park Terrace EH17 8	54-55	N5
Mortonhall Park View EH17 8	54-55	M5
Mortonhall Park Way EH17 8	54-55	M5
Mortonhall Road EH9 2	42-43	L8
Morven Street EH4 7	24-25	F11
Morvenside EH14 2	48-49	F6
Moston Terrace EH9 2	44-45	M8
Mound Place EH1 2	28-29	L10
Mound, The EH2 2	28-29	L10
Mount Grange EH9 2	42-43	L8
Mount Lodge Place EH15 2	32-33	Q10
Mount Vernon Road EH16 6	54-55	N6
Mount Vernon Road EH16 6	54-55	N6
Mountcastle Bank EH8 7	32-33	P10
Mountcastle Crescent EH8 7	22-23	P11
Mountcastle Drive North EH8 7	32-33	P10
Mountcastle Drive South EH15 3	32-33	Q9
Mountcastle Gardens EH8 7	32-33	P10
Mountcastle Green EH8 7	32-33	P10
Mountcastle Grove EH8 7	32-33	P10
Mountcastle Loan EH8 7	22-23	P11
Mountcastle Terrace EH8 7	32-33	P10
Mounthooly Loan EH10 7	62-63	L5
Muir Wood Crescent EH14 5	58-59	E5
Muir Wood Drive EH14 5	58-59	E5

Street	Page	Grid
Muir Wood Grove EH14 5	58-59	E5
Muir Wood Place EH14 5	58-59	E5
Muir Wood Road EH14 5	58-59	F5
Muirdale Terrace EH4 3	26-27	H11
Muirend Avenue EH14 5	50-51	G6
Muirhouse Avenue EH4 4	16-17	H12
Muirhouse Avenue North EH4 4	16-17	H13
Muirhouse Bank EH4 4	16-17	H12
Muirhouse Close EH4 4	16-17	H12
Muirhouse Crescent EH4 4	16-17	H13
Muirhouse Drive EH4 4	16-17	H13
Muirhouse Gardens EH4 4	16-17	H13
Muirhouse Green EH4 4	16-17	H12
Muirhouse Grove EH4 4	16-17	H13
Muirhouse Loan EH4 4	16-17	H13
Muirhouse Medway EH4 4	16-17	H13
Muirhouse Park EH4 4	16-17	H12
Muirhouse Parkway EH4 4	16-17	H13
Muirhouse Place East EH4 4	16-17	H12
Muirhouse Place West EH4 4	16-17	H12
Muirhouse Terrace EH4 4	16-17	H12
Muirhouse View EH4 4	16-17	H13
Muirhouse Way EH4 4	16-17	H12
Mulberry Place EH6 4	12-13	L13
Munro Drive EH13 0	60-61	H5
Munro Place EH3 5	18-19	L12
Murano Place EH7 5	20-21	M11
Murdoch Terrace EH11 1	42-43	K9
Murieston Crescent EH11 2	42-43	J9
Murieston Crescent Lane EH11 2	42-43	J9
Murieston Lane EH11 2	42-43	J9
Murieston Place EH11 2	42-43	J9
Murieston Road EH11 2	42-43	J9
Murieston Terrace EH11 2	42-43	J9
Murray Cottages EH12 7	38-39	F9
Murrayburn Drive EH14 2	48-49	F7
Murrayburn Gardens EH14 2	50-51	G7
Murrayburn Gate EH14 2	48-49	F6
Murrayburn Green EH14 2	50-51	G7
Murrayburn Grove EH14 2	50-51	G7
Murrayburn Park EH14 2	48-49	F7
Murrayburn Place EH14 2	48-49	F7
Murrayburn Road EH14 2	50-51	G7
Murrayfield Avenue EH12 6	26-27	I10
Murrayfield Drive EH12 6	26-27	I10
Murrayfield Gardens EH12 6	26-27	I10
Murrayfield Place EH12 6	26-27	I10
Murrayfield Road EH12 6	26-27	I10
Murrays Brae, The EH17 8	54-55	O5
Murrays, The EH17 8	64-65	O4
Musselburgh Road EH15 2	34-35	S10
Mylne's Court EH1 2	8-9	
Myreside Court EH10 5	52-53	J7
Myreside Road EH10 5	42-43	J8
Myrtle Terrace EH11 1	42-43	J9
Nantwich Drive EH7 6	22-23	P12
Napier Road EH10 5	42-43	J8
Nellfield EH16 6	54-55	N6
Nelson Street EH3 6	28-29	L11
Nether Craigour EH17 7	44-45	O7
Nether Craigwell EH8 8	30-31	M10
Nether Currie Crescent EH14 5	58-59	E5
Nether Currie Place EH14 5	58-59	E5
Nether Currie Road EH14 5	58-59	E5
Netherbank EH16 6	54-55	M5
Netherbank View EH16 6	54-55	M5
Netherby Road EH5 3	10-11	K13
New Arthur Place EH8 9	30-31	M10
New Assembly Close EH1 1	8-9	
New Belfield EH8 7	32-33	P10
New Bell's Court EH6 6	12-13	N13
New Broompark EH5 1	10-11	J14
New Broughton EH3 6	28-29	L11
New John's Place EH8 9	30-31	M9
New Lairdship Place EH11 3	38-39	F8
New Lairdship Yards EH11 3	38-39	F8
New Lane EH6 4	12-13	L13
New Market Road EH14 1	40-41	I8
New Mart Road EH14 1	40-41	H8
New Orchardfield EH6 5	20-21	M12
New Skinner's Close EH1 1	30-31	M10
New Street EH8 8	30-31	M10
New Swanston EH10 7	62-63	J5
New Tower Place EH15 1	22-23	Q11
Newbattle Terrace EH10 4	42-43	K8
Newcraighall Road EH15 3	46-47	R8
Newcraighall Road EH15 3	46-47	Q8
Newhaven Main Street EH6 4	12-13	L14
Newhaven Place EH6 4	12-13	L14
Newhaven Road EH6 4	12-13	L13
Newington Road EH9 1	30-31	M9
Newmills Avenue EH14 5	70-71	C4
Newmills Crescent EH14 5	70-71	C4
Newmills Grove EH14 5	70-71	C4
Newmills Road EH14 5	70-71	C4
Newport Street EH3 8	28-29	K10
Newtoft Street EH17 8	54-55	O5
Newtoft Street EH17 8	56-57	P5
Newton Street EH11 1	42-43	J9
Nicolson Square EH8 9	30-31	M10
Nicolson Street EH8 9	30-31	M10
Niddrie Cottages EH15 3	46-47	R8
Niddrie Farm Grove EH16 4	46-47	P8
Niddrie House Avenue EH16 4	46-47	P8
Niddrie House Drive EH16 4	46-47	Q8
Niddrie House Gardens EH16 4	46-47	P8
Niddrie House Grove EH16 4	46-47	Q8
Niddrie House Park EH16 4	46-47	P8
Niddrie House Square EH16 4	46-47	P8
Niddrie Mains Drive EH16 4	46-47	P8
Niddrie Mains Road EH16 4	46-47	P8
Niddrie Mains Terrace EH16 4	46-47	P8
Niddrie Marischal Crescent EH16 4	46-47	P8
Niddrie Marischal Drive EH16 4	46-47	P8
Niddrie Marischal Gardens EH16 4	46-47	P8
Niddrie Marischal Green EH16 4	46-47	P8
Niddrie Marischal Grove EH16 4	46-47	Q8
Niddrie Marischal Loan EH16 4	46-47	P8
Niddrie Marischal Place EH16 4	46-47	P8
Niddrie Marischal Road EH16 4	46-47	Q8
Niddrie Marischal Street EH16 4	46-47	P8
Niddrie Mill Avenue EH15 3	46-47	Q8
Niddrie Mill Crescent EH15 3	46-47	Q8
Niddrie Mill Drive EH15 3	46-47	Q8
Niddrie Mill Grove EH15 3	46-47	Q8
Niddrie Mill Place EH15 3	46-47	Q8
Niddrie Mill Terrace EH15 3	46-47	Q8
Niddry Street EH1 1	28-29	L10
Niddry Street South EH1 1	30-31	M10
Nigel Loan EH16 6	54-55	N6
Nile Grove EH10 4	42-43	K8
Noble Place EH6 8	20-21	N12
North Bank Street EH1 2	28-29	L10
North Bridge EH1 1	28-29	L10
North Bughtlin Bank EH12 8	24-25	E11
North Bughtlin Brae EH12 8	24-25	E11
North Bughtlin Gate EH12 8	24-25	E11
North Bughtlin Neuk EH12 8	24-25	E11
North Bughtlin Place EH12 8	24-25	E11
North Bughtlinfield EH12 8	24-25	E11
North Bughtlinrig EH12 8	24-25	E11
North Bughtlinside EH12 8	24-25	E11
North Cairntow EH16 4	30-31	O9
North Castle Street EH2 3	28-29	K11
North Charlotte Street EH3 6	28-29	K11
North Clyde Street Lane EH2 1	28-29	L11
North East Circus Place EH3 6	28-29	K11
North Elgin Street EH7 5	20-21	M11
North Fort Street EH6 4	12-13	M13
North Gray's Close EH1 1	8-9	
North Greens EH15 3	32-33	Q9
North Gyle Avenue EH12 8	38-39	E9
North Gyle Drive EH12 8	24-25	E10
North Gyle Farm Court EH12 8	38-39	E9
North Gyle Farm Lane EH12 8	38-39	E9
North Gyle Grove EH12 8	24-25	E10
North Gyle Loan EH12 8	24-25	E10
North Gyle Park EH12 8	24-25	E10
North Gyle Road EH12 8	24-25	E10
North Gyle Terrace EH12 8	38-39	E9
North Hillhousefield EH6 4	12-13	M13
North Junction Street EH6 6	12-13	M13
North Leith Mill EH6 6	12-13	M13
North Leith Sands EH6 4	12-13	M13
North Meggetland EH14 1	42-43	J8
North Park Terrace EH4 1	28-29	K11
North Peffer Place EH16 4	44-45	O8
North Richmond Street EH8 9	30-31	M10
North St. Andrew Street EH2 1	28-29	L11
North St. David Street EH2 1	28-29	L11
North Werber Park EH4 2	18-19	J12
North Werber Place EH4 1	18-19	J12
North Werber Road EH4 1	18-19	J12
North West Circus Place EH3 6	28-29	K11
Northcote Street EH11 2	42-43	J9
Northfield Avenue EH8 7	30-31	O10
Northfield Broadway EH8 7	32-33	P10
Northfield Circus EH8 7	30-31	O10
Northfield Crescent EH8 7	30-31	O10
Northfield Drive EH8 7	32-33	P10
Northfield Farm Avenue EH8 7	32-33	P10
Northfield Farm Road EH8 7	32-33	P10
Northfield Gardens EH8 7	32-33	P10
Northfield Grove EH8 7	32-33	P10
Northfield Park EH8 7	32-33	P10
Northfield Park Grove EH8 7	32-33	P10
Northfield Road EH8 7	30-31	O10
Northfield Square EH8 7	32-33	P10
Northfield Terrace EH8 7	30-31	O10
Northlawn Terrace EH4 6	16-17	G12
Northumberland Place EH3 6	28-29	L11
Northumberland Place Lane EH3 6	28-29	L11
Northumberland Street EH3 6	28-29	L11
Northumberland Street; NE. Lane EH3 6	28-29	L11
Northumberland Street; NW. Lane EH3 6	28-29	L11
Northumberland Street; SE. Lane EH3 6	28-29	L11
Northumberland Street; SW. Lane EH3 6	28-29	L11
Norton Park EH7 5	20-21	N11
Oak Lane EH12 6	26-27	G11
Oakfield Place EH8 9	30-31	M10
Oakville Terrace EH6 8	20-21	N12
Observatory Green EH9 3	44-45	M7
Observatory Road EH9 3	44-45	M7
Ocean Drive EH6 6	12-13	M13
Ochiltree Gardens EH16 5	44-45	O7
Ogilvie Terrace EH11 1	42-43	J8
Old Assembly Close EH1 1		8-9
Old Broughton EH3 6		28-29
Old Burdiehouse Road EH17 8		64-65
Old Church Lane EH15 3		30-31
Old Dalkeith Road EH16 4		56-57
Old Dalkeith Road EH16 4		44-45
Old Farm Avenue EH13 0		50-51
Old Farm Place EH13 0		50-51
Old Fishmarket Close EH1 1		28-29
Old Kirk Road EH12 6		26-27
Old Mill Lane EH16 5		44-45
Old Newmills Road EH14 4		70-71
Old Playhouse Close EH8 8		8-9
Old Stamp Office Close EH1 1		8-9
Old Tolbooth Wynd EH8 8		30-31
Orchard Bank EH4 2		28-29
Orchard Brae EH4 1		28-29
Orchard Brae Avenue EH4 2		28-29
Orchard Brae Gardens EH4 2		28-29
Orchard Brae Gardens West EH4 2		28-29
Orchard Brae West EH4 2		28-29
Orchard Crescent EH4 2		26-27
Orchard Drive EH4 2		26-27
Orchard Grove EH4 2		28-29
Orchard Place EH4 2		28-29
Orchard Road EH4 2		28-29
Orchard Road South EH4 3		26-27
Orchard Terrace EH4 2		28-29
Orchard Toll EH4 3		28-29
Orchardfield Avenue EH12 7		38-39
Orchardhead Loan EH16 6		54-55
Orchardhead Road EH16 6		44-45
Ormelie Terrace EH15 2		32-33
Ormidale Terrace EH12 6		26-27
Ormiston Terrace EH12 7		38-39
Orrok Park EH16 5		44-45
Orwell Place EH11 2		42-43
Orwell Terrace EH11 2		42-43
Osborne Terrace EH12 5		28-29
Oswald Court EH9 2		42-43
Oswald Road EH9 2		42-43
Oswald Terrace EH12 7		38-39
Otterburn Park EH14 1		50-51
Oxcraig Street EH5 1		10-11
Oxford Street EH8 9		30-31
Oxford Terrace EH4 1		28-29
Oxgangs Avenue EH13 9		52-53
Oxgangs Bank EH13 9		62-63
Oxgangs Brae EH13 9		62-63
Oxgangs Broadway EH13 9		62-63
Oxgangs Crescent EH13 9		52-53
Oxgangs Drive EH13 9		52-53
Oxgangs Farm Avenue EH13 9		62-63
Oxgangs Farm Drive EH13 9		62-63
Oxgangs Farm Gardens EH13 9		62-63
Oxgangs Farm Grove EH13 9		62-63
Oxgangs Farm Loan EH13 9		62-63
Oxgangs Farm Terrace EH13 9		62-63
Oxgangs Gardens EH13 9		52-53
Oxgangs Green EH13 9		52-53
Oxgangs Grove EH13 9		52-53
Oxgangs Hill EH13 9		52-53
Oxgangs Loan EH13 9		52-53
Oxgangs Medway EH13 9		62-63
Oxgangs Park EH13 9		62-63
Oxgangs Path EH13 9		62-63
Oxgangs Place EH13 9		52-53
Oxgangs Rise EH13 9		52-53
Oxgangs Road EH10 7		62-63
Oxgangs Road North EH13 9		62-63
Oxgangs Row EH13 9		62-63
Oxgangs Street EH13 9		62-63
Oxgangs Terrace EH13 9		62-63
Oxgangs View EH13 9		62-63
Paddockholm, The EH12 7		40-41
Paisley Avenue EH8 7		30-31
Paisley Close EH1 1		8-9
Paisley Crescent EH8 7		30-31
Paisley Drive EH8 7		30-31
Paisley Gardens EH8 7		30-31
Paisley Grove EH8 7		30-31
Paisley Terrace EH8 7		30-31
Palmer Place EH14 5		58-59
Palmer Road EH14 5		58-59
Palmerston Place EH12 5		28-29
Palmerston Place Lane EH12 5		28-29
Palmerston Road EH9 1		42-43
Panmure Place EH3 9		42-43
Pape's Cottages EH12 6		26-27
Park Avenue EH15 1		32-33
Park Crescent EH16 6		54-55
Park Gardens EH16 6		54-55
Park Grove EH16 6		54-55
Park Place EH6 4		12-13
Park Road EH6 4		12-13
Parker Avenue EH7 6		22-23
Parker Road EH7 6		22-23
Parker Terrace EH7 6		22-23
Parkgrove Avenue EH4 7		24-25
Parkgrove Bank EH4 7		24-25
Parkgrove Crescent EH4 7		24-25
Parkgrove Drive EH4 7		24-25
Parkgrove Gardens EH4 7		24-25
Parkgrove Green EH4 7		24-25
Parkgrove Loan EH4 7		24-25

Street	Page	Grid
...kgrove Neuk EH4 7	24-25	F11
...kgrove Path EH4 7	24-25	F11
...kgrove Place EH4 7	24-25	F11
...kgrove Road EH4 7	24-25	F11
...kgrove Row EH4 7	24-25	F11
...kgrove Street EH4 7	24-25	F11
...kgrove Terrace EH4 7	24-25	F11
...kgrove View EH4 7	24-25	F11
...khead Avenue EH11 4	50-51	G7
...khead Drive EH11 4	50-51	G7
...khead Gardens EH11 4	50-51	G7
...khead Grove EH11 4	50-51	G7
...khead Loan EH11 4	50-51	G7
...khead Place EH11 4	50-51	G7
...khead Street EH11 4	50-51	G7
...khead Terrace EH11 4	40-41	G8
...khead View EH11 4	50-51	G7
...kside Street EH8 9	30-31	M9
...kside Terrace EH16 5	30-31	M9
...kvale Place EH6 8	20-21	N12
...liament Street EH6 6	12-13	M13
...rotshot EH15 3	32-33	Q9
...sons Green Terrace EH8 7	20-21	O11
...ies Road EH14 1	50-51	I6
...riothall EH3 5	28-29	K11
...tison Street EH6 7	12-13	N13
...cock Court EH6 4	12-13	L14
...cocktail Close EH15 3	46-47	Q8
...rce Avenue EH12 8	24-25	F10
...rce Grove EH12 8	24-25	F10
...rce Road EH28 8	24-25	F10
...tville Gardens EH14 2	50-51	H7
...tville Terrace EH14 2	50-51	H7
...el Terrace EH16 4	44-45	M8
...fer Bank EH16 4	44-45	O8
...fer Place EH16 4	44-45	O8
...fer Street EH16 4	44-45	O8
...fermill Road EH16 5	44-45	N8
...ggy's Mill Road EH4 6	14-15	E13
...mbroke Place EH12 5	28-29	J10
...nnywell Cottages EH4 4	16-17	H13
...nnywell Gardens EH4 4	16-17	H13
...nnywell Grove EH4 4	16-17	H13
...nnywell Medway EH4 4	16-17	H13
...nnywell Place EH4 4	16-17	H13
...nnywell Road EH4 4	16-17	H13
...nnywell Villas EH4 4	16-17	H13
...ntecox EH16 4	46-47	P7
...ntland Avenue EH14 5	58-59	D4
...ntland Avenue EH13 0	60-61	H5
...ntland Crescent EH10 6	52-53	K6
...ntland Drive EH10 6	62-63	J5
...ntland Gardens EH10 6	52-53	K6
...ntland Grove EH10 6	52-53	K6
...ntland Place EH14 5	58-59	D4
...ntland Road EH13 0	50-51	H6
...ntland Terrace EH10 6	52-53	K6
...ntland Terrace EH10 6	52-53	K6
...ntland View EH10 6	62-63	K5
...ntland View EH14 5	58-59	D4
...ntland Villas EH14 5	58-59	F5
...drixknowe EH14 1	50-51	I7
...rth Street EH3 5	28-29	K11
...veril Terrace EH16 6	54-55	N6
...ardy Place EH1 3	28-29	L11
...r Place EH6 4	12-13	L14
...rsfield Grove EH8 7	20-21	O11
...rsfield Place EH8 7	20-21	O11
...rsfield Terrace EH8 7	20-21	O11
...rshill Lane EH8 7	20-21	O11
...rshill Place EH8 7	20-21	O11
...rshill Square East EH8 7	20-21	O11
...rshill Square West EH8 7	20-21	O11
...rshill Terrace EH8 7	30-31	O10
...rie's Close EH8 8	8-9	
...ochry Place EH7 5	20-21	N11
...sligo Road EH10 4	42-43	K8
...t Street EH6 4	12-13	M13
...tville Street EH15 2	32-33	Q10
...tville Street Lane EH15 2	32-33	Q10
...easance EH8 8	30-31	M10
...wlands Avenue EH10 5	52-53	J7
Plewlands Gardens EH10 5	52-53	J7
Plewlands Terrace EH10 5	52-53	J7
Pleydell Place EH16 6	54-55	N6
Polwarth Crescent EH11 1	42-43	J9
Polwarth Gardens EH11 1	42-43	J9
Polwarth Grove EH11 1	42-43	J8
Polwarth Park EH11 1	42-43	J9
Polwarth Place EH11 1	42-43	J9
Polwarth Terrace EH11 1	42-43	J9
Ponton Street EH3 9	42-43	K9
Poplar Lane EH6 7	12-13	N13
Portgower Place EH4 1	28-29	K11
Portland Place EH6 6	12-13	M13
Portland Street EH6 4	12-13	M13
Portland Terrace EH6 6	12-13	M13
Portobello High Street EH15 1	22-23	Q11
Portobello Road EH8 7	20-21	O11
Potterrow EH8 9	28-29	L10
Pottery, The EH15 1	22-23	Q11
Prestonfield Avenue EH16 5	44-45	N8
Prestonfield Bank EH16 5	44-45	N8
Prestonfield Crescent EH16 5	44-45	N8
Prestonfield Gardens EH16 5	44-45	N8
Prestonfield Road EH16 5	44-45	N8
Prestonfield Terrace EH16 5	44-45	N8
Priestfield Avenue EH16 5	44-45	N8
Priestfield Crescent EH16 5	44-45	N8
Priestfield Gardens EH16 5	44-45	N8
Priestfield Grove EH16 5	30-31	N9
Priestfield Road EH16 5	30-31	N9
Priestfield Road North EH16 5	30-31	N9
Primrose Bank Road EH5 3	10-11	K13
Primrose Street EH6 8	20-21	N12
Primrose Terrace EH11 1	42-43	J9
Prince Regent Street EH6 4	12-13	M13
Princes Street EH2 3	28-29	L10
Promenade Terrace EH15 1	22-23	Q11
Prospect Bank Crescent EH6 7	20-21	N12
Prospect Bank Gardens EH6 7	20-21	N12
Prospect Bank Grove EH6 7	20-21	O12
Prospect Bank Place EH6 7	20-21	O12
Prospect Bank Road EH6 7	20-21	N12
Prospect Bank Terrace EH6 7	20-21	O12
Quality Street EH4 5	16-17	G12
Quality Street Lane EH4 5	16-17	G12
Quarry Close EH8 9	30-31	M9
Quarry Cottages EH15 3	46-47	Q8
Quarrybank EH14 2	48-49	F6
Quarrybank Close EH14 2	48-49	F6
Quarrybank Court EH14 2	48-49	F6
Quarrybank End EH14 2	48-49	F6
Quarryview EH14 2	48-49	F6
Quayside Street EH6 6	12-13	M13
Queen Charlotte Lane EH6 6	12-13	N13
Queen Charlotte Street EH6 6	12-13	N13
Queen Margaret Close EH10 7	62-63	L5
Queen Street EH2 3	28-29	K11
Queen Street Gardens East EH3 6	28-29	L11
Queen Street Gardens West EH3 6	28-29	L11
Queen's Avenue EH4 2	26-27	H11
Queen's Avenue South EH4 2	26-27	I11
Queen's Bay Crescent EH15 2	32-33	R10
Queen's Crescent EH9 2	44-45	M8
Queen's Drive EH8 9	30-31	M9
Queen's Gardens EH4 2	26-27	I11
Queen's Park Avenue EH8 7	20-21	N11
Queen's Road EH4 2	26-27	I11
Queen's Walk EH16 4	46-47	P8
Queensferry Road EH4 3	26-27	I11
Queensferry Road EH4 7	24-25	F11
Queensferry Street EH3 7	28-29	K10
Queensferry Street Lane EH2 4	28-29	K10
Queensferry Terrace EH4 3	28-29	J11
Quilts Wynd EH6 5	12-13	M13
Quilts, The EH6 5	12-13	M13
Rae's Court EH16 6	54-55	N5
Raeburn Mews EH4 1	28-29	K11
Raeburn Place EH4 1	28-29	K11
Raeburn Street EH4 1	28-29	K11
Ramsay Garden EH1 2	28-29	L10
Ramsay Lane EH1 2	28-29	L10
Ramsay Place EH15 1	22-23	Q11
Randolph Cliff EH3 7	28-29	K10
Randolph Crescent EH3 7	28-29	K10
Randolph Lane EH3 7	28-29	K10
Randolph Place EH3 7	28-29	K10
Rankeillor Street EH8 9	30-31	M9
Rankin Avenue EH9 3	44-45	M7
Rankin Drive EH9 3	44-45	M7
Rankin Road EH9 3	44-45	M8
Rannoch Grove EH4 7	24-25	F11
Rannoch Place EH4 7	24-25	F11
Rannoch Road EH4 7	26-27	G11
Rannoch Terrace EH4 7	24-25	F11
Ransome Gardens EH4 7	24-25	F11
Ratcliffe Terrace EH9 1	44-45	M8
Rathbone Place EH15 1	22-23	Q11
Ravelston Dykes EH4 3	28-29	J10
Ravelston Dykes Lane EH4 3	26-27	H10
Ravelston Dykes Road EH4 3	26-27	H11
Ravelston Garden EH4 3	26-27	I10
Ravelston Heights EH4 3	26-27	I11
Ravelston House Grove EH4 3	26-27	I11
Ravelston House Loan EH4 3	26-27	I11
Ravelston House Park EH4 3	26-27	I11
Ravelston House Road EH4 3	26-27	I11
Ravelston Park EH4 3	28-29	J10
Ravelston Place EH4 3	28-29	J10
Ravelston Rise EH4 3	26-27	I10
Ravelston Terrace EH4 3	28-29	J11
Ravenscroft Gardens EH17 8	56-57	P5
Ravenscroft Place EH17 8	54-55	O5
Ravenscroft Street EH17 8	56-57	P5
Ravenswood Avenue EH16 5	44-45	O7
Redbraes Grove EH7 4	18-19	L12
Redbraes Place EH7 4	18-19	L12
Redford Avenue EH13 0	60-61	I5
Redford Bank EH13 0	60-61	I5
Redford Crescent EH13 0	60-61	I5
Redford Drive EH13 0	60-61	H5
Redford Gardens EH13 0	60-61	I5
Redford Grove EH13 0	50-51	I6
Redford Loan EH13 0	60-61	I5
Redford Neuk EH13 0	60-61	I5
Redford Place EH13 0	50-51	I6
Redford Road EH13 9	60-61	I5
Redford Terrace EH13 0	60-61	I5
Redford Walk EH13 0	60-61	I5
Redgauntlet Terrace EH16 5	44-45	N7
Redhall Avenue EH14 2	50-51	H7
Redhall Bank Road EH14 2	50-51	H7
Redhall Crescent EH14 2	50-51	H7
Redhall Drive EH14 2	50-51	H7
Redhall Gardens EH14 2	50-51	H7
Redhall Grove EH14 2	50-51	H7
Redhall House Drive EH14 1	50-51	H7
Redhall Place EH14 2	50-51	H7
Redhall Road EH14 2	50-51	H7
Redhall View EH14 2	50-51	H7
Redheughs Avenue EH12 9	38-39	E8
Redheughs Rigg EH12 9	38-39	E9
Reekie's Court EH8 9	30-31	M10
Regent Place EH7 5	20-21	N11
Regent Road EH8 8	30-31	M10
Regent Street EH15 2	32-33	Q10
Regent Terrace EH7 5	20-21	M11
Regent Terrace Lane EH7 5	20-21	M11
Regent Terrace Mews EH7 5	20-21	M11
Regent's Court EH11 2	42-43	J9
Regis Court EH4 6	14-15	E12
Register Place EH2 2	28-29	L11
Reid Terrace EH3 5	28-29	K11
Reid's Close EH8 8	30-31	M10
Relugas Gardens EH9 2	44-45	M8
Relugas Place EH9 2	44-45	M8
Relugas Road EH9 2	44-45	M8
Rennie's Isle EH6 7	12-13	M13
Research Avenue North EH14 4	48-49	D6
Research Avenue South EH14 4	48-49	D6
Restalrig Avenue EH7 6	20-21	O11
Restalrig Circus EH7 6	20-21	O12
Restalrig Crescent EH7 6	20-21	O12
Restalrig Drive EH7 6	20-21	O11
Restalrig Gardens EH7 6	20-21	O11
Restalrig Park EH7 6	20-21	N12
Restalrig Road EH6 8	20-21	N12
Restalrig Road South EH7 6	20-21	O11
Restalrig Square EH7 6	20-21	O12
Restalrig Terrace EH6 8	20-21	N12
Riccarton Avenue EH14 5	58-59	D5
Riccarton Crescent EH14 5	58-59	E5
Riccarton Drive EH14 5	58-59	D5
Riccarton Grove EH14 5	58-59	E5
Riccarton Mains Road EH14 5	58-59	E5
Richmond Lane EH8 9	30-31	M10
Richmond Place EH8 9	30-31	M10
Richmond Terrace EH11 2	28-29	K10
Riddell's Close EH1 2	8-9	
Riding Park EH4 6	14-15	E12
Riego Street EH3 9	28-29	K10
Rillbank Crescent EH9 1	42-43	L9
Rillbank Terrace EH9 1	42-43	L9
Ringwood Place EH16 6	54-55	N6
Rintoul Place EH3 5	28-29	K11
Riselaw Crescent EH10 6	52-53	K6
Riselaw Place EH10 6	52-53	K6
Riselaw Road EH10 6	52-53	K6
Riselaw Terrace EH10 6	52-53	K6
Ritchie Place EH11 1	42-43	J9
Riversdale Crescent EH12 5	40-41	I8
Riversdale Grove EH12 5	26-27	I10
Riversdale Road EH12 5	40-41	I8
Robb's Loan EH14 1	40-41	I8
Robb's Loan Grove EH14 1	40-41	I8
Robert Burns Drive EH16 6	44-45	N7
Robertson Avenue EH11 1	40-41	I9
Robertson's Close EH1 1	30-31	M10
Robertson's Court EH8 8	30-31	M10
Rocheid Park EH4 1	18-19	J12
Rochester Terrace EH10 5	42-43	K8
Rodney Street EH7 4	28-29	L11
Romero Place EH16 5	30-31	M9
Rose Park EH5 3	10-11	K13
Rose Street EH2 3	28-29	L10
Rose Street North Lane EH2 3	28-29	L10
Rose Street South Lane EH2 3	28-29	L10
Rosebank Cottages EH3 8	28-29	K10
Rosebank Gardens EH5 3	10-11	K13
Rosebank Grove EH5 3	10-11	K13
Rosebank Road EH5 3	10-11	K13

Street	Page	Grid
Rosebery Crescent EH12 5	28-29	J10
Rosebery Crescent Lane EH12 5	28-29	J10
Roseburn Avenue EH12 5	26-27	I10
Roseburn Cliff EH12 6	26-27	I10
Roseburn Crescent EH12 5	26-27	I10
Roseburn Drive EH12 5	26-27	I10
Roseburn Gardens EH12 5	26-27	I10
Roseburn Maltings EH12 5	28-29	J10
Roseburn Place EH12 5	26-27	I10
Roseburn Street EH12 5	40-41	I9
Roseburn Terrace EH12 6	28-29	J10
Rosefield Avenue EH15 1	32-33	Q10
Rosefield Avenue Lane EH15 1	32-33	Q10
Rosefield Place EH15 1	32-33	Q10
Rosefield Street EH15 1	32-33	Q10
Rosemount Buildings EH3 8	28-29	K10
Roseneath Place EH9 1	42-43	L9
Roseneath Street EH9 1	42-43	L9
Roseneath Terrace EH9 1	42-43	L9
Rosevale Place EH6 8	20-21	N12
Rosevale Terrace EH6 8	20-21	N12
Roseville Gardens EH5 3	12-13	L13
Ross Gardens EH9 3	44-45	M8
Ross Place EH9 3	44-45	M8
Ross Road EH16 5	44-45	M7
Rossie Place EH7 5	20-21	N11
Rosslyn Crescent EH6 5	20-21	M12
Rosslyn Terrace EH6 5	20-21	M12
Rothesay Mews EH3 7	28-29	J10
Rothesay Place EH3 7	28-29	K10
Rothesay Terrace EH3 7	28-29	J10
Roull Grove EH12 7	38-39	F9
Roull Place EH12 7	40-41	G9
Roull Road EH12 7	40-41	G9
Rowantree Avenue EH14 5	58-59	D4
Rowantree Grove EH14 5	58-59	D4
Roxburgh Place EH8 9	30-31	M10
Roxburgh Street EH8 9	30-31	M10
Royal Circus EH3 6	28-29	K11
Royal Crescent EH3 6	28-29	L11
Royal Mile, The EH1 1	8-9	
Royal Park Place EH8 8	20-21	N11
Royal Park Terrace EH8 8	20-21	N11
Royal Terrace EH7 5	20-21	M11
Royal Terrace Mews EH7 5	20-21	M11
Royston Mains Avenue EH5 1	10-11	I13
Royston Mains Close EH5 1	10-11	J13
Royston Mains Crescent EH5 1	10-11	I13
Royston Mains Gardens EH5 1	10-11	J13
Royston Mains Green EH5 1	10-11	I13
Royston Mains Place EH5 1	10-11	I13
Royston Mains Road EH5 1	10-11	J13
Royston Mains Street EH5 1	10-11	I13
Royston Terrace EH3 5	18-19	K12
Russell Gardens EH12 5	28-29	J10
Russell Place EH5 3	10-11	K13
Russell Road EH12 5	28-29	J10
Rustic Cottages EH13 0	50-51	H6
Rutherford Drive EH16 6	44-45	N7
Rutland Court EH1 2	28-29	K10
Rutland Court Lane EH3 8	28-29	K10
Rutland Place EH1 2	28-29	K10
Rutland Square EH1 2	28-29	K10
Rutland Street EH1 2	28-29	K10
Ryehill Avenue EH6 8	20-21	N12
Ryehill Gardens EH6 8	20-21	N12
Ryehill Grove EH6 8	20-21	N12
Ryehill Place EH6 8	20-21	N12
Ryehill Terrace EH6 8	20-21	N12
Salamander Place EH6 7	12-13	N13
Salamander Street EH6 7	12-13	N13
Salisbury Place EH9 1	30-31	M9
Salisbury Road EH16 5	30-31	M9
Salmond Place EH7 5	20-21	N11
Salvesen Crescent EH4 5	16-17	H13
Salvesen Gardens EH4 5	16-17	H13
Salvesen Grove EH4 5	16-17	H13
Salvesen Terrace EH4 5	16-17	H13
Sandford Gardens EH15 1	32-33	Q10
Sandport EH6 6	12-13	N13
Sandport Place EH6 6	12-13	M13
Sandport Street EH6 6	12-13	M13
Sauchiebank EH11 2	42-43	J9
Saughton Avenue EH11 2	40-41	I8
Saughton Crescent EH12 5	40-41	H9
Saughton Gardens EH12 5	40-41	H9
Saughton Grove EH12 5	40-41	H9
Saughton Loan EH12 5	40-41	H9
Saughton Mains Avenue EH11 3	40-41	G8
Saughton Mains Bank EH11 3	40-41	G8
Saughton Mains Cottages EH11 3	40-41	G8
Saughton Mains Drive EH11 3	40-41	G8
Saughton Mains Gardens EH11 3	40-41	G8
Saughton Mains Grove EH11 3	40-41	H8
Saughton Mains Loan EH11 3	40-41	G8
Saughton Mains Park EH11 3	40-41	G8
Saughton Mains Place EH11 3	40-41	G8
Saughton Mains Street EH11 3	40-41	G8
Saughton Mains Terrace EH11 3	40-41	G8
Saughton Park EH12 5	40-41	H9
Saughton Road EH11 3	40-41	G8
Saughton Road North EH12 7	40-41	G9
Saughtonhall Avenue EH12 5	40-41	H9
Saughtonhall Avenue West EH12 5	40-41	H9
Saughtonhall Circus EH12 5	40-41	I9
Saughtonhall Crescent EH12 5	40-41	H9
Saughtonhall Drive EH12 5	40-41	H9
Saughtonhall Gardens EH12 5	40-41	I9
Saughtonhall Grove EH12 5	40-41	I9
Saughtonhall Place EH12 5	40-41	H9
Saughtonhall Terrace EH12 5	40-41	I9
Saunders Street EH3 6	28-29	K11
Savile Place EH9 3	44-45	M8
Savile Terrace EH9 3	44-45	M8
Saxe-Coburg Place EH3 5	28-29	K11
Saxe-Coburg Street EH3 5	28-29	K11
Saxe-Coburg Terrace EH3 5	28-29	K11
School Brae EH4 6	14-15	E13
Sciennes EH9 1	30-31	M9
Sciennes Gardens EH9 1	30-31	M9
Sciennes Hill Place EH9 1	30-31	M9
Sciennes House Place EH9 1	30-31	M9
Sciennes Place EH9 1	30-31	M9
Sciennes Road EH9 1	42-43	L9
Scone Gardens EH8 7	20-21	O11
Scotland Street EH3 6	28-29	L11
Scotland Street Lane East EH3 6	28-29	L11
Scotland Street Lane West EH3 6	28-29	L11
Seacot EH7 6	20-21	O12
Seafield Avenue EH6 7	20-21	O12
Seafield Place EH6 7	20-21	O12
Seafield Road EH6 7	20-21	O12
Seafield Road East EH15 1	22-23	P12
Seafield Street EH6 7	20-21	O12
Seafield Way EH15 1	22-23	P12
Seaforth Drive EH4 2	26-27	I11
Sealcarr Street EH5 1	10-11	J14
Seaport Street EH6 6	12-13	N13
Seaview Crescent EH15 2	32-33	R10
Seaview Terrace EH15 2	32-33	R10
Seaview Terrace EH15 2	34-35	S10
Second Gait EH14 4	48-49	D6
Semple Street EH3 8	28-29	K10
Seton Place EH9 2	30-31	M9
Shaftesbury Park EH11 1	42-43	J8
Shandon Crescent EH11 1	42-43	J8
Shandon Place EH11 1	42-43	J8
Shandon Road EH11 1	42-43	J8
Shandon Street EH11 1	42-43	J8
Shandon Terrace EH11 1	42-43	J8
Shandwick Place EH3 7	28-29	K10
Sharpdale Loan EH16 5	44-45	N7
Shaw's Place EH7 4	20-21	M12
Shaw's Street EH7 4	20-21	M12
Shaw's Terrace EH7 4	20-21	M12
Sheriff Bank EH6 6	12-13	M13
Sheriff Brae EH6 6	12-13	M13
Sheriff Park EH6 6	12-13	M13
Shore EH6 6	12-13	N13
Shore Place EH6 6	12-13	N13
Shrub Mount EH15 1	22-23	Q11
Shrub Place EH7 4	20-21	M12
Shrub Place Lane EH7 4	20-21	M12
Sienna Gardens EH9 1	30-31	M9
Sighthill Avenue EH11 4	50-51	G7
Sighthill Bank EH11 4	48-49	F7
Sighthill Court EH11 4	48-49	F7
Sighthill Crescent EH11 4	48-49	F7
Sighthill Drive EH11 4	48-49	F7
Sighthill Gardens EH11 4	48-49	F7
Sighthill Green EH11 4	48-49	F7
Sighthill Grove EH11 4	50-51	G7
Sighthill Loan EH11 4	48-49	F7
Sighthill Neuk EH11 4	48-49	F7
Sighthill Park EH11 4	48-49	F7
Sighthill Place EH11 4	48-49	F7
Sighthill Rise EH11 4	48-49	F7
Sighthill Road EH11 4	48-49	F7
Sighthill Street EH11 4	48-49	F7
Sighthill Terrace EH11 4	48-49	F7
Sighthill View EH11 4	48-49	F7
Sighthill Wynd EH11 4	48-49	F7
Silverknowes Avenue EH4 5	16-17	G12
Silverknowes Bank EH4 5	16-17	G12
Silverknowes Brae EH4 5	16-17	G12
Silverknowes Court EH4 5	16-17	G12
Silverknowes Crescent EH4 5	16-17	G12
Silverknowes Dell EH4 5	16-17	H12
Silverknowes Drive EH4 5	16-17	G12
Silverknowes Eastway EH4 5	16-17	G12
Silverknowes Gardens EH4 5	16-17	G13
Silverknowes Green EH4 5	16-17	H12
Silverknowes Grove EH4 5	16-17	G13
Silverknowes Hill EH4 5	16-17	G12
Silverknowes Loan EH4 5	16-17	G12
Silverknowes Midway EH4 5	16-17	H12
Silverknowes Neuk EH4 5	16-17	H12
Silverknowes Parkway EH4 5	16-17	G13
Silverknowes Place EH4 5	16-17	G13
Silverknowes Road EH4 5	16-17	G12
Silverknowes Road East EH4 5	16-17	H12
Silverknowes Road East EH4 5	16-17	H12
Silverknowes Road South EH4 5	16-17	G12
Silverknowes Southway EH4 5	16-17	H12
Silverknowes Terrace EH4 5	16-17	G12
Silverknowes View EH4 5	16-17	H12
Silvermills EH3 5	28-29	K11
Simon Square EH8 9	30-31	M10
Sinclair Close EH11 1	42-43	J8
Sinclair Gardens EH11 1	42-43	J9
Sinclair Place EH11 1	40-41	I9
Sir Harry Lauder Road EH15 1	22-23	
Slateford Road EH14 1	40-41	
Sleigh Drive EH7 6	20-21	
Sleigh Gardens EH7 6	20-21	
Sloan Street EH6 8	20-21	
Smith's Place EH6 8	20-21	
Smithfield Street EH11 2	40-41	
Somerset Place EH6 8	20-21	
South Barnton Avenue EH4 6	16-17	
South Beechwood EH12 5	40-41	
South Bridge EH1 1	28-29	
South Charlotte Street EH2 4	28-29	
South Clerk Street EH8 9	30-31	
South College Street EH8 9	28-29	
South East Circus Place EH3 6	28-29	
South Elgin Street EH7 5	20-21	
South Elixa Place EH8 7	30-31	
South Ettrick Road EH10 5	42-43	
South Fort Street EH6 4	12-13	
South Gayfield Lane EH1 3	20-21	
South Gillsland Road EH10 5	42-43	
South Gray Street EH9 1	44-45	
South Gray's Close EH1 1	30-31	
South Groathill Avenue EH4 2	26-27	
South Gyle Broadway EH12 9	38-39	
South Gyle Crescent EH12 9	38-39	
South Gyle Crescent Lane EH12 9	38-39	
South Gyle Gardens EH12 7	38-39	
South Gyle Loan EH12 9	38-39	
South Gyle Mains EH12 9	38-39	
South Gyle Park EH12 9	38-39	
South Gyle Park EH12 9	38-39	
South Gyle Road EH12 9	38-39	
South Gyle Wynd EH12 9	38-39	
South Lauder Road EH9 2	44-45	
South Learmonth Avenue EH4 1	28-29	
South Learmonth Gardens EH4 1	28-29	
South Maybury EH12 8	38-39	
South Maybury EH12 8	38-39	
South Mellis Park EH8 7	32-33	
South Oswald Road EH9 2	42-43	
South Oxford Street EH8 9	30-31	
South Park EH6 4	12-13	
South Sloan Street EH6 8	20-21	
South St. Andrew Street EH2 2	28-29	
South St. David Street EH2 2	28-29	
South Steil EH10 5	52-53	
South Trinity Road EH5 3	10-11	
Southfield Bank EH15 1	32-33	
Southfield Farm Grove EH15 1	32-33	
Southfield Gardens East EH15 1	32-33	
Southfield Gardens West EH15 1	32-33	
Southfield Loan EH15 1	32-33	
Southfield Place EH15 1	32-33	
Southfield Road East EH15 1	32-33	
Southfield Road West EH15 1	32-33	
Southfield Square EH15 1	32-33	
Southfield Terrace EH15 1	32-33	
Southfield Villas EH15 1	32-33	
Southhouse Avenue EH17 8	54-55	
Southhouse Broadway EH17 8	64-65	
Southhouse Crescent EH17 8	54-55	
Southhouse Gardens EH17 8	64-65	
Southhouse Grove EH17 8	64-65	
Southhouse Loan EH17 8	54-55	
Southhouse Medway EH17 8	54-55	
Southhouse Path EH17 8	54-55	
Southhouse Road EH17 8	64-65	
Southhouse Square EH17 8	64-65	
Southhouse Terrace EH17 8	54-55	
Sovereign Court EH4 7	20-21	
Spa Place EH15 1	22-23	
Spence Street EH16 5	30-31	
Spencer Place EH5 3	10-11	
Spey Street EH7 4	20-21	
Spey Street Mews EH7 4	20-21	
Spey Terrace EH7 4	20-21	
Spier's Place EH6 6	12-13	
Spinney, The EH17 7	54-55	
Spittal Street EH3 9	28-29	
Spittal Street Lane EH3 9	28-29	
Spittalfield Crescent EH8 9	30-31	
Spittalfield Crescent EH8 9	30-31	
Spottiswoode Road EH9 1	42-43	
Spottiswoode Street EH9 1	42-43	
Spring Gardens EH8 8	20-21	
Springfield EH6 5	20-21	
Springfield Lane EH6 5	20-21	
Springfield Street EH6 5	20-21	
Springvalley Gardens EH10 4	42-43	
Springvalley Terrace EH10 4	42-43	
Springwell Place EH11 2	42-43	
Springwood Park EH16 6	54-55	
Spylaw Avenue EH13 0	50-51	
Spylaw Bank Road EH13 0	50-51	
Spylaw Park EH13 0	50-51	
Spylaw Road EH10 5	42-43	
Spylaw Street EH13 0	60-61	
St. Alban's Road EH9 2	44-45	
St. Andrew Square EH2 1	28-29	
St. Andrew's Place EH6 7	20-21	
St. Anthony Lane EH6 6	12-13	
St. Anthony Place EH6 6	12-13	
St. Anthony Street EH6 6	12-13	
St. Bernard's Crescent EH4 1	28-29	
St. Bernard's Row EH4 1	28-29	

Street	Pages	Grid
Catherine's Gardens EH12 7	40-41	H9
Catherine's Place EH9 1	30-31	M9
Clair Avenue EH6 8	20-21	N12
Clair Place EH6 8	20-21	N12
Clair Road EH6 8	20-21	N12
Clair Street EH6 8	20-21	N12
Clair Terrace EH10 5	52-53	J7
Colme Street EH3 6	28-29	K10
David's Place EH3 8	28-29	K10
David's Terrace EH3 8	28-29	K10
Fillan's Terrace EH10 5	52-53	K7
Giles Street EH1 2	28-29	L10
James Place EH1 3	28-29	L11
James Square EH1 3	28-29	L11
James Street EH3 8	30-31	M10
John's Avenue EH12 6	40-41	G9
John's Crescent EH12 6	40-41	G9
John's Gardens EH12 6	40-41	G9
John's Hill EH8 9	30-31	M10
John's Road EH12 7	38-39	F9
John's Terrace EH12 6	40-41	G9
Katherine's Brae EH16 6	54-55	N5
Katherine's Crescent EH16 6	54-55	N5
Katherine's Loan EH16 6	54-55	N5
Leonard's Bank EH8 9	30-31	M9
Leonard's Crag EH8 9	30-31	M9
Leonard's Hill EH8 9	30-31	M9
Leonard's Lane EH8 9	30-31	M9
Leonard's Street EH8 9	30-31	M9
Margaret's Place EH9 1	42-43	L8
Margaret's Road EH9 1	42-43	K8
Mark's Court EH15 2	32-33	Q10
Mark's Lane EH15 2	32-33	Q10
Mark's Place EH15 2	32-33	R10
Mary's Street EH1 1	30-31	M10
Ninian's Drive EH12 8	24-25	F10
Ninian's Road EH12 8	24-25	F10
Ninian's Terrace EH10 5	52-53	J7
Patrick Square EH8 9	30-31	M9
Patrick's Street EH8 9	30-31	M9
Peter's Place EH3 9	42-43	K9
Ronan's Terrace EH10 5	52-53	K7
Stephen Place EH3 5	28-29	K11
Stephen Street EH3 5	28-29	K11
Teresa Place EH10 5	42-43	J8
Thomas Road EH9 2	42-43	L8
Vincent Street EH3 6	28-29	K11
able Lane EH5 5	42-43	K8
afford Street EH3 7	28-29	K10
air Park EH12 6	26-27	I10
anedykehead EH16 6	54-55	M5
anhope Place EH12 5	28-29	J10
anhope Street EH12 5	28-29	J10
anley Place EH7 5	20-21	N11
anley Road EH6 4	12-13	L13
anley Street EH15 1	32-33	Q10
anwell Street EH6 5	20-21	M12
apeley Avenue EH7 6	22-23	P11
arbank Road EH5 3	12-13	L13
ark's Cottages EH13 9	52-53	J6
ation Brae EH15 1	32-33	Q10
ation Road EH12 7	40-41	G9
ead's Place EH6 5	20-21	M12
eel's Place EH10 4	42-43	K8
eils, The EH10 5	52-53	J7
enhouse Avenue EH11 3	40-41	H8
enhouse Avenue West EH11 3	40-41	H8
enhouse Cottages EH11 3	40-41	H8
enhouse Crescent EH11 3	40-41	H8
enhouse Cross EH11 3	40-41	H8
enhouse Drive EH11 3	40-41	G8
enhouse Gardens EH11 3	40-41	H8
enhouse Gardens North EH11 3	40-41	H8
enhouse Grove EH11 3	40-41	H8
enhouse Mill Crescent EH11 3	40-41	H8
enhouse Mill Lane EH11 3	40-41	H8
enhouse Mill Wynd EH11 3	40-41	H8
enhouse Place East EH11 3	40-41	H8
enhouse Place West EH11 3	40-41	H8
enhouse Road EH11 3	40-41	H8
enhouse Road EH11 3	40-41	H8
enhouse Street East EH11 3	40-41	H8
enhouse Street West EH11 3	40-41	G8
ennis Gardens EH17 7	54-55	O6
evenlaw's Close EH1 1	28-29	L10
evenson Avenue EH11 2	40-41	I9
evenson Drive EH11 3	40-41	H9
evenson Grove EH11 2	40-41	I9
evenson Road EH11 2	40-41	I9
evenson Terrace EH11 2	40-41	I9
ewart Avenue EH14 5	58-59	D4
ewart Crescent EH14 5	58-59	D4
ewart Gardens EH14 5	58-59	D4
ewart Place EH14 5	58-59	D4
ewart Road EH14 5	58-59	D4
ewart Terrace EH11 1	40-41	I9
ewartfield EH6 5	18-19	L12
rling Road EH5 3	10-11	K13
achan Gardens EH4 3	26-27	H11
achan Road EH4 3	26-27	H11
aiton Place EH15 2	32-33	Q10
athalmond Court EH4 8	14-15	D12
athalmond Green EH4 8	14-15	D12
athalmond Park EH4 8	24-25	D11
Strathalmond Road EH4 8	24-25	D11
Strathearn Place EH10 4	42-43	K8
Strathearn Road EH9 2	42-43	L8
Strathfillan Road EH9 2	42-43	L8
Stuart Crescent EH12 8	24-25	E10
Stuart Green EH12 8	24-25	E10
Stuart Park EH12 8	24-25	E10
Stuart Square EH12 8	24-25	E10
Stuart Wynd EH12 8	24-25	E10
Succoth Avenue EH12 6	26-27	I10
Succoth Gardens EH12 6	26-27	I10
Succoth Park EH12 6	26-27	I10
Succoth Place EH12 6	26-27	I10
Suffolk Road EH16 5	44-45	M8
Suffolk Road Lane EH16 5	44-45	M8
Sugar House Close EH8 8	8-9	
Summer Place EH3 5	18-19	L12
Summerbank EH3 6	28-29	L11
Summerfield Gardens EH6 7	20-21	N12
Summerfield Place EH6 8	20-21	N12
Summerhall EH9 1	30-31	M9
Summerhall Place EH9 1	30-31	M9
Summerhall Square EH9 1	30-31	M9
Summerside Place EH6 4	12-13	L13
Summerside Street EH6 4	12-13	L13
Summertrees Court EH16 5	44-45	N7
Sunbury Mews EH4 3	28-29	J10
Sunbury Place EH4 3	28-29	J10
Sunbury Street EH4 3	28-29	J10
Sunnybank Place EH7 5	20-21	N11
Sunnybank Terrace EH7 5	20-21	N11
Sunnyside EH7 5	20-21	N11
Sutherland Street EH12 5	28-29	J10
Swan Spring Avenue EH10 6	52-53	K6
Swanfield EH6 5	12-13	M13
Swanston Avenue EH10 7	62-63	K5
Swanston Crescent EH10 7	62-63	K5
Swanston Drive EH10 7	62-63	K4
Swanston Gardens EH10 7	62-63	K5
Swanston Green EH10 7	62-63	K5
Swanston Grove EH10 7	62-63	K4
Swanston Loan EH10 7	62-63	K5
Swanston Muir EH10 7	62-63	J5
Swanston Park EH10 7	62-63	K5
Swanston Place EH10 7	62-63	K5
Swanston Road EH10 7	62-63	J4
Swanston Row EH10 7	62-63	K5
Swanston Terrace EH10 7	62-63	K5
Swanston View EH10 7	62-63	K5
Swanston Village EH10 7	62-63	J4
Swanston Way EH10 7	62-63	K5
Sycamore Gardens EH12 7	38-39	F9
Sycamore Terrace EH12 7	40-41	G9
Sydney Place EH7 6	22-23	P11
Sydney Street EH7 6	22-23	P11
Sydney Terrace EH7 6	22-23	P11
Sylvan Place EH9 1	42-43	L9
Talisman Place EH16 6	44-45	N7
Tanfield EH3 5	18-19	L12
Tantallon Place EH9 1	30-31	M9
Tarvit Street EH3 9	42-43	K9
Tay Street EH11 1	42-43	J9
Taylor Gardens EH6 5	12-13	M13
Taylor Place EH7 5	20-21	N11
Telferton EH7 6	22-23	P11
Telford Drive EH4 2	16-17	I12
Telford Gardens EH4 2	16-17	I12
Telford Place EH4 2	16-17	I12
Telford Road EH4 2	16-17	I12
Templar's Cramond EH4 6	14-15	E12
Temple Park Crescent EH11 1	42-43	J9
Templeland Grove EH12 8	24-25	F10
Templeland Road EH12 8	24-25	F10
Tennant Street EH6 5	20-21	M12
Terrar's Croft EH8 9	30-31	M9
Teviot Place EH1 2	28-29	L10
Teviotdale Place EH3 5	28-29	K11
The Glebe EH4 6	14-15	E13
The North Walk EH10 5	52-53	K7
Third Gait EH14 4	48-49	D6
Thirlestane Lane EH9 1	42-43	L8
Thirlestane Road EH9 1	42-43	L9
Thistle Place EH11 1	42-43	K9
Thistle Street EH2 1	28-29	L11
Thistle Street Lane NE. EH2 1	28-29	L11
Thistle Street Lane NW. EH2 1	28-29	L11
Thistle Street Lane SE. EH2 1	28-29	L11
Thistle Street Lane SW. EH2 1	28-29	L11
Thomson Crescent EH14 5	58-59	E5
Thomson Drive EH14 5	58-59	E5
Thomson Grove EH14 5	58-59	E5
Thomson Road EH14 5	58-59	E5
Thorburn Grove EH13 0	60-61	I5
Thorburn Road EH13 0	60-61	H5
Thorntree Street EH6 8	20-21	M12
Thorntreeside EH6 8	20-21	N12
Thornybauk EH3 9	28-29	K10
Timber Bush EH6 6	12-13	N13
Tinto Place EH6 5	20-21	M12
Tipperlinn Road EH10 5	42-43	K8
Tobago Place EH3 8	28-29	K10
Tolbooth Wynd EH6 6	12-13	M13
Tollcross EH3 9	42-43	K9
Torphichen Place EH3 8	28-29	K10
Torphichen Street EH3 8	28-29	K10
Torphin Bank EH13 0	60-61	G5
Torphin Road EH13 0	60-61	G5
Torrance Park EH4 7	24-25	F11
Tower Place EH6 7	12-13	N13
Tower Street EH6 7	12-13	N13
Trafalgar Lane EH6 4	12-13	L13
Trafalgar Street EH6 4	12-13	M13
Traquair Park East EH12 7	40-41	G9
Traquair Park West EH12 7	40-41	G9
Trench Knowe EH10 7	62-63	K5
Tressilian Gardens EH16 6	44-45	N7
Trinity Court EH5 3	10-11	K13
Trinity Crescent EH5 3	10-11	K13
Trinity Grove EH5 3	10-11	K13
Trinity Mains EH5 3	10-11	K13
Trinity Road EH5 3	10-11	K13
Tron Square EH1 1	28-29	L10
Trunk's Close EH1 1	8-9	
Tryst Park EH10 7	62-63	J5
Turnhouse Road EH12 0	78-79	C10
Tweeddale Court EH1 1	8-9	
Tyler's Acre Avenue EH12 7	40-41	G9
Tyler's Acre Gardens EH12 7	40-41	G9
Tyler's Acre Road EH12 7	40-41	G9
Tynecastle Lane EH11 2	42-43	J9
Tynecastle Place EH11 2	42-43	J9
Tytler Gardens EH8 8	20-21	N11
Ulster Crescent EH8 7	30-31	O10
Ulster Drive EH8 7	30-31	O10
Ulster Gardens EH8 7	30-31	O10
Ulster Grove EH8 7	30-31	O10
Ulster Terrace EH8 7	30-31	O10
Union Place EH1 3	20-21	M11
Union Street EH1 3	20-21	M11
Upper Bow EH1 2	28-29	L10
Upper Coltbridge Terrace EH12 6	28-29	J10
Upper Craigour EH17 7	46-47	P7
Upper Craigour Way EH17 7	44-45	O7
Upper Cramond Court EH4 6	14-15	E12
Upper Damside EH4 3	28-29	J10
Upper Dean Terrace EH4 1	28-29	K11
Upper Gilmore Place EH3 9	42-43	K9
Upper Gilmore Terrace EH3 9	42-43	K9
Upper Gray Street EH9 1	30-31	M9
Upper Grove Place EH3 8	42-43	K9
Vallence's Entry EH8 8	8-9	
Valleyfield Street EH3 9	42-43	K9
Vanburgh Place EH6 8	20-21	N12
Vandeleur Avenue EH7 6	22-23	P11
Vandeleur Grove EH7 6	22-23	P11
Vandeleur Place EH7 6	22-23	P11
Ventnor Place EH9 2	44-45	N8
Ventnor Terrace EH9 2	44-45	M8
Vernon Cottages EH15 2	32-33	Q10
Vexhim Park EH15 3	32-33	Q10
Victor Park Terrace EH12 8	24-25	F10
Victoria Quay EH6 6	12-13	M13
Victoria Street EH1 2	28-29	L10
Viewcraig Gardens EH8 9	30-31	M10
Viewcraig Street EH8 9	30-31	M10
Viewfield Road EH14 5	50-51	G6
Viewforth EH11 1	42-43	K9
Viewforth Gardens EH10 4	42-43	K9
Viewforth Square EH10 4	42-43	K9
Viewforth Terrace EH10 4	42-43	K9
Violet Terrace EH11 1	42-43	J9
Vivian Terrace EH4 5	16-17	H12
Wakefield Avenue EH7 6	22-23	P11
Walker Street EH3 7	28-29	K10
Walker Terrace EH11 1	28-29	K10
Walkers Court EH14 2	50-51	G7
Walkers Rigg EH14 2	50-51	G7
Walkers Wynd EH14 2	50-51	G7
Walter Scott Avenue EH16 5	44-45	O7
Wardie Avenue EH5 2	10-11	K13
Wardie Crescent EH5 2	10-11	J13
Wardie Dell EH5 2	10-11	K13
Wardie Grove EH5 1	10-11	J13
Wardie House Lane EH5 3	10-11	K13
Wardie Park EH5 2	10-11	K13
Wardie Road EH5 3	10-11	K13
Wardie Square EH5 1	10-11	K13
Wardieburn Drive EH5 1	10-11	J13
Wardieburn Place East EH5 1	10-11	J13
Wardieburn Place North EH5 1	10-11	J13
Wardieburn Place South EH5 1	10-11	J13
Wardieburn Place West EH5 1	10-11	J13
Wardieburn Road EH5 1	10-11	J13
Wardieburn Street East EH5 1	10-11	J13
Wardieburn Street West EH5 1	10-11	J13
Wardieburn Terrace EH5 1	10-11	J13
Wardiefield EH5 1	10-11	J13
Wardlaw Place EH11 1	42-43	J9
Wardlaw Street EH11 1	42-43	J9
Wardlaw Terrace EH11 1	42-43	J9
Wardrop's Court EH1 2	8-9	
Warrender Park Crescent EH9 1	42-43	K9
Warrender Park Road EH9 1	42-43	L9
Warrender Park Terrace EH9 1	42-43	L9
Warriston Avenue EH3 5	18-19	L12
Warriston Crescent EH3 5	18-19	L12
Warriston Drive EH3 5	18-19	K12
Warriston Gardens EH3 5	18-19	K12

Warriston Grove EH3 5 — 18-19 K12
Warriston Place EH3 5 — 18-19 L12
Warriston Road EH7 4 — 12-13 L13
Warriston Terrace EH3 5 — 18-19 K12
Warriston's Close EH1 1 — 8-9
Washington Lane EH11 2 — 42-43 J9
Water Street EH6 6 — 12-13 N13
Waterloo Place EH1 3 — 28-29 L11
Waters Close EH6 6 — 12-13 N13
Watertoun Road EH9 3 — 44-45 M8
Watson Crescent EH11 1 — 42-43 J9
Wauchope Avenue EH16 4 — 46-47 P8
Wauchope Crescent EH16 4 — 46-47 P8
Wauchope Place EH16 4 — 46-47 P8
Wauchope Road EH16 4 — 46-47 P8
Wauchope Square EH16 4 — 46-47 P8
Wauchope Terrace EH16 4 — 46-47 P8
Waulkmill Loan EH14 5 — 58-59 D4
Waverley Bridge EH1 1 — 28-29 L10
Waverley Park EH8 8 — 20-21 N11
Waverley Park Terrace EH8 8 — 20-21 N11
Waverley Place EH7 5 — 20-21 N11
Weavers Knowe Crescent EH14 5 — 58-59 D5
Well Court EH4 3 — 28-29 K10
Wellington Place EH6 7 — 20-21 N12
Wellington Street EH7 5 — 20-21 M11
Wemyss Place EH3 6 — 28-29 K11
Wemyss Place Mews EH3 6 — 28-29 K11
Werberside Mews EH4 1 — 18-19 J12
West Adam Street EH8 9 — 30-31 M10
West Annandale Street EH7 4 — 18-19 L12
West Approach Road EH3 8 — 28-29 K10
West Bow EH1 2 — 28-29 L10
West Bowling Green Street EH6 5 — 12-13 M13
West Bryson Road EH11 1 — 42-43 J9
West Caiystane Road EH10 6 — 62-63 K5
West Camus Road EH10 6 — 62-63 K5
West Carnethy Avenue EH13 0 — 60-61 H5
West Castle Road EH10 5 — 42-43 K9
West Catherine Place EH12 5 — 28-29 J10
West Cherrybank EH6 4 — 12-13 L13
West Coates EH12 5 — 28-29 J10
West College Street EH1 1 — 28-29 L10
West Court EH16 4 — 46-47 P8
West Court EH4 3 — 26-27 I11
West Craigs Avenue EH12 8 — 38-39 D9
West Craigs Avenue EH12 8 — 38-39 D9
West Craigs Crescent EH12 8 — 38-39 D9
West Cromwell Street EH6 6 — 12-13 M13
West Crosscauseway EH8 9 — 30-31 M9
West End Place EH11 2 — 42-43 J9
West Ferryfield EH5 2 — 10-11 J13
West Gorgie Parks EH14 1 — 40-41 I8
West Granton Road EH5 1 — 10-11 J13
West Harbour Road EH5 1 — 10-11 J14
West Mains Road EH9 3 — 44-45 M7
West Maitland Street EH12 5 — 28-29 K10
West Mayfield EH9 2 — 44-45 M8
West Mill Lane EH4 3 — 28-29 K10
West Mill Road EH13 0 — 60-61 G5
West Montgomery Place EH7 5 — 20-21 M11
West Newington Place EH9 1 — 30-31 M9
West Nicolson Street EH8 9 — 30-31 M10
West Norton Place EH7 5 — 20-21 M11
West Park Place EH11 2 — 28-29 J10
West Pilton Avenue EH4 4 — 16-17 I12
West Pilton Bank EH4 4 — 16-17 H13
West Pilton Crescent EH4 4 — 16-17 H13
West Pilton Crossway EH4 4 — 10-11 I13
West Pilton Drive EH4 4 — 10-11 I13
West Pilton Gardens EH4 4 — 10-11 I13
West Pilton Green EH4 4 — 10-11 I13
West Pilton Grove EH4 4 — 16-17 I12
West Pilton Lea EH4 4 — 10-11 I13
West Pilton Loan EH4 4 — 10-11 I13
West Pilton March EH4 4 — 10-11 I13
West Pilton Park EH4 4 — 10-11 I13
West Pilton Place EH4 4 — 10-11 I13
West Pilton Rise EH4 4 — 10-11 I13
West Pilton Road EH4 4 — 10-11 I13
West Pilton Street EH4 4 — 10-11 I13
West Pilton Terrace EH4 4 — 10-11 I13
West Pilton View EH4 4 — 16-17 I12
West Port EH3 9 — 28-29 L10
West Powburn EH9 3 — 44-45 M8
West Preston Street EH8 9 — 30-31 M9
West Register Street EH2 2 — 28-29 L11
West Register Street Lane EH2 2 — 28-29 L11
West Relugas Road EH9 2 — 42-43 L8
West Richmond Street EH8 9 — 30-31 M10
West Savile Road EH16 5 — 44-45 M8
West Savile Terrace EH9 3 — 44-45 M8
West Shore Road EH5 1 — 10-11 I14
West Silvermills Lane EH3 5 — 28-29 K11
West Stanhope Place EH12 5 — 28-29 J10
West Telferton EH7 6 — 22-23 P11
West Tollcross EH3 9 — 42-43 K9
West Werberside EH4 1 — 18-19 J12
West Winnelstrae EH5 2 — 18-19 J12
West Woods EH4 1 — 18-19 J12
Westbank Loan EH15 1 — 22-23 Q11
Westbank Place EH15 1 — 22-23 Q11
Westbank Street EH15 1 — 22-23 Q11
Westburn Avenue EH14 2 — 48-49 F6
Westburn Grove EH14 2 — 48-49 F6
Westburn Middlefield EH14 2 — 48-49 F6

Westburn Park EH14 2 — 48-49 F6
Wester Broom Avenue EH12 7 — 38-39 F9
Wester Broom Drive EH12 7 — 38-39 F9
Wester Broom Gardens EH12 7 — 38-39 F9
Wester Broom Grove EH12 7 — 38-39 F9
Wester Broom Place EH12 7 — 38-39 F9
Wester Broom Terrace EH12 7 — 38-39 F9
Wester Coates Avenue EH12 5 — 28-29 J10
Wester Coates Gardens EH12 5 — 28-29 J10
Wester Coates Place EH12 5 — 28-29 J10
Wester Coates Road EH12 5 — 28-29 J10
Wester Coates Terrace EH12 5 — 28-29 J10
Wester Drylaw Avenue EH4 2 — 16-17 H12
Wester Drylaw Drive EH4 2 — 16-17 H12
Wester Drylaw Park EH4 2 — 16-17 I12
Wester Drylaw Place EH4 2 — 16-17 H12
Wester Drylaw Row EH4 2 — 26-27 I11
Wester Hailes Park EH14 3 — 50-51 G6
Wester Hailes Road EH11 4 — 48-49 F7
Wester Hill EH10 5 — 52-53 J6
Wester Steil EH10 5 — 52-53 J7
Western Corner EH12 5 — 26-27 H10
Western Gardens EH12 5 — 26-27 I10
Western Place EH12 5 — 26-27 I10
Western Terrace EH12 5 — 26-27 I10
Westfield Avenue EH11 2 — 40-41 I9
Westfield Court EH11 2 — 40-41 I9
Westfield Road EH11 2 — 40-41 I9
Westfield Street EH11 2 — 40-41 I9
Westgarth Avenue EH13 0 — 60-61 H5
Westhall Gardens EH10 4 — 42-43 K9
Westland Cottages EH17 8 — 56-57 P5
Whale Brae EH6 4 — 12-13 L13
Wheatfield Place EH11 2 — 40-41 I9
Wheatfield Road EH11 2 — 40-41 I9
Wheatfield Street EH11 2 — 42-43 J9
Wheatfield Terrace EH11 2 — 40-41 I9
Whins Place EH15 1 — 22-23 Q11
White Dales EH10 7 — 62-63 L5
White House Close EH8 8 — 8-9
White Park EH11 1 — 42-43 J9
Whitehouse Loan EH10 4 — 42-43 K9
Whitehouse Road EH4 6 — 14-15 E12
Whitehouse Terrace EH9 2 — 42-43 L8
Whitingford EH6 5 — 12-13 L13
Whitson Crescent EH11 3 — 40-41 H9
Whitson Grove EH11 3 — 40-41 H9
Whitson Place East EH11 3 — 40-41 H9
Whitson Place West EH11 3 — 40-41 H9
Whitson Road EH11 3 — 40-41 H9
Whitson Terrace EH11 3 — 40-41 H9
Whitson Walk EH11 3 — 40-41 H9
Whitson Way EH11 3 — 40-41 H9
Whyte Place EH7 5 — 20-21 N11
Wilfrid Terrace EH8 7 — 20-21 O11
William Jameson Place EH15 1 — 22-23 Q11
William Street EH3 7 — 28-29 K10
William Street; NE. Lane EH3 7 — 28-29 K10
William Street; NW. Lane EH3 7 — 28-29 K10
William Street; SE. Lane EH3 7 — 28-29 K10
William Street; SW. Lane EH3 7 — 28-29 K10
Williamfield Square EH15 1 — 32-33 Q10
Willow Tree Place EH14 5 — 70-71 C4
Willowbank Row EH6 4 — 12-13 L13
Willowbrae Avenue EH8 7 — 30-31 O10
Willowbrae Gardens EH8 7 — 30-31 O10
Willowbrae Road EH8 7 — 30-31 O10
Wilson's Court EH8 8 — 8-9
Wilson's Park EH15 1 — 22-23 Q11
Wilton Road EH16 5 — 44-45 M8
Windmill Lane EH8 9 — 30-31 M9
Windsor Place EH15 2 — 32-33 Q10
Windsor Street EH7 5 — 20-21 M11
Windsor Street Lane EH7 5 — 20-21 M11
Winton Drive EH10 7 — 62-63 L4
Winton Gardens EH10 7 — 62-63 L4
Winton Grove EH10 7 — 62-63 K5
Winton Loan EH10 7 — 62-63 L4
Winton Park EH10 7 — 62-63 K4
Winton Terrace EH10 7 — 62-63 K4
Wishaw Terrace EH7 6 — 20-21 N11
Wisp Green EH15 3 — 46-47 Q8
Wolrige Road EH16 6 — 54-55 N6
Wolseley Crescent EH8 7 — 20-21 O11
Wolseley Gardens EH8 7 — 20-21 O11
Wolseley Place EH8 7 — 20-21 O11
Wolseley Terrace EH8 7 — 20-21 O11
Woodburn Terrace EH10 4 — 42-43 K8
Woodfield Avenue EH13 0 — 60-61 G5
Woodfield Park EH13 0 — 60-61 G5
Woodhall Avenue EH14 5 — 58-59 F5
Woodhall Bank EH13 0 — 60-61 G5
Woodhall Drive EH14 5 — 58-59 F5
Woodhall Grove EH13 0 — 60-61 G5
Woodhall Millbrae EH14 5 — 60-61 G5
Woodhall Road EH13 0 — 60-61 G5
Woodhall Terrace EH14 5 — 58-59 F5
Woodlands Grove EH15 3 — 32-33 P10
Woodside Terrace EH15 3 — 32-33 R10
Woodstock Place EH16 6 — 44-45 N7
Woodville Terrace EH6 8 — 20-21 N12
World's End Close EH1 1 — 8-9
Wright's Houses EH10 4 — 42-43 K9
Wyvern Park EH9 2 — 42-43 L8

Yardheads EH6 6 — 12-13 M13

Yeaman Place EH11 1 — 42-43 J9
Yewlands Crescent EH16 6 — 54-55
Yewlands Gardens EH16 6 — 54-55
York Lane EH1 3 — 28-29 L
York Place EH1 3 — 28-29 L
York Road EH5 3 — 10-11 K
Young Street EH2 4 — 28-29 K
Young Street Lane North EH2 4 — 28-29 K
Young Street Lane South EH2 4 — 28-29 K

Zetland Place EH5 3 — 10-11 K

BALERNO
Addiston Crescent EH14 7 — 70-71
Addiston Grove EH14 7 — 70-71
Addiston Park EH14 7 — 70-71

Bavelaw Gardens EH14 7 — 70-71
Bavelaw Road EH14 7 — 70-71
Bridge Road EH14 7 — 70-71
Burnside Park EH14 7 — 70-71

Cairns Drive EH14 7 — 70-71
Cairns Gardens EH14 7 — 70-71
Clayhills Grove EH14 7 — 70-71
Clayhills Park EH14 7 — 70-71
Cockburn Crescent EH14 7 — 70-71
Cockburnhill Road EH14 7 — 70-71
Crosswood Avenue EH14 7 — 70-71
Crosswood Crescent EH14 7 — 70-71

Dalmahoy Crescent EH14 7 — 70-71
Deanpark Avenue EH14 7 — 70-71
Deanpark Bank EH14 7 — 70-71
Deanpark Brae EH14 7 — 70-71
Deanpark Court EH14 7 — 70-71
Deanpark Gardens EH14 7 — 70-71
Deanpark Grove EH14 7 — 70-71
Deanpark Place EH14 7 — 70-71
Deanpark Square EH14 7 — 70-71
East Hannahfield EH14 7 — 70-71

Glenbrook Road EH14 7 — 70-71
Green, The EH14 7 — 70-71
Greenfield Crescent EH14 7 — 70-71
Greenfield Road EH14 7 — 70-71

Harlaw March EH14 7 — 70-71
Harlaw Road EH14 7 — 70-71
Highlea Circle EH14 7 — 70-71
Highlea Grove EH14 7 — 70-71
Horsburgh Bank EH14 7 — 70-71
Horsburgh Gardens EH14 7 — 70-71
Horsburgh Grove EH14 7 — 70-71

Johnsburn Green EH14 7 — 70-71
Johnsburn Haugh EH14 7 — 70-71
Johnsburn Park EH14 7 — 70-71
Johnsburn Road EH14 7 — 70-71

Lade, The EH14 7 — 70-71
Ladycroft EH14 7 — 70-71
Larchfield EH14 7 — 70-71
Larchfield Neuk EH14 7 — 70-71
Lovedale Avenue EH14 7 — 70-71
Lovedale Crescent EH14 7 — 70-71
Lovedale Gardens EH14 7 — 70-71
Lovedale Grove EH14 7 — 70-71
Lovedale Road EH14 7 — 70-71

Main Street EH14 7 — 70-71
Main Street EH14 7 — 70-71
Malleny Avenue EH14 7 — 70-71
Malleny Millgate EH14 7 — 70-71
Mansfield Road EH14 7 — 70-71
Marchbank Drive EH14 7 — 70-71
Marchbank Gardens EH14 7 — 70-71
Marchbank Grove EH14 7 — 70-71
Marchbank Place EH14 7 — 70-71
Marchbank Way EH14 7 — 70-71
Millbank EH14 7 — 70-71

Quarry Howe EH14 7 — 70-71

Ravelrig Gait EH14 7 — 70-71
Ravelrig Hill EH14 7 — 70-71
Ravelrig Park EH14 7 — 70-71
Ravelrig Road EH14 7 — 70-71

Slaeside EH14 7 — 70-71
Station Loan EH14 7 — 70-71

Threipmuir Avenue EH14 7 — 70-71
Threipmuir Gardens EH14 7 — 70-71
Threipmuir Place EH14 7 — 70-71
Turner Avenue EH14 7 — 70-71
Turner Park EH14 7 — 70-71

Whitelea Crescent EH14 7 — 70-71
Whitelea Road EH14 7 — 70-71

BILSTON
Allermuir Avenue EH25 9 — 72-73
Brookfield Terrace EH25 9 — 72-73

aerketton Avenue EH25 9 — 72-73 M1
astlelaw Crescent EH25 9 — 72-73 M1

skgrove Drive EH25 9 — 72-73 M1

eadow Place EH25 9 — 72-73 M1
loorfoot View EH25 9 — 72-73 M1
yrtle Crescent EH25 9 — 72-73 M1

entland Court EH25 9 — 72-73 M1

tanley Avenue EH25 9 — 72-73 M1

ONNYRIGG

lmond Crescent EH19 3 — 74-75 Q1
rgyll Place EH19 2 — 74-75 P1
uld Orchard EH19 3 — 74-75 R2

aird's Way EH19 3 — 74-75 R1
eech Loan EH19 3 — 74-75 Q1
ellfield View EH19 3 — 74-75 R2
rixwold Bank EH19 3 — 74-75 R1
rixwold Drive EH19 3 — 74-75 R1
rixwold Neuk EH19 3 — 74-75 R1
rixwold Park EH19 3 — 74-75 R1
rixwold Rise EH19 3 — 74-75 R1
rixwold View EH19 3 — 74-75 R1
roomieknowe EH19 1 — 74-75 Q2
roomieknowe Gardens EH19 2 — 74-75 Q2
roomieknowe Park EH19 2 — 66-67 Q3

ameron Crescent EH19 2 — 74-75 P1
ampview Road EH19 3 — 74-75 Q2
herry Road EH19 3 — 74-75 Q1
hesters Court EH19 3 — 74-75 Q1
hesters Grove EH19 3 — 74-75 Q1
hesters View EH19 3 — 74-75 Q1
hestnut Grove EH19 3 — 74-75 Q1
hurch Road EH18 1 — 66-67 P3
ockpen Avenue EH19 3 — 74-75 Q1
ockpen Crescent EH19 3 — 74-75 Q1
ockpen Drive EH19 3 — 74-75 Q1
ockpen Place EH19 3 — 74-75 Q1
ockpen Terrace EH19 3 — 74-75 R1
ockpen Terrace EH19 3 — 74-75 Q1
ockpen View EH19 3 — 74-75 Q1
uguen Place EH18 1 — 66-67 Q3

alhousie Avenue EH19 2 — 74-75 Q1
alhousie Avenue West EH19 2 — 74-75 P1
alhousie Drive EH19 2 — 74-75 Q1
alhousie Gardens EH19 2 — 74-75 Q1
alhousie Place EH19 2 — 74-75 P1
alhousie Road East EH19 2 — 74-75 Q1
alhousie Road West EH19 2 — 74-75 Q1
alkeith Western Bypass EH18 1 — 66-67 R3
e Quincey Road EH18 1 — 74-75 P1
ickson Grove EH19 3 — 74-75 Q2
obbie's Road EH19 2 — 74-75 Q2
ouglas Crescent EH19 2 — 74-75 Q2
undas Park EH19 3 — 74-75 R2
undas Street EH19 3 — 74-75 Q2
urham Bank EH19 3 — 74-75 R1
urham Grove EH19 3 — 74-75 Q1
urham Place EH19 3 — 74-75 Q1

ldindean Place EH19 2 — 74-75 Q2
ldindean Road EH19 2 — 74-75 Q2
ldindean Terrace EH19 2 — 74-75 Q2
lm Row EH18 1 — 66-67 Q3
skbank Road EH19 3 — 74-75 R2
skdale Court EH19 2 — 74-75 Q2
skdale Drive EH19 2 — 74-75 Q2
skdale Terrace EH19 2 — 74-75 Q2
vans Gardens EH19 3 — 74-75 R2

arm Avenue EH18 1 — 74-75 P1

lebe Place EH18 1 — 66-67 P3
olf Course Road EH19 2 — 74-75 Q2
ordon Avenue EH19 2 — 74-75 P1
reen Lane EH19 3 — 74-75 P2
rove End EH18 1 — 74-75 Q2

awthornden Avenue EH19 2 — 74-75 Q2
awthornden Gardens EH19 2 — 74-75 Q2
azel Drive EH19 3 — 74-75 Q1
igh Street EH19 3 — 74-75 Q2
igh Street EH18 1 — 66-67 Q3
illhead EH19 2 — 74-75 Q2
olly Terrace EH19 3 — 74-75 Q1
opefield Park EH19 2 — 74-75 Q1
opefield Place EH19 2 — 74-75 Q1
opefield Terrace EH19 2 — 74-75 Q2
unter Terrace EH19 2 — 74-75 Q2

ames Leary Way EH19 3 — 74-75 R2

evock Road EH18 1 — 74-75 R2

aird Terrace EH19 3 — 74-75 R1
asswade Road EH18 1 — 66-67 P3
inden Park EH19 2 — 74-75 Q2
eyden Place EH19 2 — 74-75 Q2

Lime Place EH19 3 — 74-75 Q1
Lothian Street EH19 3 — 74-75 Q2
Lower Broomieknowe EH18 1 — 74-75 Q2

MacLean Place EH18 1 — 74-75 P1
Martin Grove EH19 3 — 74-75 R2
Maryfield Place EH19 3 — 74-75 R2
Mason Place EH18 1 — 74-75 P1
Mavisbank Place EH18 1 — 74-75 P1
McQuade Street EH19 3 — 74-75 R2
Melville View EH18 1 — 74-75 Q2
Methven Terrace EH18 1 — 74-75 P1
Moffat Avenue EH19 3 — 74-75 Q1
Moorfoot Place EH19 3 — 74-75 Q1
Moorfoot View EH19 3 — 74-75 Q1
Myredale EH19 3 — 74-75 R1

Park Crescent EH19 2 — 74-75 Q2
Park Road EH19 2 — 74-75 Q2
Parsonspool EH19 3 — 74-75 R1
Pendreich Avenue EH19 2 — 74-75 R2
Pendreich Drive EH19 2 — 74-75 R2
Pendreich Grove EH19 2 — 66-67 R3
Pendreich Terrace EH19 2 — 74-75 R2
Pendreich View EH19 2 — 74-75 R2
Pentland Road EH19 2 — 74-75 P1
Polton Avenue Road EH19 2 — 74-75 P1
Polton Bank EH18 1 — 72-73 O1
Polton Bank Terrace EH18 1 — 74-75 P1
Polton Court EH19 3 — 74-75 Q2
Polton Gardens EH18 1 — 74-75 Q2
Polton Place EH19 3 — 74-75 Q2
Polton Road EH18 1 — 74-75 Q2
Polton Road West EH18 1 — 74-75 P1
Polton Street EH19 3 — 74-75 Q1
Polton Terrace EH18 1 — 74-75 Q2
Poplar Terrace EH19 3 — 74-75 Q1
Pryde Avenue EH19 2 — 74-75 Q2
Pryde Terrace EH19 2 — 74-75 Q2

Quarryfoot Gardens EH19 2 — 74-75 Q2
Quarryfoot Green EH19 2 — 74-75 R2
Quarryfoot Place EH19 2 — 74-75 Q2

Rae's Gardens EH19 2 — 74-75 Q2
Ramsay Place EH18 1 — 74-75 P1
Rockville Terrace EH19 2 — 74-75 Q2
Rose Avenue EH19 3 — 74-75 R1
Rose Cottages EH19 3 — 74-75 R1
Rose Gardens EH19 3 — 74-75 R1
Rose Grove EH19 3 — 74-75 R1
Rose Neuk EH19 3 — 74-75 R1
Rose Park EH19 3 — 74-75 R1
Rose Path EH19 3 — 74-75 R1
Rose Place EH19 3 — 74-75 R1
Rose Terrace EH19 3 — 74-75 R1
Rose Way EH19 3 — 74-75 R1
Rosewell Road EH19 3 — 74-75 P1
Rowan Gardens EH19 3 — 74-75 Q1

School Green EH18 1 — 66-67 Q3
Scollon Avenue EH19 3 — 74-75 R2
Seaforth Terrace EH19 2 — 74-75 P1
Sherwood Avenue EH19 3 — 74-75 R1
Sherwood Court EH19 3 — 74-75 R1
Sherwood Crescent EH19 3 — 74-75 R1
Sherwood Drive EH19 3 — 74-75 R1
Sherwood Loan EH19 3 — 74-75 R1
Sherwood Loan EH19 3 — 74-75 R1
Sherwood Park EH19 3 — 74-75 R1
Sherwood Place EH19 3 — 74-75 R1
Sherwood Terrace EH19 3 — 74-75 R1
Sherwood View EH19 3 — 74-75 R1
Sherwood Walk EH19 3 — 74-75 R1
Sherwood Way EH19 3 — 74-75 R1
Skeltiemuir Avenue EH19 3 — 74-75 Q1
Skeltiemuir Court EH19 3 — 74-75 Q1
Skeltiemuir Grove EH19 3 — 74-75 Q1
South Melville EH18 1 — 66-67 R3
St. Anne's Avenue EH18 1 — 74-75 P1
Stevenson Place EH18 1 — 72-73 O1

Union Park EH19 3 — 74-75 Q2
Upper Broomieknowe EH18 1 — 74-75 Q2

Viewbank Avenue EH19 2 — 66-67 R3
Viewbank Drive EH19 2 — 74-75 R2
Viewbank Road EH19 2 — 74-75 Q2
Viewbank View EH19 2 — 74-75 R2
Viewfield EH19 2 — 74-75 R2
Viewpark Gardens EH19 2 — 74-75 Q2

Wadingburn Lane EH18 1 — 66-67 P3
Wadingburn Road EH18 1 — 74-75 P2
Walker Place EH19 3 — 74-75 P1
Waverley Court EH19 3 — 74-75 R2
Waverley Crescent EH19 3 — 74-75 R2
Waverley Drive EH19 3 — 74-75 R2
Waverley Park EH19 3 — 74-75 R2
Waverley Road EH19 3 — 74-75 R2
Waverley Terrace EH19 3 — 74-75 R2
West Mill Court EH18 1 — 66-67 Q3
West Mill Road EH18 1 — 74-75 Q2
West Mill Wynd EH18 1 — 74-75 Q2
Willow Avenue EH19 3 — 74-75 Q1

Wishart Avenue EH19 3 — 74-75 R2
Wolsey Avenue EH19 3 — 74-75 R1

DALKEITH/ESKBANK

Abbey Road EH22 3 — 68-69 T3
Allan Terrace EH22 1 — 68-69 T4
Ancrum Bank EH22 3 — 68-69 S3
Ancrum Road EH22 3 — 68-69 S3
Andrew Dodds Avenue EH22 5 — 76-77 U2
Angres Court EH22 1 — 56-57 R6
Arthur View Crescent EH22 1 — 56-57 Q6
Arthur View Terrace EH22 1 — 56-57 Q6
Avenue Road EH22 3 — 68-69 S3

Backdean Road EH22 1 — 56-57 Q6
Beechgrove Avenue EH22 1 — 66-67 R3
Bellfield Avenue EH22 3 — 68-69 S3
Bevan Lee Court EH22 2 — 68-69 U4
Bogwood Road EH22 5 — 76-77 U2
Bonnyrigg Road EH22 3 — 68-69 S3
Bridgend EH22 1 — 68-69 S4
Bridgend Court EH22 1 — 68-69 T4
Broadhurst Road EH22 4 — 76-77 U2
Broomhill Drive EH22 3 — 68-69 S3
Broomhill Park EH22 3 — 68-69 S3
Bruce Gardens EH22 2 — 68-69 T3
Bruntons Close EH22 1 — 68-69 T4
Buccleuch Street EH22 1 — 68-69 T4
Burnside Avenue EH22 4 — 76-77 U2
Burnside Crescent EH22 4 — 76-77 U2

Campview EH22 1 — 56-57 Q6
Campview Avenue EH22 1 — 56-57 Q6
Campview Crescent EH22 1 — 56-57 R6
Campview Gardens EH22 1 — 56-57 Q6
Campview Grove EH22 1 — 56-57 R6
Campview Terrace EH22 1 — 56-57 Q6
Carrick Crescent EH22 4 — 76-77 U2
Cemetery Road EH22 3 — 68-69 S4
Circle, The EH22 1 — 56-57 Q6
Clarinda Gardens EH22 2 — 68-69 U3
Conifer Road EH22 5 — 76-77 U2
Coronation Place EH22 5 — 76-77 U2
Cortleferry Drive EH22 3 — 68-69 S3
Cortleferry Grove EH22 3 — 68-69 S3
Cortleferry Park EH22 3 — 68-69 S3
Cortleferry Terrace EH22 3 — 68-69 S3
Cowden Crescent EH22 2 — 68-69 U4
Cowden Grove EH22 2 — 68-69 U4
Cowden Lane EH22 2 — 68-69 U4
Cowden Park EH22 2 — 68-69 U4
Cowden Terrace EH22 2 — 68-69 U4
Cowden View EH22 2 — 68-69 U4
Crame Terrace EH22 3 — 68-69 S3
Croft Street EH22 3 — 68-69 T4

Dalhousie Road EH22 3 — 76-77 S2
Danderhall Crescent EH22 1 — 56-57 Q6
Drum View Avenue EH22 1 — 56-57 Q6
Duke Street EH22 1 — 68-69 T4
Dundas Crescent EH22 3 — 68-69 S3
Dundas Grove EH22 3 — 68-69 S3
Dundas Road EH22 3 — 68-69 S3

Easthouses Court EH22 4 — 76-77 U2
Easthouses Place EH22 4 — 68-69 U3
Easthouses Road EH22 4 — 76-77 U2
Easthouses Way EH22 4 — 68-69 U3
Edinburgh Road EH22 1 — 68-69 T4
Edmonstone Avenue EH22 1 — 56-57 Q6
Edmonstone Drive EH22 1 — 56-57 Q6
Edmonstone Road EH22 1 — 56-57 Q6
Edmonstone Terrace EH22 1 — 56-57 Q6
Elmfield Court EH22 1 — 68-69 T4
Elmfield Park EH22 1 — 68-69 T4
Elmfield Road EH22 1 — 68-69 T4
Esk Glades EH22 1 — 68-69 T4
Esk Place EH22 1 — 68-69 S4
Eskbank Road EH22 3 — 68-69 S3
Eskbank Terrace EH22 3 — 68-69 S3
Eskbank Toll EH22 3 — 68-69 S3
Eskdaill Court EH22 1 — 68-69 T4
Eskdaill Street EH22 1 — 68-69 T4
Eskfield Grove EH22 3 — 66-67 R3
Eskside Court EH22 1 — 68-69 S4
Eskview Grove EH22 1 — 68-69 S4
Eskview Villas EH22 3 — 68-69 S3

Forthview Crescent EH22 1 — 56-57 Q6

Gibraltar Court EH22 1 — 68-69 T4
Gibraltar Gardens EH22 1 — 68-69 T4
Gibraltar Road EH22 1 — 68-69 T4
Gibraltar Terrace EH22 1 — 68-69 T4
Gibson Drive EH22 2 — 68-69 U4
Gilmerton Road EH22 1 — 66-67 R4
Glebe Street EH22 1 — 68-69 S4
Glenesk Crescent EH22 3 — 68-69 S3
Gordon Street EH22 4 — 76-77 U2

Hawthorn Crescent EH22 5 — 76-77 U2
Hepburn Drive EH22 2 — 68-69 U3
High School Close EH22 1 — 68-69 T4
High Street EH22 1 — 68-69 T4
Hunt Close EH22 1 — 68-69 T4
Hursted Avenue EH22 4 — 76-77 U2

Street	Page	Grid
Ironmills Road EH22 1	68-69	S4
James Lean Avenue EH22 2	68-69	T4
Jarnac Court EH22 1	68-69	T4
Jean Armour Drive EH22 2	68-69	U3
Kaimes View EH22 1	56-57	Q6
Kerr Avenue EH22 3	68-69	S3
Kippielaw Drive EH22 4	68-69	U3
Kippielaw Gardens EH22 4	68-69	U3
Kippielaw Medway EH22 4	68-69	U3
Kippielaw Park EH22 5	76-77	U2
Kippielaw Road EH22 4	68-69	U3
Kippielaw Walk EH22 4	68-69	U3
Komarom Place EH22 2	68-69	U4
Langlaw Road EH22 5	76-77	U2
Lansbury Court EH22 1	68-69	T4
Larkfield Drive EH22 3	66-67	R3
Larkfield Road EH22 3	68-69	S3
Lasswade Road EH22 3	66-67	R3
Lauder Road EH22 2	68-69	U3
Laurelbank EH22 2	68-69	U3
Lawfield Road EH22 5	76-77	U2
Leighton Crescent EH22 4	76-77	U2
London Road EH22 1	68-69	T4
Lothian Bank EH22 3	68-69	S3
Lothian Drive EH22 4	76-77	U2
Lothian Road EH22 1	68-69	T4
Lothian Street EH22 1	68-69	T4
Lugton Brae EH22 1	68-69	S4
Martin Place EH22 3	68-69	S3
Maryburn Road EH22 4	76-77	U2
Maulsford Avenue EH22 1	56-57	Q6
Maxton Court EH22 1	68-69	T4
Mayfield Road EH22 4	76-77	U2
Melville Road EH22 3	68-69	S3
Melville Terrace EH22 3	68-69	S3
Millerhill Road EH22 1	56-57	R6
Mitchell Street EH22 1	68-69	S4
Muirpark EH22 3	68-69	S3
Musselburgh Road EH22 1	68-69	T4
Myrtle Grove EH22 5	76-77	U2
New Meadowspott EH22 3	68-69	S3
Newbattle Abbey Crescent EH22 3	76-77	S2
Newbattle Gardens EH22 3	68-69	T3
Newbattle Road EH22 3	68-69	S3
Newmills Road EH22 1	68-69	T4
Newmills Terrace EH22 1	68-69	T4
Newton Church Road EH22 1	56-57	R6
Newton Street EH22 4	76-77	U2
Newton Village EH22 1	56-57	R6
North Wynd EH22 1	68-69	T4
Old Dalkeith Road EH22 1	68-69	S4
Old Edinburgh Road EH22 1	68-69	S4
Orchard View EH22 3	66-67	R3
Pankhurst Loan EH22 2	68-69	U4
Park Crescent EH22 4	76-77	U2
Park Road EH22 3	68-69	S3
Parkhead Park EH22 4	76-77	U2
Parkhead Place EH22 4	76-77	U2
Parkside Court EH22 3	68-69	S4
Parkside Place EH22 3	68-69	T4
Pentland View EH22 2	68-69	U3
Pettigrews Close EH22 1	68-69	T4
Place Charente EH22 2	68-69	U4
Primrose Crescent EH22 2	68-69	U3
Primrose Terrace EH22 2	68-69	U3
Redcroft Street EH22 1	56-57	Q6
Reed Drive EH22 4	76-77	T2
Roanshead Road EH22 4	76-77	U2
Robert Burns Mews EH22 2	68-69	U4
Robertson's Close EH22 1	68-69	T4
Salters Green EH22 2	68-69	U4
Salters Road EH22 2	68-69	U4
Salters Terrace EH22 2	68-69	U4
Shadepark Crescent EH22 1	68-69	T4
Shadepark Drive EH22 1	68-69	T4
Shadepark Gardens EH22 1	68-69	T4
Shaw Place EH22 5	76-77	U2
Smithy Green Avenue EH22 1	56-57	Q6
South Street EH22 1	68-69	T4
Spalding Crescent EH22 2	68-69	T4
Speedwell Avenue EH22 1	56-57	Q6
Square, The EH22 1	56-57	Q6
St. Andrew Street EH22 1	68-69	T4
Station Road EH22 3	68-69	S3
Stewart Grove EH22 1	56-57	Q6
Strawberry Bank EH22 3	68-69	S3
Tait Street EH22 1	68-69	T4
Taylor Place EH22 2	68-69	U3
Thornyhall EH22 2	68-69	U4
Torsonce Road EH22 3	68-69	S3
Toscana Court EH22 1	56-57	Q6
Walker Crescent EH22 3	66-67	R3
Waverley Road EH22 3	68-69	S3
Weir Crescent EH22 3	68-69	S3
Westfield Court EH22 3	68-69	S3
Westfield Drive EH22 3	68-69	S3
Westfield Grove EH22 3	68-69	S3
Westfield Park EH22 3	68-69	S3
White Hart Street EH22 1	68-69	T4
White's Close EH22 1	68-69	T4
Whitehill Drive EH22 2	68-69	U3
Whitehill Grove EH22 2	68-69	U3
Whitehill Lodge EH22 2	68-69	U3
Whitehill Road EH22 1	46-47	R8
Wilson Avenue EH22 2	68-69	U4
Wishart Place EH22 3	68-69	S3
Wisp, The EH22 1	56-57	Q6
Woodburn Avenue EH22 2	68-69	U4
Woodburn Bank EH22 2	68-69	U4
Woodburn Drive EH22 2	68-69	T4
Woodburn Gardens EH22 2	68-69	U4
Woodburn Grove EH22 2	68-69	U3
Woodburn Loan EH22 2	68-69	U3
Woodburn Medway EH22 2	68-69	U3
Woodburn Park EH22 2	68-69	U4
Woodburn Place EH22 2	68-69	U3
Woodburn Road EH22 2	68-69	T4
Woodburn Street EH22 2	68-69	U4
Woodburn Terrace EH22 2	68-69	U4
Woodburn View EH22 2	68-69	U3
Woolmet Crescent EH22 1	56-57	Q6

LOANHEAD

Street	Page	Grid
Academy Lane EH20 9	72-73	O2
Arbuthnot Road EH20 9	72-73	O2
Braeside Road EH20 9	72-73	O2
Burghlee Crescent EH20 9	72-73	O2
Burghlee Terrace EH20 9	72-73	O2
Burnbank EH20 9	72-73	N2
Burndene Drive EH20 9	64-65	N3
Church Street EH20 9	72-73	O2
Clerk Street EH20 9	72-73	O2
Dalum Court EH20 9	72-73	N2
Dalum Drive EH20 9	72-73	N2
Dalum Grove EH20 9	72-73	N2
Dalum Loan EH20 9	72-73	N2
Dryden Avenue EH20 9	72-73	N2
Dryden Crescent EH20 9	72-73	N2
Dryden Glen EH20 9	72-73	M2
Dryden Road EH20 9	72-73	M2
Dryden Terrace EH20 9	72-73	N2
Dryden View EH20 9	72-73	N2
Edgefield Place EH20 9	72-73	O2
Edgefield Road EH20 9	64-65	O3
Engine Road EH20 9	72-73	O2
Fountain Place EH20 9	72-73	N2
Fowler Crescent EH20 9	72-73	O2
Fowler Square EH20 9	72-73	O2
Gaynor Avenue EH20 9	72-73	N2
George Avenue EH20 9	72-73	N2
George Crescent EH20 9	72-73	O2
George Drive EH20 9	72-73	N2
George Terrace EH20 9	72-73	N2
Harnes Court EH20 9	72-73	O2
Hawthorn Gardens EH20 9	64-65	N3
Herd Terrace EH20 9	72-73	N2
High Street EH20 9	72-73	O2
High Street EH20 9	72-73	O2
Hunter Avenue EH20 9	72-73	O2
Hunter Court EH20 9	72-73	O2
Hunter Terrace EH20 9	72-73	O2
Inveravon Road EH20 9	64-65	N3
Kennington Avenue EH20 9	72-73	N2
Kennington Terrace EH20 9	72-73	N2
Langloan Road EH20 9	64-65	N3
Lasswade Road EH20 9	72-73	O2
Lawrie Terrace EH20 9	72-73	N2
Loan, The EH20 9	72-73	N2
Loanhead Road EH20 9	64-65	N3
Lomond Walk EH20 9	64-65	N3
Lorne Grove EH20 9	64-65	N3
Mavisbank EH20 9	72-73	O2
Mayburn Avenue EH20 9	64-65	N3
Mayburn Bank EH20 9	72-73	N2
Mayburn Court EH20 9	72-73	N2
Mayburn Crescent EH20 9	64-65	N3
Mayburn Drive EH20 9	64-65	N3
Mayburn Grove EH20 9	72-73	N2
Mayburn Hill EH20 9	72-73	N2
Mayburn Loan EH20 9	64-65	N3
Mayburn Terrace EH20 9	64-65	N3
Mayburn Vale EH20 9	72-73	N2
Mayburn Walk EH20 9	72-73	N2
Mayfield Crescent EH20 9	72-73	O2
Mayshade Road EH20 9	64-65	N3
McKinlay Terrace EH20 9	72-73	N2
McNeill Avenue EH20 9	72-73	N2
McNeill Place EH20 9	72-73	N2
McNeill Terrace EH20 9	72-73	N2
Muirfield Gardens EH20 9	72-73	O2
Nivensknowe Road EH20 9	72-73	M2
Paradykes Avenue EH20 9	72-73	N
Park Avenue EH20 9	72-73	N
Park Crescent EH20 9	72-73	N
Park View EH20 9	72-73	N
Polton Road EH20 9	72-73	O
Station Road EH20 9	72-73	O
Straiton Mains EH20 9	64-65	N
Straiton Road EH20 9	64-65	N
Traprain Terrace EH20 9	72-73	O
Wheatfield Grove EH20 9	72-73	N
Wheatfield Loan EH20 9	64-65	N
Wheatfield Walk EH20 9	72-73	N

MUSSELBURGH

Street	Page	Grid
Albert Terrace EH21 7	36-37	V
Ashgrove EH21 7	36-37	V
Ashgrove EH21 7	36-37	V
Ashgrove View EH21 7	36-37	V
Balcarres Place EH21 7	34-35	U1
Balcarres Road EH21 7	34-35	U1
Beach Lane EH21 6	34-35	T1
Bellfield Avenue EH21 6	34-35	T
Bellfield Court EH21 6	34-35	T
Beulah EH21 7	36-37	V
Bog Park Road EH21 6	34-35	U
Bridge Street EH21 6	34-35	U
Brunton Court EH21 6	34-35	U
Bush Street EH21 6	34-35	T1
Bush Terrace EH21 6	34-35	T
Caird's Row EH21 6	34-35	T1
Campie Gardens EH21 6	34-35	T
Campie Lane EH21 6	34-35	T
Campie Road EH21 6	34-35	T
Carberry Grove EH21 8	36-37	U
Carberry Road EH21 7	36-37	V
Carlyle Place EH21 6	34-35	U
Champigny Court EH21 7	36-37	V
Clayknowes Avenue EH21 6	34-35	T
Clayknowes Court EH21 6	34-35	S
Clayknowes Drive EH21 6	34-35	S
Clayknowes Place EH21 6	34-35	T
Clayknowes Way EH21 6	34-35	T
Craighall Terrace EH21 7	36-37	V
Crookston Court EH21 7	36-37	V
Crookston Court EH21 8	36-37	V
Dalrymple Crescent EH21 6	34-35	U
Dalrymple Loan EH21 7	34-35	U
Dambrae EH21 7	34-35	U
Dambrae EH21 7	34-35	U
Delta Place EH21 7	36-37	U
Denholm Avenue EH21 6	36-37	V
Denholm Road EH21 6	34-35	S
Denholm Way EH21 6	35-35	S
Double Dykes EH21 7	36-37	U
Downie Place EH21 6	34-35	U
Edenhall Bank EH21 7	36-37	V
Edenhall Crescent EH21 7	36-37	V
Edenhall Road EH21 7	36-37	V
Edinburgh Road EH21 6	34-35	S1
Esk Mill Villas EH21 7	34-35	U
Eskdale Mews EH21 7	34-35	U
Eskside East EH21 7	34-35	U
Eskside West EH21 6	34-35	T
Eskview Avenue EH21 6	34-35	T
Eskview Crescent EH21 6	34-35	T
Eskview Grove EH21 6	34-35	T
Eskview Road EH21 6	34-35	T
Eskview Terrace EH21 6	34-35	T
Fairways EH21 6	36-37	T
Ferguson Court EH21 6	36-37	U
Ferguson Drive EH21 6	36-37	T
Ferguson Gardens EH21 6	36-37	U
Ferguson Green EH21 6	36-37	T
Ferguson View EH21 6	36-37	T
Fisher's Wynd EH21 6	34-35	T
Goose Green Avenue EH21 7	34-35	U1
Goose Green Crescent EH21 7	34-35	U1
Goose Green Place EH21 7	34-35	U
Goose Green Road EH21 7	34-35	U1
Gracefield Court EH21 6	34-35	T
Greenfield Park EH21 6	36-37	U
Grove Street EH21 7	34-35	U
Grove, The EH21 7	36-37	V
Harbour Road EH21 6	34-35	T
Hercus Loan EH21 6	34-35	T
High Street EH21 7	34-35	U
Inveresk Road EH21 6	34-35	U
Inveresk Village EH21 7	34-35	U
James Street EH21 7	34-35	U
Kerr's Wynd EH21 7	34-35	U
Kilwinning Street EH21 7	34-35	U
Kilwinning Street EH21 7	34-35	U
Kilwinning Terrace EH21 7	34-35	U

Street	Page	Grid
adywell EH21 6	34-35	U9
adywell Way EH21 6	34-35	U9
ewisvale Avenue EH21 7	36-37	V9
ewisvale Court EH21 7	36-37	V9
inkfield Court EH21 7	36-37	V9
inkfield Road EH21 7	36-37	V9
inks Avenue EH21 6	34-35	T10
inks Street EH21 6	34-35	U9
inks View EH21 6	34-35	U10
ochend Road North EH21 6	34-35	T9
ochend Road South EH21 6	34-35	T9
oretto Court EH21 6	36-37	T8
aitland Avenue EH21 6	34-35	T9
aitland Park Road EH21 6	34-35	T9
aitland Street EH21 6	34-35	T9
all Avenue EH21 7	34-35	U9
ansfield Avenue EH21 7	34-35	U9
ansfield Court EH21 7	34-35	U9
ansfield Place EH21 7	34-35	U9
ansfield Road EH21 7	34-35	U9
arket Street EH21 6	34-35	T9
ayfield Avenue EH21 6	36-37	T8
ayfield Crescent EH21 6	36-37	T8
ayfield Park EH21 6	36-37	T8
ayfield Place EH21 6	36-37	T8
illhill EH21 7	34-35	U9
illhill Lane EH21 7	34-35	U9
illhill Wynd EH21 7	34-35	U9
onktonhall Place EH21 6	36-37	T8
onktonhall Terrace EH21 6	36-37	T8
ountjoy Terrace EH21 6	34-35	U10
ucklets Avenue EH21 6	36-37	T8
ucklets Court EH21 6	36-37	T8
ucklets Crescent EH21 6	36-37	T8
ucklets Drive EH21 6	36-37	T8
ucklets Place EH21 6	36-37	T8
usselburgh Bypass EH21 8	46-47	R8
ew Street EH21 6	34-35	T9
Newbigging EH21 7	34-35	U9
Newbigging EH21 7	34-35	U9
Newbigging EH21 7	34-35	U9
Newcraighall Drive EH21 8	46-47	R8
Newcraighall Road EH21 8	34-35	S9
Newhailes Avenue EH21 6	34-35	T9
Newhailes Crescent EH21 6	34-35	S9
Newhailes Road EH21 6	34-35	S9
North High Street EH21 6	34-35	T9
Olive Bank Road EH21 6	34-35	T9
Park Avenue EH21 7	36-37	V9
Park Court EH21 7	36-37	V9
Park Gardens EH21 7	36-37	V9
Park Grove Place EH21 7	36-37	V9
Park Grove Terrace EH21 7	36-37	V9
Park Lane EH21 7	36-37	V9
Park View EH21 7	36-37	V9
Park View EH21 8	46-47	R8
Parsonage EH21 7	34-35	U9
Pinkie Avenue EH21 7	36-37	V9
Pinkie Drive EH21 7	36-37	V9
Pinkie Hill Crescent EH21 7	36-37	V9
Pinkie Place EH21 7	36-37	V9
Pinkie Road EH21 7	36-37	V9
Pinkie Terrace EH21 7	36-37	V9
Promenade EH21 6	34-35	T10
Riverside Gardens EH21 6	34-35	T9
Rothesay Place EH21 7	34-35	U9
Shorthope Street EH21 7	34-35	U9
Smeaton Grove EH21 7	36-37	U8
South Street EH21 6	34-35	T9
St. Michael's Avenue EH21 7	34-35	U9
Station Road EH21 7	34-35	T9
Stoneybank Avenue EH21 6	36-37	T8
Stoneybank Court EH21 6	34-35	T9
Stoneybank Crescent EH21 6	36-37	T8
Stoneybank Drive EH21 6	34-35	T9
Stoneybank Gardens EH21 6	34-35	T9
Stoneybank Gardens North EH21 6	34-35	T9
Stoneybank Gardens South EH21 6	36-37	T8
Stoneybank Grove EH21 6	36-37	T8
Stoneybank Place EH21 6	36-37	T8
Stoneybank Road EH21 6	36-37	T8
Stoneybank Terrace EH21 6	36-37	T8
Stoneyhill Avenue EH21 6	34-35	T9
Stoneyhill Court EH21 6	34-35	T9
Stoneyhill Crescent EH21 6	34-35	T9
Stoneyhill Drive EH21 6	34-35	T9
Stoneyhill Farm Road EH21 6	34-35	T9
Stoneyhill Grove EH21 6	34-35	T9
Stoneyhill Place EH21 6	34-35	T9
Stoneyhill Rise EH21 6	34-35	T9
Stoneyhill Road EH21 6	34-35	T9
Stoneyhill Steading EH21 6	34-35	T9
Stoneyhill Terrace EH21 6	34-35	T9
Stoneyhill Wynd EH21 6	34-35	T9
Victoria Terrace EH21 7	36-37	V9
Wanless Court EH21 6	34-35	U9
Watt's Close EH21 6	34-35	T9
Wedderburn Terrace EH21 7	36-37	U8
West Holmes Gardens EH21 6	34-35	T9
Whitehill Avenue EH21 6	34-35	T9
Whitehill Farm Road EH21 6	36-37	T8
Whitehill Gardens EH21 6	36-37	T8
Whitehill Street EH21 8	34-35	S9
Windsor Gardens EH21 7	36-37	V9
Windsor Park EH21 7	36-37	V9
Windsor Park Drive EH21 7	36-37	V9
Windsor Park Place EH21 7	36-37	V9
Windsor Park Terrace EH21 7	36-37	V9
Woodside Gardens EH21 7	36-37	V9

INDEX TO PLACES OF INTEREST : EDINBURGH

Place	Page	Grid
Haven Townhouse EH 6 4	12-13	L13
obeyhill Baptist Church EH 7 5	20-21	M11
obeyhill Methodist Church EH 7 5	20-21	N11
obeyhill Primary Sch. EH 8 8	20-21	N11
BC Cinema EH 3 8	28-29	K10
BC Multiplex Cinema EH14 2	48-49	F6
bercorn Sports Club EH 8 7	30-31	O10
cademy Sports Centre, The EH 3 5	18-19	K12
cheson House EH 8 8	30-31	M10
dam Hotel EH12 5	28-29	J10
dam House (Examination Halls) EH 1 1	28-29	L10
ddison Hotel EH12 6	26-27	I10
dria Hotel EH 7 5	20-21	M11
ton Hotel EH12 5	28-29	K10
lsa Craig Hotel EH 7 5	20-21	M11
nslie Park Leisure Centre EH 5 2	10-11	J13
bany Hotel EH 1 3	28-29	L11
bert Place P.O. EH 7 5	20-21	M11
ermuir Court EH13 9	52-53	J6
ermuir Outdoor Education Centre EH14 1	50-51	I6
lison House Hotel EH 9 2	44-45	M8
mond Court East EH 4 6	14-15	E12
mond Court West EH 4 6	14-15	E12
merican Consulate General EH 7 5	20-21	M11
nimal Diseases Research Association EH17 7	54-55	O6
pex European Hotel EH12 5	28-29	J10
pex International Hotel EH 1 2	28-29	L10
postolic Church EH 8 9	30-31	M10
rchers Hall EH 8 9	30-31	M9
dmillan Bowling Club EH11 2	42-43	J9
gus Hotel EH12 5	28-29	J10
gyle Backpackers Hotel EH 9 1	42-43	L9
gyle House EH 3 9	28-29	L10
thur View Hotel EH 9 2	44-45	M8
thur's Seat EH16 5	30-31	N9
sda, Hutchison Court EH14 1	40-41	I8
sda, The Jewel EH15 3	32-33	R9
shley EH28 8	78-79	B8
shlyn Hotel EH 3 5	18-19	K12
ssembly Rooms EH 2 2	28-29	L10
stley Ainslie Hospital EH 9 2	42-43	L8
ugustine United Congregational Church EH 1 1	28-29	L10
ustrian Consulate EH 4 2	26-27	I11
venue Hotel EH16 5	26-27	I10
von Hotel EH16 5	30-31	M9
& Q, Stevenson Rd EH11 2	40-41	I9
& Q, Warriston Rd EH 7 4	18-19	L12
aberton Golf Course EH14 5	58-59	F5
Baberton Mains Farm EH14 2	48-49	F6
Bainfield Bowling & Social Club EH14 1	40-41	I8
Balfour House EH 6 5	20-21	M12
Balgreen Bowling Club EH11 3	40-41	I9
Balgreen Library EH11 3	40-41	I9
Balgreen Primary Sch. EH11 3	40-41	I9
Balgreen Road P.O. EH11 3	40-41	I9
Balm Well EH16 6	54-55	N5
Balm Well, The EH16 6	54-55	N5
Balmoral Hotel EH 2 2	28-29	L10
Bangholm Loan Medical Centre EH 5 3	12-13	L13
Bank Hotel EH 1 1	28-29	L10
Bank of Scotland HQ EH 1 2	28-29	L10
Baptist Church EH11 3	40-41	H8
Barclay Church (C of S) EH10 4	42-43	K9
Barnardo's Blackford Brae Project EH 9 2	42-43	L8
Barnton Court EH 4 6	14-15	E12
Barnton Park Lawn Tennis Club EH 4 6	16-17	G12
Barnton P.O. EH 4 6	14-15	E12
Barnton Thistle Hotel EH 4 6	24-25	E11
BBC Scotland EH 2 1	28-29	L11
Bedford House Hotel EH15 2	32-33	R10
Bedlam Theatre EH 1 2	28-29	L10
Beechcroft Hotel EH12 6	26-27	I10
Beechwood Bowling Club EH12 5	40-41	I9
Belford Youth Hostel EH 4 3	28-29	J10
Bellevue Chapel EH 7 4	28-29	L11
Bellevue Medical Centre EH 7 4	20-21	M11
Beresford Hotel EH12 5	28-29	J10
Beverley Hotel EH12 6	26-27	I10
Big ' W ', The EH15 3	32-33	R9
Bingham P.O. EH15 3	32-33	Q9
Birnie's Court EH 4 4	16-17	H13
Blackford Avenue P.O. EH 9 2	42-43	L8
Blackhall Bowling Club EH 4 3	26-27	I11
Blackhall Lawn Tennis Club EH 4 3	26-27	I11
Blackhall Library EH 4 3	16-17	H12
Blackhall Primary Sch. EH 4 3	26-27	H11
Blackhall Primary Sch. EH 4 3	26-27	H11
Blackhall United Free Church EH 4 2	26-27	H11
Blood Donor Centre EH 3 9	28-29	L10
Boisdale Hotel EH12 5	28-29	J10
Bonaly Primary Sch. EH13 0	60-61	H5
Bonaly Tower EH13 0	60-61	H4
Bonham Hotel EH 3 7	28-29	K10
Bonnington Primary Sch. EH 6 5	20-21	M12
Boroughmuir Rugby Football Club EH14 1	42-43	J8
Boroughmuir Secondary Sch. EH10 4	42-43	K9
Boswall Drive P.O. EH 5 2	10-11	K13
Braeburn Coach House EH14 6	58-59	E4
Braid Bowling Club EH10 6	52-53	L7
Braid Hills Golf Club EH10 6	52-53	K6
Braid Hills Golf Range EH16 6	54-55	M6
Braid Hills Hotel EH10 6	52-53	K6
Braid Tennis Club EH10 6	52-53	L7
Brass Rubbing Centre EH 1 1	30-31	M10
Bristo Baptist Church EH 4 3	28-29	J11
Bristo Memorial Parish Church EH16 4	44-45	O8
Britannia Visitor Centre EH 6 6	12-13	M14
British Energy EH12 9	38-39	D8
British Geological Survey EH 9 3	44-45	M7
British Philatelic Bureau EH 3 5	28-29	K11
Broomhall P.O. EH12 7	38-39	F9
Broomhouse Primary Sch. EH11 3	40-41	G8
Broomview House EH11 4	48-49	F7
Broughton High Sch. EH 4 1	28-29	J11
Broughton Primary Sch. EH 7 4	18-19	L12
Broughton St Mary's Parish Church EH 3 6	28-29	L11
Brunstane Bowling Club EH15 2	32-33	R10
Brunstane Primary Sch. EH15 3	32-33	R9
Brunswick Hotel EH 7 5	20-21	M11
Bruntsfield Evangelical Church EH10 4	42-43	K9
Bruntsfield Health Centre EH10 4	42-43	K9
Bruntsfield Hotel EH10 4	42-43	K9
Bruntsfield Links Golf Club EH 4 6	14-15	F12
Bruntsfield Links Hotel EH 9 1	42-43	K9
Bruntsfield Park Hotel EH 9 1	42-43	K9
Bruntsfield Primary Sch. EH10 4	42-43	K9
Bruntsfield Youth Hostel EH10 4	42-43	K9
Buckstone Primary Sch. EH10 6	62-63	L5
Buckstone Terrace P.O. EH10 6	52-53	K6
Bughtlin Market EH12 8	24-25	E10
Burdiehouse Church EH16 6	54-55	N5
Burdiehouse Mains Farm EH17 8	64-65	N4
Burdiehouse Primary Sch. EH17 8	64-65	N4
Bus Station, Edinburgh EH 1 3	28-29	L11
Bute House EH 2 4	28-29	L10
Caerketton Court EH13 9	52-53	J6
Cairn Hotel EH 7 5	20-21	M11
Cairnpark Sch. EH14 1	50-51	I7
Cairns Memorial Church EH11 2	42-43	J9
Calder Crossway P.O. EH11 4	48-49	E7
Calder Junction EH14 4	48-49	E7
Caledonian Bowling Club EH11 2	42-43	J9
Caledonian Hotel EH 1 2	28-29	K10
Cameo Cinema EH 3 9	42-43	K9
Camera Obscura & Outlook Tower EH 1 2	28-29	L10
Cameron House Prestonfield Bowling Club EH16 5	44-45	N8
Cameron Toll Shopping Centre EH16 5	44-45	N8
Cammo Country Park EH 4 8	24-25	D11
Cammo Home Farm EH 4 8	24-25	D11
Camore Hotel EH 6 7	12-13	N13

Canaan Lodge EH10 4   42-43   K8
Canadian Consulate EH 1 2   28-29   K10
Canon Court EH 3 5   18-19   L12
Canongate Kirk (C of S) EH 8 8   30-31   M10
Canongate Tolbooth EH 8 8   30-31   M10
Canonmills Baptist Church EH 3 5   18-19   L12
Canonmills Sch. EH 7 4   28-29   L11
Capelaw Court EH13 9   52-53   J6
Capital House EH 3 9   28-29   K10
Capital Moat House Hotel EH12 6   26-27   G11
Cargilfield Secondary Sch. EH 4 6   14-15   E12
Carlton Cricket Club EH 9 2   42-43   L8
Carlton Highland Hotel EH 1 1   28-29   L10
Carrick Knowe Bowling Club EH12 7   38-39   F8
Carrick Knowe Golf Club EH12 5   40-41   H9
Carrick Knowe Parish Church EH12 7   40-41   G9
Carrick Knowe P.O. EH12 7   40-41   G8
Carrick Knowe Primary Sch. EH12 7   40-41   G9
Castle Gogar EH12 9   78-79   C10
Castle Rock Hostel EH 1 2   28-29   L10
Castlebrae High Sch. EH16 4   46-47   P8
Castleview House EH17 7   44-45   O7
Cat Nick EH 8 9   30-31   M10
Catholic Church of St. Teresa EH16 4   46-47   P8
Ceilidh-Donia Hotel EH16 5   30-31   N9
Centre Court EH14 1   50-51   I7
Chalmers Hospital EH 3 9   28-29   L10
Champions Ten Pin Bowling EH 7 4   20-21   M11
Chancelot Mills EH 6 6   12-13   M14
Channings Hotel EH 4 1   28-29   J11
Charlotte Chapel (Baptist) EH 2 4   28-29   K10
Charteris Memorial Church (C of S) EH 8 9   30-31   M10
Chesser House (City of Edinburgh) EH11 3   40-41   H8
Chinese Consulate EH12 7   40-41   G9
Christ Church Morningside EH10 4   42-43   K8
Christian Centre Ministries EH 4 3   28-29   K11
Christopher North House Hotel EH 3 6   28-29   K11
Church Hill Theatre EH10 4   42-43   K8
Church of Christ EH17 8   54-55   O5
Church of God EH11 2   42-43   J9
Church of Jesus Christ of
Latter-Day Saints EH10 5   42-43   J8
Church of St Catherine EH16 6   54-55   N5
Church of Scotland, Hailesland Place
EH14 2   50-51   G7
Church of Scotland Morningside United
EH10 4   42-43   K8
Church of St. Andrew and St. George
EH 2 2   28-29   L11
Church of the Nazarene EH 4 7   24-25   F11
Church of the Nazarene EH11 2   42-43   J9
Citadel Church EH 6 6   12-13   M13
City Art Centre EH 1 1   28-29   L10
City Chambers EH 1 1   28-29   L10
City Hospital EH10 5   52-53   J6
City Observatory EH 7 5   20-21   M11
Civic Amenity Site EH12 0   24-25   D10
Civic Amenity Site EH16 4   44-45   O7
Civil Service Sports Club EH 4 5   16-17   H13
Clan Campbell Hotel EH 7 5   20-21   M11
Clan Tartan Centre EH 6 5   12-13   M13
Claremont Hotel EH 7 4   18-19   L12
Claremont Park P.O. EH 6 8   20-21   N12
Claymore Hotel EH 7 5   20-21   M11
Clermiston Baptist Church EH 4 7   24-25   F11
Clermiston Health Clinic EH 4 7   24-25   F11
Clermiston Kingdom Hall of
Jehovah's Witness EH 4 7   24-25   F11
Clermiston P.O. EH 4 7   24-25   F11
Clermiston Primary Sch. EH 4 7   24-25   F11
Clerwood House EH12 6   26-27   G10
Clifton Hotel EH12 5   28-29   K10
Clovenstone Primary Sch. EH14 3   50-51   G6
Cluny Parish Church EH10 6   52-53   K7
Cluny Parish Church Centre EH10 6   52-53   K7
Clydesdale Bank Plaza EH 1 2   28-29   K10
Cobbinshaw House EH11 4   48-49   F7
Coillesdene House EH15 2   32-33   R10
Colinton Bowling Club EH13 0   60-61   I5
Colinton Castle Sports Club EH14 1   50-51   H6
Colinton Lawn Tennis Club EH13 0   60-61   H5
Colinton Library EH13 0   60-61   H5
Colinton Mains Bowling Club EH13 9   52-53   J6
Colinton Mains Drive P.O. EH13 9   52-53   J6
Colinton Mains Parish Church EH13 9   52-53   J6
Colinton Parish Church EH13 0   50-51   H6
Colinton P.O. EH13 0   60-61   H5
Colinton Primary Sch. EH13 0   50-51   I6
Coltbridge Bowling Club EH12 6   28-29   J10
Comely Bank P.O. EH 4 1   28-29   J11
Comiston Primary Sch. EH13 9   62-63   J5
Commodore Hotel EH 4 5   16-17   G13
Corstorphine Bowling Club EH12 7   40-41   G9
Corstorphine Hospital EH12 6   40-41   G9
Corstorphine Lawn Tennis Club EH12 6   26-27   G10
Corstorphine Library EH12 7   40-41   G9
Corstorphine Old Parish Church EH12 7   40-41   G9
Corstorphine Police Station EH12 7   38-39   F9
Corstorphine P.O. EH12 6   40-41   G9
Corstorphine Primary Sch. EH12 7   38-39   F9
Counan Hall EH 3 9   30-31   M9
Court of Session & High Court EH 1 1   28-29   L10
Craigentinny Avenue P.O. EH 7 6   22-23   P11
Craigentinny Bowling Club EH 7 6   22-23   P11
Craigentinny Golf Club EH 7 6   22-23   P12
Craigentinny Primary Sch. EH 7 6   20-21   O11

Craigentinny Road P.O. EH 7 6   22-23   P11
Craigleith Hill P.O. EH 4 2   26-27   I11
Craigleith Retail Park EH 4 2   26-27   I11
Craiglockhart Parish Church EH14 1   50-51   I7
Craiglockhart P.O. EH14 1   50-51   I7
Craiglockhart Primary Sch. EH11 1   42-43   J8
Craiglockhart Tennis and Sports Centre
EH14 1   50-51   I7
Craigmillar Castle EH16 4   44-45   O7
Craigmillar Court EH16 4   44-45   O8
Craigmillar Lawn Tennis Club EH16 5   44-45   N7
Craigmillar Library EH16 4   46-47   P8
Craigmillar Medical Centre EH16 4   46-47   P8
Craigmillar Park Bowling Club EH16 5   44-45   M8
Craigmillar Park Church EH16 5   44-45   M8
Craigmillar Park Golf Club EH 9 3   44-45   M7
Craigmillar Police Station 'D' Division
EH16 4   44-45   O8
Craigmillar P.O. EH16 4   44-45   O8
Craigmillar Primary Sch. EH16 4   46-47   P8
Craigmount High Sch. EH12 8   24-25   E10
Craigmuir Primary Sch. EH 4 4   10-11   I13
Craigroyston Health Clinic EH 4 4   16-17   I12
Craigroyston House EH 4 5   16-17   H13
Craigroyston Secondary Sch. EH 4 4   16-17   H12
Cramond Boat Club EH 4 6   14-15   E13
Cramond Brig Hotel EH 4 6   14-15   D12
Cramond House EH 4 6   14-15   F13
Cramond Infant Sch. EH 4 6   14-15   E13
Cramond Kirk EH 4 6   14-15   E13
Cramond P.O. EH 4 6   14-15   E13
Cramond Primary Sch. EH 4 6   14-15   E13
Cramond Roman Fort EH 4 6   14-15   F13
Cramond Tower EH 4 6   14-15   F13
Crewe Medical Centre EH 5 2   10-11   I13
Crewe Road North P.O. EH 5 2   10-11   I13
Crewe Toll Fire Station EH 4 2   16-17   I12
Cruise Ship Terminal EH 6 6   12-13   M14
Culane House Hotel EH 6 8   20-21   N12
Cumberland Hotel EH12 5   28-29   J10
Currie Baptist Church EH14 5   58-59   E4
Currie Bowling Club EH14 5   58-59   D4
Currie High Sch. EH14 5   58-59   D4
Currie Kirk EH14 6   58-59   E4
Currie Library EH14 5   58-59   E4
Currie P.O. EH14 5   58-59   E4
Curriehill Health Centre EH14 5   58-59   E4
Curriehill Primary Sch. EH14 5   58-59   E4
Curriehill Station EH14 4   58-59   D5
Currievale Farm EH14 4   58-59   D5
Dalkeith Road P.O. EH16 5   44-45   N8
Dalmeny Church EH 6 5   20-21   M12
Dalry Congregational Church EH11 2   42-43   K9
Dalry Primary Sch. EH11 2   42-43   J9
Dalry Road P.O. EH11 2   42-43   J9
Dalry Swimming Centre EH11 2   42-43   K9
Daniel Stewarts & Melville College EH 4 3   28-29   J11
Danish Consulate General EH 7 5   20-21   M11
David Horne Hostel EH16 5   44-45   N8
Davidsons Mains Medical Centre EH 4 5   16-17   G12
Davidsons Mains Parish Church EH 4 5   16-17   G12
Davidsons Mains P.O. EH 4 5   16-17   G12
Davidsons Mains Primary Sch. EH 4 5   16-17   G12
Deacon Brodie's Tavern EH 1 2   28-29   L10
Deaconess House
(Lothian Region Health Board) EH 8 9   30-31   M10
Dean Bowling Club EH 4 1   28-29   K11
Dean Gallery EH 4 3   28-29   J10
Dean Hotel EH 4 1   28-29   K11
Dean Parish Church EH 4 3   28-29   J11
District Court EH 1 1   28-29   L10
Dominion Cinema EH10 4   42-43   K8
Donaldson's College For The Deaf EH12 5   28-29   J10
Dorstan Hotel EH16 5   30-31   N9
Dreghorn Barracks EH13 9   60-61   I5
Dreghorn Junction EH10 7   62-63   J4
Drifters Youth Hostel EH 3 9   42-43   K9
Drum Farm EH17 8   56-57   Q5
Drum Riding Centre EH17 8   56-57   Q5
Drumbank Farm EH16 4   56-57   Q6
Drumbrae Primary Sch. EH 4 7   24-25   F10
Drummond High Sch. EH 7 4   28-29   L11
Drummond Lawn Tennis Club EH 3 6   28-29   L11
Drylaw Church EH 4 2   16-17   I12
Drylaw House EH 4 2   16-17   H12
Drylaw Police Station EH 4 2   16-17   I12
Drylaw Secondary Sch. EH 4 2   16-17   I12
Duddingston Golf Club EH15 3   32-33   P9
Duddingston House EH15 1   32-33   P9
Duddingston House Courtyard EH15 1   32-33   P9
Duddingston House Courtyard EH15 3   32-33   P9
Duddingston House Courtyard EH15 1   32-33   P9
Duddingston Kirk EH15 3   30-31   O9
Duddingston Primary Sch. EH15 1   32-33   P10
Dudley Bowling Club EH 6 4   12-13   L13
Dugald Stewart's Monument EH 7 5   20-21   M11
Duke Street Congregational Church EH 6 8   20-21   N12
Dumbryden P.O. EH14 2   50-51   G7
Dumbryden Primary Sch. EH14 2   50-51   G7
Duncan Street Baptist Church EH 9 1   44-45   M8
Duncan Street Dental Centre EH 9 1   44-45   M8
Dundee Street P.O. EH11 1   42-43   J9
Dunstane House Hotel EH12 5   28-29   J10
Dunsyre House EH11 4   48-49   F7

Duthus Lodge Hotel EH12 5   28-29   J10
Dynamic Earth EH 8 8   30-31   M10
East Craigie Farm EH 4 6   14-15   D13
East Craigs P.O. EH12 8   24-25   E10
East Craigs Primary Sch. EH12 8   24-25   E10
East Hermiston Farm EH14 4   48-49   E8
Easter Kinleith Farm EH14 6   58-59   F3
Easter Norton EH28 8   78-79   B10
Easter Road Stadium (Hibernian FC)
EH 7 5   20-21   N11
Eastern General Hospital EH 6 7   20-21   O11
Ebenezer United Free Church EH 6 5   12-13   M13
Edinburgh Academical Sports Centre
EH 4 1   28-29   K11
Edinburgh Academy Preparatory Sch.
EH 3 5   18-19   K12
Edinburgh Academy, The EH 3 5   28-29   K11
Edinburgh Airport Police Station EH12 9   78-79   A10
Edinburgh Backpackers Hostel EH 1 1   28-29   L10
Edinburgh Bowling Club EH 8 9   30-31   M9
Edinburgh Caravan Club Site EH 4 5   16-17   H13
Edinburgh Castle EH 1 2   28-29   L10
Edinburgh Central Library EH 1 1   28-29   L10
Edinburgh College of Art EH 3 9   28-29   L10
Edinburgh Dog & Cat Home EH15 1   22-23   P10
Edinburgh Experience, The EH 7 5   20-21   M11
Edinburgh Festival Centre EH 1 2   28-29   L10
Edinburgh Festival Theatre EH 8 9   28-29   L10
Edinburgh Fort Retail Park EH15 3   46-47   Q8
Edinburgh Hebrew Congregation EH16 5   30-31   M9
Edinburgh International Conference Centre
EH 3 8   28-29   K10
Edinburgh Leisure EH 9 1   42-43   L8
Edinburgh Playhouse Theatre EH 1 3   20-21   M11
Edinburgh Turnhouse Airport EH12 9   78-79   A10
Edinburgh West End Bowling Club EH 3 9   42-43   K9
Edinburgh Zoo EH12 6   40-41   G9
Edinburgh's Telford College EH 5 2   10-11   J13
Edinburgh's Telford College EH 6 8   18-19   J12
Edinburgh's Telford College EH 4 2   18-19   J12
Edmonstone Cottage EH16 4   56-57   P6
Eglinton Hotel EH12 5   28-29   J10
Eglinton Youth Hostel EH12 5   28-29   J10
Elder Memorial Free Church EH 6 5   20-21   M12
Ellersly House Hotel EH12 6   26-27   I10
Ellwyn Hotel EH 7 6   22-23   P11
Evang. Gemeinde Deutscher Sprache
(German Speaking Congregat EH 9 1   42-43   L8
Fairmile Marie Curie Centre EH10 7   62-63   L5
Fairmilehead Parish Church EH10 7   62-63   K4
Fairmilehead P.O. EH10 7   62-63   K4
Fala Court EH16 6   54-55   N5
Ferniehill Evangelical Church EH17 7   56-57   P6
Fernieside Primary Sch. EH17 7   56-57   P6
Ferranti Bowling Club EH 3 5   18-19   K12
Ferry Road P.O. EH 6 4   12-13   M13
Ferryfield House EH 5 2   18-19   J12
Ferryhill Primary Sch. EH 4 2   16-17   I13
Fettes College EH 4 1   18-19   J12
Fettes College Preparatory EH 4 1   18-19   J12
Fidra Court EH 4 4   16-17   H13
Filmhouse, The EH 3 9   28-29   K10
Finnish Consulate EH 2 2   28-29   L11
Firrhill High Sch. EH14 1   50-51   I7
Firrhill Medical Centre EH13 9   50-51   I6
Fisherrow Yacht Club,,34-35   T10
Flora Stevenson Primary Sch. EH 4 1   28-29   J11
Forecourt Leisure EH 6 5   20-21   M12
Forestry Commission EH12 7   40-41   G9
Former Royal Yacht Britannia, The EH 6 6   12-13   M14
Forrest Road P.O. EH 1 2   28-29   L10
Forrester High Sch. EH12 9   38-39   F9
Fort House EH 6 4   12-13   M14
Fort Primary Sch. EH 6 4   12-13   M14
Forte Post House Hotel EH12 6   40-41   G9
Forteviot House EH17 7   54-55   O5
Forth Corinthian Yacht Club EH 5 1   10-11   J14
Fountain Brewery Bowling Club EH14 1   40-41
Fountainbridge Library EH11 1   42-43   J9
Fox Covert R C Primary Sch. EH12 8   26-27   G10
Frederick House Hotel EH 2 1   28-29   L11
Frederick Street P.O. EH 2 1   28-29   L11
Free Buccleuch & Greyfriars (C of S)
EH 8 9   30-31   M10
Free Church of Scotland EH 1 2   28-29   L10
Freelands EH28 8   78-79   A10
Freemasons Hall EH 2 3   28-29   L11
French Consulate General EH 3 7   28-29   K11
Fringe Society EH 1 1   28-29   L10
Fruitmarket Gallery EH 1 1   28-29   L10
Fun Park EH15 1   22-23   Q10
Garvald Court EH16 6   54-55   N5
Gayfield Square Police Station
'B' Division EH 1 3   20-21   M11
GEC-Marconi Avionics EH12 9   38-39   F9
GEC-Marconi Avionics EH 5 2   18-19   J12
General P.O. EH 1 3   28-29   L11
George Heriot's Rugby Football Club
EH 3 5   18-19   K12
George Heriot's Secondary Sch. EH 3 9   28-29   L10
George Hotel EH 2 2   28-29   L11
George Square Lecture Theatre EH 8 9   42-43

Place	Pages	Grid
orge Watson's College EH10 5	42-43	K8
orge Watson's Primary Sch. EH10 5	42-43	J8
orgian House, The EH 2 4	28-29	K10
rman Consulate EH12 5	28-29	J10
lsland Hotel EH10 5	42-43	J8
merton Bowling Club EH17 8	56-57	P5
merton Clinic EH17 8	54-55	O5
merton Dykes P.O. EH17 8	54-55	O5
merton Library EH17 8	54-55	O5
merton Miners Welfare	56-57	P5
ociety & Social Club EH17 8		
merton Parish Church EH17 8	56-57	P5
merton P.O. EH17 8	56-57	P5
merton Primary Sch. EH17 8	54-55	O5
more Place Free Presbyterian Church	42-43	K9
EH 3 9		
dstone's Land EH 1 2	28-29	L10
enalmond Court EH11 4	48-49	F7
enfield Hotel EH 9 2	44-45	M8
enisla Hotel EH16 5	44-45	N7
enogle Swim Centre EH 3 5	28-29	K11
enora Hotel EH 9 2	28-29	J10
enorchy Hotel EH 9 2	44-45	M8
envarloch Crescent P.O. EH16 6	54-55	N6
gar Mains Farm EH12 9	78-79	C10
gar Mount EH12 9	78-79	B9
gar Park Curling Club EH12 9	78-79	C9
gar Park House EH12 9	38-39	D9
gar Roundabout EH12 9	38-39	D9
garbank EH12 9	48-49	D7
garbank House EH12 9	48-49	D7
garburn Golf Club EH12 9	78-79	B8
garburn Hospital EH12 9	78-79	C9
garburn Poultry Farm EH12 9	38-39	D8
denacre Bowling Club EH 3 5	18-19	L12
denacre P.O. EH 3 5	18-19	K12
f Tavern EH12 4	42-43	K9
gie Gospel Hall EH11 2	40-41	I9
gie Mills Bowling Club EH11 2	40-41	I9
gie Mission EH11 2	40-41	I9
gie P.O. EH11 3	40-41	H8
icemount High Sch. EH16 6	54-55	O5
icemount P.O. EH17 8	54-55	N5
icemount Primary Sch. EH16 6	54-55	N5
icemount Sports Centre EH17 8	54-55	N5
nge Club, The EH 4 1	28-29	K11
nge Hotel EH 9 2	42-43	L8
nge Road P.O. EH 9 1	30-31	M9
nton Baptist Church EH 5 2	10-11	I13
nton Congregational Church EH 5 2	10-11	J13
nton Harbour P.O. EH 5 1	10-11	J14
nton House EH 5 1	16-17	H13
nton Library EH 5 2	10-11	J13
nton Methodist Church EH 5 2	10-11	I13
nton Parish Church EH 5 2	10-11	I11
nton P.O. EH 4 4	10-11	I13
nton Primary Sch. EH 5 2	10-11	J13
yfield House EH11 4	48-49	F7
ysmill Sch. EH14 1	50-51	I7
at Junction Street P.O. EH 6 5	12-13	M13
at Mills DIY EH12 8	38-39	E9
ek Consulate EH 3 7	28-29	K10
enbank Church of Scotland EH10 6	52-53	K7
endykes House EH16 4	46-47	P8
endykes P.O. EH16 4	46-47	P8
endykes Primary Sch. EH16 4	46-47	P8
ens Hotel EH12 5	28-29	J10
enside Hotel EH 7 5	20-21	M11
enside Parish Church EH 7 5	20-21	M11
enway Centre, The EH14 3	48-49	F6
yfriars Kirk (C of S) EH 1 2	46-47	P8
yfriars Kirk (C of S) EH 1 2	28-29	L10
svenor Club EH12 5	28-29	K10
svenor Gardens Hotel EH12 5	28-29	J10
nnet Court EH 4 4	16-17	H13
e Centre, The EH12 9	38-39	E9
emuir Primary Sch. EH12 7	38-39	F9
es Hotel EH14 2	48-49	F6
esland Primary Sch. EH14 2	50-51	G6
cyon Hotel EH 7 5	20-21	M11
npton Hotel EH12 6	26-27	I10
p Hotel, The EH12 8	38-39	E9
y Ramsden's EH 6 4	12-13	L14
khill Court EH 7 6	20-21	N12
market Depot EH12 5	40-41	I9
market Hotel EH12 5	28-29	J10
market Station EH12 5	28-29	J10
ald House Hotel EH 3 8	42-43	K9
ot-Watt Research Park EH14 4	48-49	D6
iot-Watt University EH14 4	48-49	D6
rmiston EH14 4	48-49	D7
rmiston Court EH11 4	48-49	F7
rmiston Farm EH14 4	48-49	D7
rmiston Gait EH11 4	38-39	E8
rmiston Gait Junction EH11 4	48-49	E7
rmiston House EH14 4	48-49	D7
mitage Park Primary Sch. EH 6 8	20-21	N12
h Court EH 1 1	28-29	L10
h Street Youth Hostel EH 1 1	30-31	M10
side Bowling Club EH 7 5	20-21	M11
wood EH12 6	26-27	G10
on National Hotel EH 4 3	28-29	J10
oric Scotland HQ EH 9 1	30-31	M9
day Inn Crowne Plaza EH 1 1	28-29	L10
day Inn Express EH 6 6	12-13	M13

Place	Pages	Grid
Holiday Inn Garden Court EH 4 3	26-27	I11
Holy Cross Episcopal Church EH 4 5	16-17	G12
Holy Cross R C Church EH 5 3	12-13	L13
Holy Cross R C Primary Sch. EH 6 4	30-31	O9
Holy Cross Rugby & Cricket Clubs EH 5 2	18-19	K12
Holyrood Court EH 8 8	30-31	M10
Holyrood Palace EH 8 8	30-31	M10
Holyrood P.O. EH 8 8	30-31	M10
Holyrood R C High Sch. EH15 3	30-31	O9
Holyrood R C High Sch. EH15 3	30-31	O9
Hope Street P.O. EH 2 4	28-29	K10
Howard Hotel EH 3 6	28-29	L11
Howdenhall Police Station 'B' Division	54-55	N5
EH16 6		
Hunters Tryst EH13 9	62-63	J5
Hunters Tryst Primary Sch. EH13 9	52-53	J6
Huntly House Museum EH 8 8	30-31	M10
Hutchison House EH14 1	40-41	I8
Hutchison P.O. EH14 1	40-41	I8
Ibis Hotel EH 1 1	28-29	L10
Icelandic Consulate EH 6 5	20-21	M12
Inch Christian Centre EH16 5	44-45	N7
Inchcolm Court EH 4 4	10-11	I13
Inchgarvie Court EH 4 4	10-11	I13
Inchkeith Court EH 7 4	20-21	M12
Inchmickery Court EH 4 4	16-17	H13
Inchview Primary Sch. EH 4 4	16-17	I12
Ingliston Showground EH28 8	78-79	A10
Inverleith Parish Church EH 3 5	18-19	K12
Iona Hotel EH 9 2	42-43	K8
Italian Consulate General EH 3 7	28-29	K10
Jack Kane Sports Centre EH16 4	46-47	Q8
James Gillespie's High Sch. EH 9 1	42-43	L9
James Gillespie's Primary Sch. EH 9 1	42-43	L9
Japanese Consulate General EH 3 7	28-29	K10
Jenners EH 2 2	28-29	L10
Jessfield Bowling Club EH15 1	32-33	Q10
Jewel & Esk Valley College EH15 2	32-33	R9
Jewel Miners Bowling Club EH15 3	32-33	Q9
Jocks Lodge EH 6 8	20-21	O11
John Knox' House EH 1 1	30-31	M10
Joppa EH15 2	32-33	R10
Joppa Tennis Courts EH15 2	32-33	R10
Juniper Green Bowling Club EH14 5	58-59	F5
Juniper Green Parish Church EH14 5	58-59	F5
Juniper Green EH14 5	58-59	F5
Juniper Green Primary Sch. EH14 5	58-59	F5
Jurys Inn Hotel EH 1 1	30-31	M10
Kaimes Special Sch. EH16 6	54-55	O5
Kildonan Lodge Hotel EH16 5	44-45	N8
King James Thistle Hotel EH 1 3	28-29	L11
King's Theatre EH 3 9	42-43	K9
Kingdom Hall of Jehovah's Witnesses	16-17	I12
EH 4 4		
Kingdom Hall of Jehovah's Witnesses	32-33	Q10
EH15 2		
Kingdom Hall of Jehovah's Witnesses	56-57	P5
EH17 8		
Kings Manor Hotel EH15 2	32-33	R9
Kingsinch Sch. EH16 5	44-45	N7
Kingsknowe Golf Club EH14 2	50-51	H6
Kingsknowe P.O. EH14 2	50-51	H6
Kingsknowe Station EH14 2	50-51	H7
Kingston House Hotel EH16 5	44-45	O7
Kinnauld Farm EH14 5	58-59	D4
Kirkgate Church EH 6 6	12-13	N13
Lady Nairne Hotel EH 8 7	32-33	P10
Ladywell House EH12 7	38-39	F9
Lasswade Junction EH17 8	66-67	P4
Lauriston Castle EH 4 5	16-17	G13
Lauriston Farm Restaurant EH 4 5	16-17	G13
Laverockdale House EH13 0	60-61	H5
Learmonth Hotel EH 4 1	28-29	J11
Leith Academy EH 6 8	20-21	N12
Leith Baptist Church EH 6 4	12-13	M13
Leith Bowling Club EH 6 7	20-21	N12
Leith Franklin Academicals Cricket Club	20-21	N12
EH 6 7		
Leith Hospital EH 6 6	12-13	M13
Leith Library EH 6 4	12-13	M13
Leith Methodist Church EH 6 7	20-21	N12
Leith Links Bowling Green EH 6 7	12-13	N13
Leith Police Station 'D' Division HQ EH 6 7	12-13	N13
Leith P.O. EH 6 8	12-13	N13
Leith Primary Sch. EH 6 7	20-21	N12
Leith Victoria Swim Centre EH 6 5	12-13	M13
Leith Walk EH 6 8	20-21	M12
Leith Walk Primary Sch. EH 7 5	20-21	M11
Leith Waterworld EH 6 8	20-21	M12
Lennie Cottages EH12 0	78-79	C10
Liberton Bowling Club EH16 6	54-55	N6
Liberton Fire Station EH16 6	44-45	N7
Liberton Gardens P.O. EH16 6	54-55	N6
Liberton Golf Club EH16 5	44-45	O7
Liberton High Sch. EH17 7	54-55	O6
Liberton Hospital EH16 6	54-55	N6
Liberton Kirk EH16 6	54-55	N6
Liberton Mains Farm EH16 6	54-55	N6
Liberton Northfield Parish Church EH16 5	54-55	N6
Liberton Primary Sch. EH16 5	44-45	N7
Liberton Tower EH16 6	54-55	M6

Place	Pages	Grid
Links House Hotel EH 6 8	20-21	N12
Links Primary Sch. EH 6 7	12-13	N13
Lismore Primary Sch. EH15 3	32-33	P9
Little France House EH17 7	54-55	O6
Loaning Crescent Bowling Club EH 7 6	20-21	O11
Lochend House EH 7 6	20-21	O11
Lochend P.O. EH 7 6	20-21	O12
Lochview Court EH 8 8	30-31	M10
Lodge Hotel EH12 5	28-29	J10
Lomond Park Lawn Tennis Club EH 5 3	10-11	K13
London Road Church EH 7 5	20-21	M11
London Road Foundry Bowling Club	22-23	P11
EH 7 6		
London Street P.O. EH 1 3	28-29	L11
London Street Primary Sch. EH 7 4	28-29	L11
Longstone Bowling & Social Club EH14 2	50-51	H7
Longstone P.O. EH14 2	50-51	H7
Longstone Primary Sch. EH14 2	50-51	H7
Lorne Primary Sch. EH 6 8	20-21	M12
Lothian & Borders Fire Brigade HQ EH 3 9	28-29	L10
Lothian & Borders Fire Brigade Museum	28-29	L10
EH 3 9		
Lothian & Borders Police HQ EH 4 1	28-29	J11
Lothianburn Golf Club EH10 7	62-63	K4
Lothianburn Junction EH10 7	62-63	K4
Lovat Hotel EH 3 5	18-19	L12
Lutton Place Bowling Club EH 8 9	30-31	M9
Lygon Hotel EH16 5	44-45	N8
Lymphoy House EH14 6	58-59	D4
Lyncliff Hotel EH 7 5	20-21	M11
Magdalen Chapel EH 1 1	28-29	L10
Magdalene Drive P.O. EH15 3	32-33	Q9
Maitland Bowling Club EH 4 5	16-17	H12
Maitland Hotel EH 2 4	28-29	K10
Makro EH11 4	38-39	F8
Malcomstone Farm EH14 4	58-59	D5
Malmaison Hotel EH 6 7	12-13	N13
Marina Hotel EH 3 5	18-19	K12
Marrakech Hotel EH 3 6	28-29	L11
Mary Erskine Sch., The EH 4 3	26-27	H11
Marytree House EH17 7	54-55	O6
May Court EH 4 4	16-17	H13
Maybury Stakis Casino EH12 8	38-39	E9
Mayfield Bowling Club EH 9 2	44-45	M8
Mayfield Road P.O. EH 9 3	44-45	M8
Mayfield Salisbury Parish Church EH 9 2	44-45	M8
McDonald Road Fire Station EH 7 4	20-21	M12
McDonald Road Library EH 7 4	20-21	M11
Mckenzie Medical Centre EH 8 9	30-31	M10
McNair Hotel EH 6 7	12-13	N13
Meadowbank Sports Centre EH 7 6	20-21	N11
Meadowfield Farm EH12 0	24-25	D10
Meadowhead Farm EH16 6	54-55	M6
Meadows East Bowling Club EH 9 1	30-31	M9
Meadows West Bowling Club EH 3 9	42-43	L9
Medwin House EH11 4	48-49	F7
Mega Bowl EH15 3	46-47	R8
Melvin House Hotel EH 3 7	28-29	K10
Merchants of Edinburgh Golf Club EH10 5	52-53	J7
Merchiston Bowling & Tennis Club EH11 1	42-43	J9
Merchiston Castle Sch. EH13 0	50-51	H6
Merith House Hotel EH 6 8	20-21	N12
Methodist Central Halls EH 3 9	42-43	K9
Middle Kinleith Farm EH14 6	58-59	E4
Middle Norton EH28 8	78-79	A9
Milestone House (AIDS Hospice) EH14 1	50-51	I6
Mill Lane Health Clinic EH 6 6	12-13	M13
Millburn Tower EH12 9	38-39	D8
Mills Mount Barracks EH 1 2	28-29	L10
Milton Road West P.O. EH15 1	32-33	Q9
Minto Hotel EH 9 1	44-45	M8
Minto Hotel EH 1 1	28-29	L10
Moat House EH14 1	40-41	I8
Moidart House EH 4 5	58-59	E4
Monaco Consulate EH 2 3	28-29	K10
Moncrieffe House EH17 7	54-55	O6
Moray House EH 8 8	30-31	M10
Moray House College of Education EH 8 8	30-31	M10
Moray House College of Education EH 4 6	14-15	F13
Moredun EH17 7	54-55	O6
Moredun Library EH17 7	56-57	P6
Moredun P.O. EH17 7	56-57	P6
Moredun Primary Sch. EH17 7	52-53	K6
Moredun Research Institute EH17 7	54-55	O6
Morningside Baptist Church EH10 4	42-43	K8
Morningside Braid Parish Church EH10 4	42-43	K8
Morningside Library EH10 4	42-43	K8
Morningside Medical Practice EH10 4	42-43	K8
Morningside P.O. EH10 4	42-43	K8
Morton House EH10 7	62-63	L4
Morton Mains EH10 7	64-65	M4
Morton Mains Farm EH10 7	62-63	L4
Mortonhall Caravan Park EH16 6	54-55	M5
Mortonhall Crematorium EH16 6	54-55	M5
Mortonhall Golf Club EH10 6	52-53	K6
Mortonhall Tennis Club EH10 6	52-53	K7
Mosque and Islamic Centre EH 8 9	30-31	M10
Mosque Anwar-e-Madina EH 7 4	20-21	M11
Mount Royal Hotel EH 2 2	28-29	L10
Mountcastle Clinic EH15 3	32-33	Q9
Muirhouse Library EH 4 4	16-17	H13
Muirhouse Medical Group EH 4 4	16-17	H12
Muirhouse P.O. EH 4 4	16-17	H13
Muirhouse Primary Sch. EH 4 4	16-17	H12
Murray Home, The EH17 7	54-55	O6

Murrayburn Primary Sch. EH11 4 — 50-51 G7
Murrayfield (S.R.U Ground) EH12 5 — 40-41 I9
Murrayfield Episcopal Church EH12 6 — 26-27 I10
Murrayfield Golf Course EH12 6 — 26-27 H10
Murrayfield Hospital (BUPA) EH12 6 — 26-27 H10
Murrayfield Hotel EH12 6 — 26-27 I10
Murrayfield Ice Rink EH12 5 — 40-41 I9
Murrayfield Lawn Tennis Club EH12 5 — 26-27 I10
Murrayfield Parish Church EH12 6 — 26-27 I10
Murrayfield P.O. EH12 6 — 26-27 I10
Museum of Childhood EH 1 1 — 30-31 M10

Napier University; Colinton EH10 5 — 48-49 D6
Napier University; Craighouse Campus EH10 5 — 52-53 J7
Napier University; Craiglockhart Campus EH14 1 — 50-51 I7
Napier University; Sighthill EH11 4 — 48-49 F7
National Gallery of Scotland EH 2 2 — 28-29 L10
National Library of Scotland EH 1 1 — 28-29 L10
National Map Library Of Scotland EH 9 1 — 30-31 M9
National Monument EH 7 5 — 20-21 M11
National Museums of Scotland EH 1 1 — 28-29 L10
National Trust for Scotland HQ EH 2 4 — 28-29 K10
National War Memorial EH 1 2 — 28-29 L10
Navaar Hotel EH 9 2 — 44-45 M8
Nelson's Monument EH 7 5 — 20-21 M11
Nether Currie Health Clinic EH14 5 — 58-59 E5
Nether Currie Primary Sch. EH14 5 — 58-59 E5
Netherlands Consulate EH 2 2 — 28-29 L11
New Club, The EH 2 2 — 28-29 L10
New Register House EH 1 3 — 28-29 L11
New Royal Infirmary of Edinburgh (Open 2001) EH16 4 — 46-47 P7
Newhaven Church EH 6 4 — 12-13 L13
Newhaven Heritage Museum EH 6 4 — 12-13 L14
Newhaven Main Street P.O. EH 6 4 — 12-13 L14
Newhaven Road P.O. EH 6 4 — 12-13 L13
Newington Library EH 9 2 — 44-45 M8
Newington P.O. EH 8 9 — 30-31 M9
Newkirkgate P.O. EH 6 6 — 20-21 M12
Next Generation Club EH 6 6 — 12-13 L14
Nicholson Square Methodist Church EH 8 9 — 30-31 M10
Nicolson Street P.O. EH 8 9 — 30-31 M10
Niddrie Primary Sch. EH16 4 — 46-47 Q8
Nirvana Hotel EH11 2 — 42-43 J9
Nisbet Court EH 7 6 — 20-21 N12
North Junction Street P.O. EH 6 6 — 12-13 M13
North Leith Parish Church EH 6 4 — 12-13 M13
Northern Bowling Club EH 3 5 — 18-19 L12
Northfield House Hotel EH16 6 — 54-55 O5
Northfield P.O. EH 8 7 — 32-33 P10
Northumberland Hotel EH16 5 — 44-45 N8
Northview Court EH 4 4 — 16-17 H13
Norton Mains EH28 8 — 78-79 A9
Norton Park P.O. EH 7 5 — 20-21 M11
Norway Royal Consulate General EH 2 3 — 28-29 L10
Nova Hotel EH10 4 — 42-43 K9

Oddfellows Hall EH 1 2 — 28-29 L10
Odeon Cinema EH 8 9 — 30-31 M9
Old Kirk Parish Church EH 4 4 — 16-17 I12
Old Saughton P.O. EH11 3 — 40-41 G8
Old St. Ninians Christian Fellowship EH10 4 — 42-43 K8
Old St. Paul's Church (Episcopal) EH 1 1 — 28-29 L10
Old Waverley Hotel EH 2 2 — 28-29 L10
Orwell Lodge Hotel EH11 1 — 42-43 J8
Orwell Primary Sch. EH11 2 — 42-43 J9
Osbourne Hotel EH 1 3 — 28-29 L11
Our Lady's R C Church EH14 5 — 58-59 E4
Oxcars Court EH 4 4 — 16-17 H13
Oxgangs Library EH13 9 — 62-63 J5
Oxgangs Police Station 'C' Division EH13 9 — 62-63 J5
Oxgangs P.O. EH13 9 — 62-63 J5
Oxgangs Primary Sch. EH13 9 — 50-51 I6

Palmerston Place Church (C of S) EH12 5 — 28-29 K10
Parkgrove Medical Centre EH 4 7 — 24-25 F11
Parkside Bowling Club EH16 5 — 30-31 M9
Parkview Hotel EH 6 8 — 20-21 N12
Parliament House EH 1 1 — 28-29 L10
Parliament House EH 7 5 — 20-21 M11
Parliament House Hotel EH 1 3 — 20-21 M11
Parsons Green Primary Sch. EH 8 7 — 30-31 O10
PC World EH12 8 — 38-39 F9
Peffermill Court EH16 4 — 44-45 O8
Peffermill Primary Sch. EH16 4 — 44-45 O8
Pentecox EH16 4 — 46-47 P7
Pentland Medical Centre EH14 5 — 58-59 D4
People's Story EH 8 8 — 30-31 O10
Perseverse Court EH 6 6 — 12-13 M13
Petsmart EH15 3 — 46-47 R8
Philippine Consulate EH 2 3 — 28-29 K11
Piershill Library EH 8 7 — 20-21 O11
Piershill Sch. EH 8 7 — 30-31 O10
Pilrig Bowling Club EH 6 5 — 20-21 M12
Pilrig Park Primary Sch. EH 6 5 — 20-21 M12
Pilrig Toll P.O. EH 6 5 — 20-21 M12
Pirie's Hotel EH 3 9 — 28-29 J10
Pirniehall Primary Sch. EH 4 4 — 10-11 I13
Pitz Five-a-Side Complex EH11 4 — 38-39 F8
Pitz Five-a-Side Complex EH15 1 — 22-23 Q11
Pleasance Theatre EH 8 9 — 30-31 M10
Point Hotel EH 3 9 — 28-29 K10

Polish Consulate EH 3 5 — 18-19 K12
Polwarth Gardens P.O. EH11 1 — 42-43 K9
Polwarth Parish Church EH11 1 — 42-43 J8
Port Royal Golf Range EH28 8 — 78-79 A9
Portcullis Gate EH 1 2 — 28-29 L10
Portobello Baptist Church EH15 1 — 32-33 Q10
Portobello Bowling Club EH15 1 — 32-33 Q10
Portobello Congregational Church EH15 2 — 32-33 Q10
Portobello Golf Club EH15 1 — 32-33 Q10
Portobello Group Medical Practice EH15 2 — 32-33 Q10
Portobello High Sch. EH15 1 — 32-33 P10
Portobello Indoor Bowls & Leisure Club EH15 1 — 22-23 Q11
Portobello Library EH15 1 — 32-33 Q10
Portobello Old & Windsor Place Parish Church EH15 2 — 32-33 Q10
Portobello Police Station EH15 1 — 32-33 Q10
Portobello P.O. EH15 1 — 32-33 Q10
Portobello Spiritualist Church EH15 1 — 22-23 Q11
Portobello Swimming Pool EH15 2 — 32-33 Q10
Portobello Town Hall EH15 1 — 32-33 Q10
Portuguese Consulate EH 6 6 — 12-13 N13
Postal Bowling Club EH 8 7 — 20-21 O11
Powderhall Bowling Club EH 7 4 — 18-19 L12
Preston Street Primary Sch. EH16 5 — 30-31 M9
Prestonfield Clinic EH16 5 — 44-45 N8
Prestonfield Golf Club EH16 5 — 44-45 N9
Prestonfield House Hotel EH16 5 — 30-31 N9
Prestonfield Primary Sch. EH16 5 — 44-45 N8
Princes Street East Backpackers Hostel EH 2 2 — 28-29 L11
Princes Street West Backpackers Hostel EH 2 4 — 28-29 K10
Princess Alexandra Eye Pavilion EH 3 9 — 62-63 L5
Princess Margaret Rose Hospital EH10 7 — 62-63 L5
Prospectbank Sch. EH 6 8 — 20-21 N12

Quaker Meeting House EH 1 2 — 28-29 L10
Queen Margaret College EH12 8 — 24-25 F10
Queen Margaret University College EH 6 8 — 20-21 N12
Queen's Hall EH 8 9 — 30-31 M9
Queens Park Bowling Club EH 8 8 — 30-31 N10
Queensberry Bowling Club EH 5 1 — 10-11 J13

Radio Forth EH 1 3 — 28-29 L11
Raeburn House Hotel EH 4 1 — 28-29 K11
Raeburn Place P.O. EH 4 1 — 28-29 K11
Ratho Byres EH28 8 — 78-79 A8
Ravelston Golf Club EH 4 3 — 26-27 H11
Redford Barracks EH13 0 — 50-51 I6
Redholme House Hotel EH10 5 — 42-43 J8
Regent Bowling Club EH 8 8 — 20-21 M11
Regent House Hotel EH 1 3 — 28-29 L11
Register House EH 1 3 — 28-29 L11
Registers of Scotland EH 8 7 — 20-21 O11
Reid Memorial Church EH 9 3 — 44-45 M8
Restalrig House EH 7 6 — 20-21 O11
Riccarton Mains EH14 4 — 48-49 E6
Richmond Craigmillar Parish Church EH16 4 — 46-47 P8
Richmond House Hotel EH 7 5 — 20-21 M11
Ritz Bar & Grill EH12 9 — 38-39 D8
Ritz Hotel EH12 5 — 28-29 K10
Robert Burns Hotel EH15 2 — 32-33 R10
Robert Burns Monument EH 8 8 — 20-21 M11
Rockville House Hotel EH15 2 — 34-35 S10
Roddinglaw Works EH12 9 — 78-79 C8
Rose Garden Medical Centre EH 6 6 — 12-13 M13
Rosebank EH14 6 — 58-59 E4
Rosebery Hotel EH12 5 — 28-29 J10
Roseburn Primary Sch. EH12 5 — 40-41 I9
Rosehall Hotel EH16 5 — 30-31 N9
Ross Theatre EH 2 2 — 28-29 L10
Rothesay Hotel EH 3 7 — 28-29 K10
Roxburghe Hotel EH 2 4 — 28-29 K10
Roxstone House Hotel EH12 6 — 26-27 I10
Royal (Dick Vet) Sch. of Veterinary Studies EH 9 1 — 30-31 M9
Royal Abbey Hotel EH 7 5 — 20-21 M11
Royal Air Forces (Edinburgh) Club EH 7 5 — 20-21 M11
Royal Bank of Scotland EH12 9 — 38-39 E8
Royal Bank of Scotland HQ EH 2 2 — 28-29 L11
Royal Blind Sch. EH 9 1 — 44-45 M8
Royal Botanic Garden Edinburgh EH 3 5 — 18-19 K12
Royal British Hotel EH 2 2 — 28-29 L11
Royal Burgess Club House EH 4 6 — 14-15 E12
Royal Circus Hotel EH 3 6 — 28-29 K11
Royal Commonwealth Pool EH16 5 — 30-31 M9
Royal Edinburgh Hospital EH10 5 — 42-43 K8
Royal Ettrick Hotel EH10 5 — 42-43 J8
Royal Forth Yacht Club EH 5 1 — 10-11 J14
Royal High Primary Sch. EH 8 7 — 30-31 O10
Royal High Sch. EH 4 6 — 14-15 F12
Royal Hospital for Sick Children EH 9 1 — 42-43 L9
Royal Hotel EH15 1 — 32-33 Q10
Royal Infirmary EH 3 9 — 42-43 L9
Royal Lyceum Theatre EH 3 9 — 28-29 K10
Royal Mail HQ Scotland EH 3 9 — 28-29 L10
Royal Mail Sorting Office EH 7 5 — 20-21 M11
Royal Mail Sorting Office EH11 4 — 48-49 E7
Royal Mile Backpackers EH 1 1 — 30-31 M10
Royal Mile Primary Sch. EH 8 8 — 20-21 M11
Royal Observatory, The EH 9 3 — 52-53 L7
Royal Overseas League EH 2 3 — 28-29 L10
Royal Scot Hotel EH12 8 — 38-39 F9

Royal Scots Club EH 3 6 — 28-29 L
Royal Scottish Academy EH 2 2 — 28-29 L
Royal Society of Edinburgh EH 2 2 — 28-29 L
Royal Terrace Hotel EH 7 5 — 20-21 M
Royal Victoria Hospital EH 4 2 — 28-29 J
Royston Primary Sch. EH 5 2 — 10-11 J
Rudolph Steiner Sch. EH10 5 — 42-43
Russian Federation, Consulate General EH 3 7 — 28-29 K
Rutland Hotel EH 1 2 — 28-29 K

Sacred Heart of Jesus Church (R C) EH 3 9 — 28-29 L
Safeway EH 4 1 — 28-29 J
Safeway EH 4 6 — 16-17 G
Safeway EH 8 7 — 28-29 O
Safeway EH10 7 — 62-63
Safeway EH 5 2 — 18-19 J
Sainsbury's EH 4 2 — 26-27
St Aidan's EH 6 1 — 40-41
St Andrew Steel Works Bowling Club EH 7 5 — 20-21 N
St Andrew's Catholic Church EH 4 3 — 28-29 J
St Andrew's Church EH 4 4 — 16-17 H
St Andrew's Church EH 4 7 — 26-27 G
St Andrew's House EH 1 3 — 28-29 M
St Andrew's Parish Church EH 6 8 — 20-21 N
St Anne's Parish Church EH12 6 — 40-41
St Anthony's Chapel (Ruin) EH 8 8 — 30-31 N
St Augustine's R C High Sch. EH12 9 — 38-39
St Barnabas Church EH17 7 — 56-57
St Bernard's Well EH 3 6 — 28-29 K
St Catherine's Argyle Church EH 9 1 — 42-43
St Catherine's R C Primary Sch. EH16 6 — 54-55
St Columba's (Free Church) EH 1 2 — 28-29 L
St Columba's by the Castle (Epis) EH 1 2 — 28-29 L
St Columba's Hospice EH 5 3 — 10-11 K
St Columba's R C Church EH 9 1 — 30-31
St Crispin's Sch. EH 9 3 — 44-45
St Cuthbert's (C of S) EH 1 2 — 28-29 K
St Cuthbert's Church EH14 1 — 40-41
St Cuthbert's Episcopal Church EH13 0 — 60-61
St Cuthbert's R C Primary Sch. EH14 1 — 40-41
St David's Broomhouse Church EH11 3 — 40-41
St David's Church EH 5 3 — 10-11
St David's R C Primary Sch. EH 4 4 — 16-17
St Fillan's Church EH10 6 — 52-53
St Francis Primary Sch. EH16 4 — 16-17
St George's Sch. for Girls (Primary) EH12 6 — 28-29 J
St George's Sch. for Girls (Secondary) EH12 6 — 28-29 J
St George's West Church (C of S) EH 2 4 — 28-29 K
St Giles Cathedral (C of S) EH 1 1 — 28-29 L
St Giles Parish Church EH 9 2 — 42-43
St Giles Primary Sch. EH 3 8 — 40-41
St Gregory the Great Catholic Church EH16 5 — 44-45
St Hilda's Church EH13 9 — 62-63
St James Episcopal Church EH 6 7 — 12-13 N
St James House EH 1 3 — 28-29
St James Parish Church EH15 1 — 32-33 C
St James Scottish Episcopal Church EH 3 5 — 18-19 K
St James Shopping Centre EH 1 3 — 28-29
St John Ogilvie Church EH11 4 — 48-49
St John the Baptist R C Church EH12 8 — 24-25 F
St John the Evangelist R C Church EH15 1 — 32-33
St John Vianney R C Church EH17 7 — 56-57
St John Vianney R C Primary Sch. EH16 6 — 44-45
St John's Church EH13 9 — 62-63
St John's Church (Episcopal) EH 2 4 — 28-29 K
St John's R C Primary Sch. EH15 1 — 32-33 C
St John's Road P.O. EH12 7 — 38-39
St Joseph's Catholic Church EH11 3 — 40-41
St Joseph's R C Primary Sch. EH11 3 — 40-41
St Katharine's Centre EH16 6 — 54-55
St Leonard's Police Station 'B' Division HQ EH 8 9 — 30-31
St Margaret & Leonard's Catholic Church EH 8 9 — 30-31
St Margaret's EH 7 5 — 20-21
St Margaret's & St Denis Sch. EH16 5 — 44-45
St Margaret's Catholic Church EH 4 5 — 16-17 C
St Margaret's Chapel EH 1 2 — 28-29
St Margaret's Garrison Church EH13 0 — 60-61
St Margaret's Parish Church EH 7 6 — 20-21 C
St Margaret's Tower Chapel EH 9 1 — 42-43
St Margaret's Well EH 8 8 — 30-31
St Mark's (Unitarian) EH 1 3 — 28-29
St Mark's Street P.O. EH 1 1 — 30-31
St Mark's R C Church EH13 9 — 52-53
St Mark's R C Primary Sch. EH13 9 — 36-37
St Mark's Episcopal Church EH15 2 — 32-33
St Martin's Church EH15 3 — 32-33
St Martin's Church EH11 2 — 42-43
St Mary Magdalene R C Church EH15 3 — 32-33
St Mary's Cathedral (Episcopal) EH 3 9 — 28-29
St Mary's Metropolitan Cathedral (R C) EH 1 3 — 28-29
St Mary's Music Sch. EH12 5 — 28-29
St Mary's Street P.O. EH 1 1 — 30-31
St Michael & All Saints (Episcopal) EH 3 9 — 42-43
St Michael's Parish Church EH11 1 — 42-43
St Nicholas Church EH11 4 — 48-49
St Nicholas Sch. EH11 4 — 40-41
St Ninian & Triduana R C Church EH 7 6 — 20-21

linian's Church EH12 8	38-39	F9
linian's Episcopal Church EH 4 1	28-29	J11
linian's R C Primary Sch. EH 7 6	20-21	O11
linian's R C Primary Sch. EH 7 6	36-37	V9
atrick's Church (R C) EH 1 1	30-31	M10
aul's & St George's Episcopal Church EH 1 3	28-29	L11
aul's R C Church EH 4 4	16-17	H12
eter's Episcopal Church EH 8 9	30-31	M9
eter's R C Church EH10 4	42-43	K8
eter's R C Primary Sch. EH10 4	42-43	K8
hilip's EH 7 4	18-19	L12
hilip's Joppa Parish Church EH15 2	32-33	R10
alvador's Church EH11 3	40-41	H8
erf's Parish Church EH 5 3	10-11	K13
erf's Sch. EH12 5	28-29	J10
stephen's Church (C of S) EH 3 6	28-29	K11
stephen's Comely Bank Parish Church EH 4 1	28-29	K11
homas's Church EH12 8	38-39	E9
homas's Junction Road Parish Church EH 6 5	12-13	M13
incent's Chapel EH 3 5	28-29	K11
sbury View Hotel EH16 5	30-31	M9
vation Army EH11 2	40-41	I8
ghton House (Scottish Office) EH11 3	40-41	G8
ghton Prison EH11 3	40-41	H8
ghton Sports Pavilion EH11 3	40-41	H8
ghtonhall Congregational Church EH12 5	40-41	H9
ghtonhall Drive P.O. EH12 5	26-27	H10
ennes Primary Sch. EH 9 1	42-43	L9
t FM EH 6 7	12-13	N13
tch Whisky Heritage Centre EH 1 2	28-29	L10
tmid EH 6 8	20-21	N12
tsman Publications EH 8 8	30-31	M10
tt Monument EH 2 2	28-29	L10
ttish Agricultural Museum EH28 8	78-79	A9
ttish Agricultural Science Agency 24-25 EH12 8		E10
ttish Equitable HQ EH12 9	38-39	E9
ttish Health Service (C S A) EH 5 3	10-11	K13
ttish National Gallery of Modern Art	28-29	J10
ttish National Portrait Gallery EH 2 1	28-29	L11
ttish Natural Heritage HQ EH 9 2	42-43	L8
ttish Executive EH 6 6	12-13	M13
ttish Office EH14 1	40-41	I8
ttish Parliament (Temp) / C of S	28-29	L10
ssembly Halls EH 1 2		
ttish Parl. Committee Bldg. (Temp) EH 1 1	28-29	L10
ttish Parliament Offices (Temp) EH 1 1	28-29	L10
ttish Poetry Library EH 1 1	30-31	M10
ttish Record Office EH11 4	38-39	E8
ttish Tartans Museum, The EH 2 2	28-29	L10
ttish Tourist Board EH 4 3	28-29	J11
ttish United Services Museum EH 1 2	28-29	L10
ttish Widows EH16 5	30-31	M9
ttish Widows HQ EH 3 8	28-29	K10
pture Union Scotland EH13 9	62-63	J5
field Bowling Club EH 6 7	20-21	N12
field Crematorium EH 6 7	20-21	O12
field Road P.O. EH15 1	22-23	Q11
haven Hotel EH15 2	32-33	R10
enth-Day Adventist Church EH 1 1	28-29	L10
jalal Mosque Islamic Centre EH 7 4	20-21	M11
ndon Place P.O. EH11 1	42-43	J9
ep's Heid Inn EH15 3	30-31	O9
r Discount Warehouse EH15 3	46-47	R8
raton Grand Hotel EH 3 9	28-29	K10
riff Court and Crown Office EH 1 1	28-29	L10
nthill Bowling Club EH11 4	48-49	F7
nthill Fire Station EH11 4	48-49	F7
nthill Health Centre EH11 4	48-49	F7
nthill Hotel EH11 4	48-49	F7
nthill Library EH11 4	48-49	F7
nthill P.O. EH11 4	50-51	G7
nthill Primary Sch.EH11 4	48-49	F7
net Library EH 1 1	16-17	H12
h Temple EH 6 6	12-13	M13
erknowes Golf Club EH 4 5	16-17	G13
erknowes Primary Sch. EH 4 4	16-17	H12
erknowes Riding Sch. EH 4 5	16-17	H13
pson Memorial Maternity Pavilion EH 3 9	42-43	L9
pson's Hotel EH 3 9	28-29	L10
eford Bowling Club EH14 1	50-51	I7
eford Longstone Parish Church EH14 2	50-51	H7
eford Station EH14 1	40-41	I8
rise Christian Fellowship EH13 9	62-63	J5
th Gyle Station EH12 7	38-39	E9
th Leith Baptist Church EH 6 5	20-21	M12
th Morningside Primary Sch.EH10 5	52-53	K7
thfield Hall EH15 3	32-33	Q9
thfield Hospital EH16 6	54-55	O6
tra Court EH16 6	54-55	N5
anish Consulate General EH 2 3	28-29	K11
ingwell House Health Centre EH11 2	42-43	J9
kis Edinburgh Airport Hotel EH28 8	78-79	B10
kis Edinburgh Grosvenor Hotel EH12 5	28-29	K10
ndard Life Bank HQ EH 3 8	28-29	K10
ndard Life HQ EH 3 5	18-19	L12
tion House EH 1 1	28-29	L10

Stationery Office, The EH12 9	38-39	E8
Stenhouse Community Bowling Club X EH11 3	40-41	H8
Stenhouse Cross P.O. EH11 3	40-41	H8
Stenhouse Primary Sch. EH11 3	40-41	H8
Stepping Stones Theatre EH 1 1	28-29	L10
Stevenson College EH11 4	38-39	F8
Stevenson College EH11 3	40-41	H8
Stewartfield Industrial Estate EH 6 5	18-19	L12
Stewarts-Melville Club House EH 5 2	18-19	J12
Stockbridge Health Centre EH 3 6	28-29	K11
Stockbridge Library EH 3 5	28-29	K11
Stockbridge Parish Church EH 3 5	28-29	K11
Stockbridge P.O. EH 3 6	28-29	K11
Stockbridge Primary Sch. EH 3 5	28-29	K11
Strachan P.O. EH 4 2	26-27	H11
Straiton Junction EH17 8	64-65	N4
Strathearn Road P.O. EH 9 1	42-43	L8
Struan Hotel EH12 7	40-41	G9
Succoth Court EH12 6	26-27	I10
Suffolk Hall Hotel EH16 5	44-45	M8
Summerside Bowling Club EH 6 4	12-13	L13
Surgeons Hall EH 8 9	30-31	M10
Swanston Golf Club EH10 7	62-63	J4
Swanston House EH10 7	62-63	K4
Swedish Consulate EH 2 2	28-29	L10
Swiss Consular Agency EH 2 1	28-29	L11
Tabernacle Independent Baptist Church EH 6 6	12-13	M13
Tanfield Bowling Club EH 4 1	28-29	K11
Tattoo Office EH 1 1	28-29	L10
Telephone House EH11 2	40-41	I9
Tennent Caledonian Breweries EH12 9	38-39	E8
Terrace Hotel EH 7 5	20-21	M11
Tesco EH 7 4	18-19	L12
Tesco EH14 2	50-51	G7
Textile World EH 6 5	20-21	M12
Thain Inn EH 3 8	42-43	K9
The Inch P.O. EH16 5	44-45	N7
The Tron EH 1 1	28-29	L10
Thistle Court Hotel EH12 5	28-29	J10
Thistle Foundation Chapel EH16 4	46-47	P8
Thistle Hotel EH 3 7	28-29	K10
Thistle Inn Hotel EH 1 2	28-29	L10
Thomas Morton Hall EH 6 4	12-13	M13
Thrums Hotel EH 9 1	30-31	M9
Tipperlinn Bowling Club EH10 5	42-43	J8
Tollcross Fire Station EH 3 9	42-43	K9
Tollcross P.O. EH 3 9	42-43	K9
Tollcross Primary Sch. EH 3 9	42-43	K9
Torphin Hill Golf Club EH13 0	60-61	G5
Torphin Holding EH13 0	60-61	G4
Tourist Information Centre EH 2 2	28-29	L10
Tower Farm Riding Stables EH16 6	54-55	M6
Towerbank Primary Sch. EH15 1	22-23	Q11
Toys R Us EH15 3	46-47	R8
Tramways Bowling Club EH 6 5	20-21	M12
Travel Inn EH 6 6	12-13	L14
Travel Inn, Edinburgh City EH 3 8	28-29	K10
Traverse Theatre EH 1 2	28-29	L10
Trinity Academy EH 6 4	12-13	L13
Trinity Academy Annex EH 6 4	12-13	L13
Trinity Bowling Club EH 5 3	10-11	K13
Trinity Primary Sch. EH 6 4	12-13	L13
Tron Church EH17 7	56-57	P6
True Jesus Church EH 4 1	28-29	J11
Turnhouse Golf Club Ltd EH12 0	42-43	J9
Tyncastle Stadium (Heart of Midlothian FC) EH11 2	42-43	J9
Tynecastle High Sch. EH11 2	42-43	J9
Tynecastle P.O. EH11 2	42-43	J9
UCI EH15 3	46-47	R8
Ukrainian Church EH 6 8	20-21	M12
United Free Church of Scotland EH12 7	38-39	F9
University Conference Centre EH 8 9	28-29	L10
University of Edinburgh Residence EH 9 1	42-43	K9
University of Edinburgh; High Sch. Yards EH 8 9	30-31	M10
University of Edinburgh; King's Buildings EH 9 3	44-45	M7
University of Edinburgh; Library EH 8 9	42-43	L9
University of Edinburgh; Management Sch. EH 8 9	28-29	L10
University of Edinburgh; McEwan Hall EH 1 2	28-29	L10
University of Edinburgh; Medical Sch. EH 8 9	28-29	L10
University of Edinburgh; New College EH 1 2	28-29	L10
University of Edinburgh; Old College EH 8 9	28-29	L10
University of Edinburgh; Pleasance Sports Centre EH 8 9	30-31	M10
University of Edinburgh; Pollock Halls of Residence EH16 5	30-31	M9
University of Edinburgh; St Cecilia's Hall EH 1 1	30-31	M10
University of Edinburgh; Student's Union EH 8 9	28-29	L10
Usher Hall EH 1 2	28-29	K10
Victoria Park Bowling Club EH 6 4	12-13	L13
Victoria Park Hotel EH 6 4	12-13	L13

Victoria Primary Sch. EH 6 4	12-13	L14
Virgin Multiplex EH11 1	42-43	K9
W M Co, The EH 4 2	18-19	J12
Walton Hotel EH 3 6	28-29	L11
War Memorial Clock EH 3 8	28-29	K10
Wardie Bowling Club EH 5 2	10-11	K13
Wardie Hotel EH 5 1	10-11	K14
Wardie Parish Church EH 5 3	10-11	K13
Wardie Primary Sch. EH 5 3	10-11	K13
Warrender Park P.O. EH 9 1	42-43	L9
Warriston Crematorium EH 7 4	18-19	L12
Warriston P.O. EH 3 5	18-19	L12
Watsonian Football Club EH10 5	42-43	J8
Watsonian Rugby Football Club EH10 5	42-43	J8
Wauchope House EH16 4	46-47	P8
Waverley Lawn Tennis Squash & Sports Club EH16 5	44-45	M8
Waverley Market EH 2 2	28-29	L10
Waverley Station EH 1 1	28-29	L10
Weir Court EH11 4	48-49	F7
Wells O' Wearie EH16 5	30-31	N9
West Craigs Farm EH12 8	24-25	D10
West Craigs Industrial Estate EH12 0	24-25	D10
West Edge Farm EH17 8	64-65	O4
West End Hotel EH12 5	28-29	K10
West End Police Station 'C' Division HQ EH 3 8	28-29	K10
West Maitland Street P.O. EH12 5	28-29	K10
West Pilton Neighbourhood Centre EH 4 4	10-11	I13
West Pilton P.O. EH 4 4	16-17	H13
West Preston Street Clinic EH 8 9	30-31	M9
West Register House EH 2 4	28-29	K10
Westburn Primary Sch. EH11 4	48-49	F7
Westbury Hotel, The EH12 8	38-39	F9
Wester Hailes Baptist Church EH14 3	50-51	G6
Wester Hailes Education Centre EH14 2	48-49	F7
Wester Hailes Health Centre EH14 2	48-49	F6
Wester Hailes Library EH14 2	48-49	F6
Wester Hailes Police Station 'C' Division EH14 2	50-51	G7
Wester Hailes Station EH14 3	48-49	F6
Wester Melville Farm EH17 8	66-67	P3
Wester Row EH14 4	48-49	D7
Westerlea Day Sch. EH12 6	26-27	I10
Western Bar EH 3 9	28-29	L10
Western General Hospital EH 4 2	26-27	I11
Westfield Court EH11 2	40-41	I9
Westside Plaza EH14 2	48-49	F6
Wheatfield P.O. EH11 2	40-41	I9
Whinpark Medical Centre EH11 3	40-41	G8
White Hart Inn EH 1 2	28-29	L10
Whitefoord Bowling Club EH 8 8	30-31	M10
Whitefoord House EH 8 8	30-31	M10
Whitehouse & Grange Bowling Club EH 9 2	42-43	L8
Whitelaw Farm EH14 5	48-49	E6
Wickes EH15 3	46-47	R8
Wilkie House EH 1 1	28-29	L10
Willowbrae Bowling Club EH 8 7	30-31	O10
Willowbrae Hotel EH 8 7	32-33	P10
Willowpark Sch. EH11 2	40-41	I9
Wilson Memorial Church EH 7 6	22-23	P11
Witchery by the Castle, The EH 1 2	28-29	L10
Woodhall Mains EH13 0	58-59	F5
Woodhall Riding Sch. EH13 0	60-61	G5
Writers' Museum, The EH 1 2	28-29	L10

BALERNO

Balerno Bowling Club EH14 7	70-71	C3
Balerno High Sch. EH14 7	70-71	C3
Balerno Library EH14 7	70-71	C3
Balerno Parish Church (C of S) EH14 7	70-71	C3
Balerno Police Station 'C' Division EH14 7	70-71	C3
Balerno P.O. EH14 7	70-71	C3
Bankhead House EH14 7	70-71	B3
Barnardo's EH14 7	70-71	B3
Dean Park Primary Sch. EH14 7	70-71	C2
Goodtrees EH14 7	70-71	B2
Harmeny Sch. EH14 7	70-71	C2
Larch Grove House EH14 7	70-71	B3
Malleny Cottages EH14 7	70-71	C3
Malleny House EH14 7	70-71	C3
St Joseph's Catholic Church EH14 7	70-71	C3
St Mungo's Episcopal Church EH14 7	70-71	C3

BILSTON

Bilston Church EH25 9	72-73	M1
Bilston Miners Bowling Club EH25 9	72-73	M1
Bilston P.O. EH25 9	72-73	M1
Bilston Primary Sch. EH25 9	72-73	M1
Langhill Farm EH25 9	72-73	M1

BONNYRIGG

Bonnyrigg Bowling Club EH19 2	74-75	Q2
Bonnyrigg Health Centre EH19 2	74-75	Q2
Bonnyrigg Leisure Centre EH19 2	74-75	Q2
Bonnyrigg Library EH19 3	74-75	Q2
Bonnyrigg Parish Church EH19 2	74-75	Q2

Bonnyrigg Police Station 'E' Division EH19 2   74-75   Q2
Bonnyrigg P.O. EH19 2   74-75   Q2
Bonnyrigg Primary Sch. EH19 3   74-75   R1
Broomhill House EH18 1   66-67   R3
Broomieknowe Golf Club EH19 2   74-75   Q2

Cherry Road Resource Centre EH19 3   74-75   Q1

Dobbie's Garden World EH18 1   66-67   R4

Edinburgh & Lasswade Riding Centre EH18 1   74-75   P2
Edinburgh Butterfly World EH18 1   66-67   R4

Gilmerton Junction EH18 1   66-67   Q4

Primary Sch. EH19 2   74-75   P1
Sch. EH19 3   74-75   Q1

Kevock Vale Caravan Park (Residential) EH18 1   74-75   Q2
Kings Acre Golf Club EH18 1   66-67   Q4

Lasswade High Sch. EH19 2   74-75   Q2
Lasswade Parish Church EH18 1   66-67   Q3
Lasswade P.O. EH18 1   66-67   Q3
Lasswade Primary Sch. EH19 2   74-75   R2
Lasswade Rugby Football Club EH19 3   74-75   Q1

Mavisbank EH18 1   72-73   O2
Melville Castle EH18 1   66-67   R3
Melville Golf Course EH18 1   66-67   R3
Melville Golf Range EH18 1   66-67   R3
Melville Grange Farm EH18 1   66-67   Q4
Melville Mains EH18 1   66-67   Q4
Middlemills EH18 1   66-67   Q3
Montrose Stables EH18 1   74-75   P1

Nazareth Nursing Home EH19 2   66-67   Q3

Pittendreich House EH18 1   66-67   Q3
Polton Bowling Club EH18 1   72-73   O1
Polton House EH18 1   74-75   P2
Poltonhall P.O. EH19 2   74-75   Q1

St Leonard's Scottish Episcopal Church EH18 1   74-75   Q2
St Mary's R C Primary Sch. EH19 3   74-75   Q1
Sherwood Industrial Est EH19 3   74-75   R2
South Melville Farmhouse EH18 1   66-67   R3
Springfield Farm EH18 1   74-75   P1
Springfield House EH18 1   74-75   P1

DALKEITH/ESKBANK

Archview Lodge EH22 2   68-69   T3

Bogwood P.O. EH22 5   76-77   U2

Campend Farm EH22 1   56-57   R5
Cauldcoats Farm EH22 1   46-47   Q7
Church of Jesus Christ of Latter-Day Saints EH22 1   68-69   S3
County Hotel, The EH22 1   68-69   T4

Dalkeith Baptist Church EH22 1   68-69   T4
Dalkeith Bowling Club EH22 1   68-69   S4
Dalkeith Bus Station EH22 1   68-69   S4
Dalkeith Fire Station EH22 3   68-69   T3
Dalkeith High Sch. EH22 1   68-69   T4
Dalkeith House EH22 2   68-69   T4
Dalkeith Lawn Tennis Club EH22 3   68-69   S3
Dalkeith Leisure Centre EH22 2   68-69   T4
Dalkeith Library & Art Centre EH22 1   68-69   T4
Dalkeith Medical Centre EH22 1   68-69   T4
Dalkeith Police Station 'E' Division HQ EH22 3   68-69   S3
Dalkeith Water Tower EH22 3   68-69   S4
Danderhall Leisure Centre EH22 1   56-57   R6
Danderhall Library EH22 1   56-57   R6
Danderhall Miners' Welfare and Social Club EH22 1   56-57   Q6
Danderhall P.O. EH22 1   56-57   Q6
Danderhall Primary Sch. EH22 1   56-57   Q6

Easthouses Bowling Club EH22 4   76-77   U2
Easthouses Church EH22 5   76-77   U2
Easthouses P.O. EH22 4   76-77   U2
Eskbank Hotel EH22 3   68-69   S3

Eskbank P.O. EH22 3   68-69   S3

Hardengreen Business Park EH22 3   68-69   S3
Hardengreen Industrial Estate EH22 3   68-69   S3
Hillcrest House EH22 1   46-47   Q7
Hilltown EH22 1   46-47   R7
Hilltown Farm Cottages EH22 1   46-47   R7

Jewel & Esk Valley College EH22 3   68-69   S3
Justinlees Inn EH22 3   68-69   S3

King's Park Primary Sch. EH22 3   68-69   T4
Kingdom Hall of Jehovah's Witnesses EH22 1   68-69   T4

Langlaw Primary Sch. EH22 5   76-77   U2
Lugton Special Sch. EH22 2   68-69   S4

Medic Centre EH22 1   56-57   R6
Midlothian Council Offices EH22 1   68-69   T4
Midlothian Indoor Bowling Club EH22 1   68-69   S4

Newbattle Abbey College EH22 3   68-69   T3
Newbattle Golf Club EH22 3   68-69   T3
Newbattle High Sch. EH22 4   76-77   U2
Newbattle Parish Church EH22 3   68-69   T3
Newton Parish Church EH22 1   56-57   R6
Newton Village EH22 1   56-57   R6
Royal Mail; Dalkeith Delivery Office EH22 1   68-69   S4

St David's Church EH22 3   68-69   S3
St David's R C High Sch. EH22 3   68-69   T3
St David's R C Primary Sch. EH22 2   68-69   U3
St John's & Kings Park Parish Church EH22 1   68-69   S4
St Mary's Episcopal Church EH22 1   68-69   T4
St Nicholas Buccleuch Parish Church EH22 1   68-69   T4
Scottish Fire Service EH22 3   68-69   T3
Shawfair EH22 1   46-47   R7
Sheriffhall Farm EH22 1   68-69   S4
Sheriffhall Roundabout EH22 1   56-57   R5

Thornybank Industrial Estate EH22 2   68-69   U4
Todhills Farm EH22 1   56-57   Q5

Westfield Special Sch. EH22 2   68-69   S4
Woodburn P.O. EH22 2   68-69   T4
Woodburn Primary Sch. EH22 2   68-69   U4

LOANHEAD

Ashgrove House EH20 9   64-65   N3

Blairesk Hall EH20 9   72-73   O2
Burghlee Farm EH20 9   72-73   N1

Costco, Loanhead EH20 9   72-73   N2

Edgefield Road Industrial Estate EH20 9   64-65   O3
Edgefield Toll Farm EH20 9   64-65   O3
Enterprise Centre, Loanhead EH20 9   72-73   M2

Ikea EH20 9   72-73   N2

Loanhead Bowling Club EH20 9   72-73   N2
Loanhead Clinic EH20 9   72-73   N2
Loanhead Farm EH20 9   72-73   O2
Loanhead Hospital EH20 9   72-73   O2
Loanhead Leisure Centre EH20 9   72-73   N2
Loanhead Library EH20 9   72-73   N2
Loanhead Miners Bowling Club EH20 9   72-73   O2
Loanhead Police Station 'E' Division EH20 9   72-73   O2
Loanhead P.O. EH20 9   72-73   O2
Loanhead Primary Sch. EH20 9   72-73   O2
Loanhead Swimming Pool EH20 9   72-73   N2
Loanhead West Church EH20 9   72-73   N2

Nivensknowe Caravan Park (Residential) EH20 9   72-73   M2

Old Pentland EH20 9   64-65   M3

Paradykes Primary Sch. EH20 9   72-73   N2
Pentland Caravan Park (Residential) EH20 9   72-73   M2
Pentland Industrial Estate EH20 9   72-73   M2

Pentland Mains Farm EH20 9   72-73
Pentland Nurseries EH20 9   72-73

Sainsbury's EH20 9   64-65
St Margaret's Farm EH20 9   64-65
St Margaret's R C Church EH20 9   72-73
St Margaret's R C Sch. EH20 9   72-73
Straighton Cottages EH20 9   64-65
Straiton Caravan Park (Residential) EH20 9   64-65
Straiton Farm EH20 9   64-65
Straiton Pond EH20 9   64-65
Straiton Retail Park EH20 9   64-65

MUSSELBURGH

Apostolic Church, The EH21 6   34-35

B & Q, Newcraighall Rd EH21 8   46-47
Bridge Christian Centre, The EH21 6   34-35
Brunton Hall EH21 6   34-35

Campie Primary Sch. EH21 6   34-35
Church of God in Musselburgh, The EH21 7   34-35

Edenhall Hospital EH21 7   36-37
Eskbridge Medical Centre EH21 6   34-35

Fisherrow Coast Mission EH21 6   34-35
Fisherrow Industrial Estate EH21 6   34-35
Fisherrow Links Pitch & Putt EH21 6   34-35
Fisherrow P.O. EH21 6   34-35

Gospel Hall EH21 6   34-35

Inveresk House EH21 7   34-35

Living Well Health Club EH21 8   46-47
Loretto Junior Sch. EH21 6   34-35
Loretto R C Primary Sch. EH21 7   34-35
Loretto Sch. EH21 7   34-35

Monktonhall P.O. EH21 6   34-35
Musselburgh Arms Hotel EH21 7   34-35
Musselburgh Baptist Church EH21 7   34-35
Musselburgh Bowling Club EH21 7   34-35
Musselburgh Bowling Greens EH21 6   34-35
Musselburgh Burgh Primary Sch. EH21 7   34-35
Musselburgh Fire Station EH21 7   34-35
Musselburgh Golf Club EH21 7   36-37
Musselburgh Grammar Sch. EH21 7   36-37
Musselburgh Library EH21 6   34-35
Musselburgh Links The Old Golf Course (Public) EH21 7   34-35
Musselburgh Museum of Dolls & Art Exhibits EH21 7   34-35
Musselburgh Police Station 'E' Division EH21 7   34-35
Musselburgh P.O. EH21 7   34-35
Musselburgh Racecourse EH21 7   34-35
Musselburgh Rugby Club EH21 6   34-35
Musselburgh Sports Centre EH21 7   34-35
Musselburgh Station EH21 8   36-37
Musselburgh Town Hall EH21 7   34-35

Newcraighall Fire Station EH21 8   46-47
Newcraighall P.O. EH21 8   46-47
Newhailes Mansion House (NTS) EH21 6   34-35
Niddrie Bowling Club EH21 8   34-35
North Esk Parish Church EH21 6   34-35

Our Lady of Loretto Catholic Church EH21 7   34-35

Pinkie Mains EH21 7   36-37

Ravelston House Hotel EH21 6   34-35

St Anne's Convent EH21 7   36-37
St Peter's EH21 7   34-35
St Peter's Primary Sch. EH21 7   36-37
St Peter's Primary Sch. EH21 7   36-37
Stoneyhill Primary Sch. EH21 6   34-35

Wanton Walls Farm EH21 8   34-35
Wedderburn House EH21 7   36-37
Whitehill Mains Farm EH21 8   46-47